PARALEGAL SUCCESS

PARALEGAL SUCCESS

GOING FROM GOOD TO GREAT IN THE NEW CENTURY

DEBORAH BOGEN

Prentice Hall
Upper Saddle River, New Jersey 07458

Library of Congress Cataloging-in-Publication Data

Bogen, Deborah
    Paralegal success : going from good to great in the new century /
Deborah Bogen.
      p. cm. — (Prentice Hall paralegal series)
    Includes index.
    ISBN 0-13-095193-5
    1. Legal assistants—United States—Handbooks, manuals, etc.
I. Title. II. Series.
KF320.L4B64 2000
340'.023'73—dc21
                                              99-12032
                                                CIP

Acquisitions Editor: Elizabeth Sugg
Editorial Assistant: Delia Uherec
Director of Production and Manufacturing: Bruce Johnson
Managing Editor: Mary Carnis
Editorial/Production Supervision and
   Interior Design: Inkwell Publishing Services
Cover Director: Jayne Conte
Manufacturing Buyer: Edward O'Dougherty

© 2000 by Prentice-Hall, Inc.
Upper Saddle River, New Jersey 07458

Printed in the United States of America

10 9 8 7 6 5 4 3 2 1

ISBN 0-13-095193-5

PRENTICE-HALL INTERNATIONAL (UK) LIMITED, *London*
PRENTICE-HALL OF AUSTRALIA PTY. LIMITED, *Sydney*
PRENTICE-HALL CANADA INC., *Toronto*
PRENTICE-HALL HISPANOAMERICANA, S.A., *Mexico*
PRENTICE-HALL OF INDIA PRIVATE LIMITED, *New Delhi*
PRENTICE-HALL OF JAPAN, INC., *Tokyo*
PRENTICE-HALL OF SOUTHEAST ASIA PTE. LTD., *Singapore*
EDITORA PRENTICE-HALL DO BRASIL, LTDA., *Rio de Janeiro*

For Jim
my husband, my hero, my heart

CONTENTS

PREFACE

I'm a working paralegal. I've been a paralegal for fifteen years. After all those years—and after writing articles and teaching seminars and giving speeches and winning awards and even after signing a contract to write this book—the central focus of my working life is the day-to-day work of a paralegal.

Every morning I drink two cups of coffee, swallow my vitamins, eat a cup of yogurt, grab a banana for the road, and head to the office to deal with lawyers, clients, secretaries, courts, deadlines, evaluations, lunch meetings, legal briefs, missing memos, discovery demands, boxes of documents, process servers, calendaring systems, telephone calls, opposing counsel, E-mail communiques, library research, dead filing, proofreading, fax exchanges, strategy conferences, trial preparation, educational seminars, city ordinances, contracts, evidence gathering, database and fact organization, witness preparation, conflicts of interest rules, worklogs, summer clerks, client receptions and a million other things.

I live and work in the legal trenches. During my tenure I've learned that a paralegal's life can be boring and enervating, or it can be demanding, exciting, surprising, rewarding, energizing, and educational. I opted for career number two and have been lucky enough to run into strong mentors, excellent teachers, good friends, and valuable colleagues who've taught me, trained me, and helped me discover things about the practice of law that have made me a first-string paralegal. Much of what I've learned is in this book.

Paralegal Success is designed to teach you a hundred real-life concepts that will make a difference in your paralegal career, from how to handle your time sheets to how to handle someone who is lying to a senior partner about you. This book is based not only on my experience, but on the collective knowledge of some of the best paralegals and attorneys in the country. It will help you deal with both the obvious factors related to your professional career and the subtle and often invisible factors that have a real and definite impact on whether you end up happy and productive in your work. I think this is a thoughtful book, but it's not a theoretical book. It's a hands-on, here's how you do it, paralegal career book. It tells you how to do the things that will lead to success.

Some of the ideas you'll read about here will be uplifting: There really are outstanding individuals out there who will do the right thing when it counts. Some ideas will be more discouraging, like the fact that sometimes you can be quite right and loyal and deserving of good treatment and still have to tolerate bad behavior on the part of folks who have more law office clout than you do. This book will teach you how to deal with the bad and the good, and how to manage a secretary, support staff, cantankerous clients, several lawyers, and yourself—and get the job done right, the first time.

Finally, this book is based on the principle that you are in charge of your own career and that you are willing to invest in yourself and work hard to make that career rewarding and successful. The information you will find here will help you become a true professional, with top-notch skills and a resume to match. It's a solid resource with tools to help you assess your skills, your employer, and your chances for success in a particular legal setting. It includes information about how to become a specialist, how to change your job without changing firms, and how to transplant your paralegal skills to a new professional domain. There are many of kinds of successful paralegal careers. This book is about how to create the one that's really right for you.

ACKNOWLEDGMENTS

I wish to thank Michael Senneff and Phillip Kelly, who hired me fresh out of school and taught me that ethical behavior and the highest standards of professionalism are the keys to both an honorable and a successful career.

I owe an even greater debt to my boss, mentor, and friend, Ken MacVey, who's a terrific lawyer and a gifted teacher. Ken extends the best kind of intellectual collegiality to paralegals who are committed to excellence. He's an advocate and supporter of professional growth. A great deal of what I've learned in the past ten years I've learned from him.

I'm also grateful to Clark Alsop, Wynne Furth, and Chris Carpenter, all of whom have been professional models, teachers, and friends. Their insights into how things work within a law office and how to work with clients in the real world have been invaluable. Thanks also to Doyle Letbetter, whose willingness to listen and to talk straight has made a difference. All these people have helped me become a better paralegal and have affected crucial career decisions along the way.

I'm indebted to many people in the greater paralegal community. Diane Petropulos, Coordinator of the Sonoma State University Attorney Assistant Program, introduced me to this profession fifteen years ago. I am personally grateful to her for that and we are all indebted to her for the work she has done on behalf of the profession at the local, state, and national levels. Susan Nauss Exon, Director of Law and Public Policy at University of California Extension, Riverside, has practiced both as a paralegal and as a lawyer. As an educator she is a source of encouragement and inspiration, working energetically to promote the profession and to help individual students reach their potential.

Legal Assistant Today magazine convinced me that writing for paralegals is a good idea. I'm grateful to past editors Gina Gladwell and Nicole Kording as well as to present editors Daryl Teshima, Natasha Emmons, and Leanne Cazares. In addition, *LAT* has graciously allowed me to reprint in this book some material originally published there.

It's essential in putting a book together to be able to talk about everything—from the most important concepts to the most mundane detail—with someone smart who will listen generously and respond insightfully and honestly. I owe great thanks to Jim Bogen for being that someone, and even more importantly for reminding me on a regular basis that my goal in writing this book is to help serious paralegals become the truly skilled professionals behind those glossy resumes.

Finally, I want to thank Elizabeth Sugg at Prentice Hall, who believed me when I said I could write a good book. I hope I haven't let her down.

FURTHER ACKNOWLEDGMENTS

Robert Mittelstaedt of Pillsbury, Madison & Sutro, San Francisco, California; Stan Yamamoto and Carolyn Confer of the City of Riverside City Attorney's Office, Riverside, California; and Paul Shimoff of McPeters, McAlearney, Shimoff & Hatt of Redlands, California were all kind enough to provide helpful comments on qualities they value in top-notch paralegals. Their insights added to the book and I'm grateful for their help.

I'm also grateful to the following organizations for permission to reprint some of their materials:

National Association of Legal Assistants for permission to reprint its definition of a "legal assistant/paralegal" as well as the "NALA Code of Ethics."

National Federation of Paralegal Associations, Inc. for permission to reprint its definition of "paralegal/legal assistant" as well as the NFPA "Model Code of Ethics and Professional Responsibility and Guidelines for Enforcement."

The American Bar Association for permission to reprint its definition of "paralegal/legal assistant" as well as the "ABA Model Guidelines for Utilization of Legal Assistant Services."

PARALEGAL SUCCESS

GOING FROM GOOD TO GREAT: WHAT'S THE BIG DEAL?

Every time I teach a *Going from Good to Great* seminar I draw this line on the chalkboard:

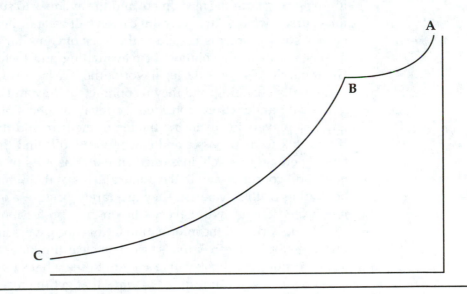

Performance Curve

This is a performance curve. Between points C and B lies a continuum that represents the distance—and the difference—between a "not much good at all" paralegal and a "darn good" one. It's a pretty long curve and along that stretch there's room for a number of variations on the paralegal theme. Above the halfway mark you'll find many strong performers, and there's certainly nothing to be ashamed of in occupying any of the upper stretch. In fact, the last inch of the CB line is quality territory.

Then there's that little curve at the end, from B to A, sharper and quite short. That curve represents the difference between a good paralegal and a top-notch professional—an envelope-pushing, cream-of-the-crop, off-the-everyday-charts paralegal. Much of what goes on in the career of a terrific paralegal takes place in that top bit. The territory's exciting, but the terrain is not very well documented.

This book is about going the distance from good to stellar, but it starts where we all start: day one, new kid on the block. It takes you through the maze of options and the potential minefield of unknowns that are part of a developing professional career. It shows you how to design an exciting, rewarding job that's customized to your personality, your professional strengths, and your lifestyle.

There are different kinds of great paralegal careers. What they all have in common is that they are the result of smart thinking, independent analysis, the ability to observe what's actually going on, and the willingness to respond in a creative and energetic fashion. Great paralegals have worked out career programs in which success is the result not only of ability and hard work, but also of incorporating the needs and requirements of the law firm and the paralegal's personal life and temperament.

There's no magic to this process. It involves taking personal responsibility for exploring both the meaning of and the avenues to success. It means defining for yourself what your successful career will be and then pursuing it. While the base of such a career is as solid as the Rock of Gibraltar, it also involves being in a constant state of evolution, of reevaluating and recreating your own career. Great paralegals know the legal world, the larger world, and their own lives are continually changing, and they respond creatively and often passionately.

Great paralegals are considered critical members of their firms' legal teams and key players in advancing the life of the firm and the interests of its clients. If you talk to their bosses and coworkers you'll find that these legal assistants have been aggressively interested in many aspects of the law, in their clients' goals and concerns, and in the political lives of their employers almost from the beginning of their careers. They are rarely passive and they've educated and reeducated themselves at every step on their professional journey.

Hard work and the information in this book will land you firmly on the AB line, developing a career that's based on clear thinking, aggressive analysis, and self-direction. This book will teach you to see what's going on in your work environment so you can respond in ways that get the results you want. Success is about high standards, a love of excellence, the pleasure of teamwork, a strong sense of responsibility, the willingness to cross old boundaries, tenacity, persistence, and the value of maintaining a strong personal life. Success can be defined in a number of ways; you must think things through and define what you count as success in your career. This book offers tools that will help you perform that analysis and develop the skills and opportunities that will carry the day.

Most importantly, this book is about remembering that your career belongs to you—not to a law firm or to a lawyer or a corporation. It's yours, and you are responsible for its upkeep and for moving it forward, which is terrific news. Here's how to do it.

THE NEW YOU: WHAT DOES IT MEAN TO BE A PARALEGAL?

In 1986 I received an Attorney Assistant Certificate from Sonoma State University in California. The graduation ceremony was the culmination of two and a half years of night classes, endless hours of study, and a wonderful but taxing internship that I'd completed while raising two children and working as a school secretary. I'd already interviewed for and accepted a promising position with one of the best firms in my area, and was amazed and delighted to learn that my income would double the day I started. Waiting in my straight-backed chair to receive the certificate I'd worked so hard for, I knew I'd accomplished something, become something, but in all honesty I wasn't sure what.

If you are a new paralegal you may be in a similar situation. Don't worry. Like so many of the rest of us, you will learn a lot about your role as paralegal on the job. You'll also help create it. This is still a new profession. There is no standard role or set of skills or group of job responsibilities shared by all paralegals. You are entering a profession in which you can expect to play an important role in the continuing evolution of the definition of a paralegal.

THE EMERGENCE OF THE PARALEGAL

We paralegals have an honorable heritage. The first paralegal jobs were created to support social justice. In fact, the first use of non-lawyer assistants occurred in government legal teams in the early 1960s, when government lawyers took on the legal battles of Americans suffering racial and other kinds of discrimination. Using non-lawyer assistants was a cost-effective way to meet the demands of this socially conscious legal work. At some unrecorded point people began to call these workers *legal assistants* and *paralegals*.

These terms were later adopted by lawyers in private law firms to describe individuals, often former legal secretaries, who were performing in their law practices at a level that was obviously more substantive than clerical. It's a reasonable guess that the desire to collect a professional fee for such services may have been a factor in the designation, but the intelligence and willingness to undertake new responsibilities of these pioneering paralegals should not be underestimated or undervalued.

In fact, the impressive quality of the work done by early legal assistants led to the training and hiring of more individuals to work as paralegals and to the eventual establishment of educational programs designed to produce assistants who came to their first jobs with background legal knowledge and training. Paralegal education program graduates were ready to be of real assistance to lawyers from the first day on the job. Many lawyers began looking to local educational programs to supply them with able job candidates.

Since the 1960s the paralegal field has grown dramatically. A number of national associations have been formed to support the profession and further educate paralegals. These organizations play a strong role in addressing issues raised in the profession and in the larger legal community by the emergence of the paralegal.

Several national organizations have adopted definitions for the terms *legal assistant* and *paralegal*. The two largest national paralegal associations are the National Association of Legal Assistants (NALA) and the National Federation of Paralegal Associations (NFPA). Here's how they define these terms:

National Association of Legal Assistants:

Legal assistants, also known as paralegals, are a distinguishable group of persons who assist attorneys in the delivery of legal services. Through formal education, training and experience, legal assistants have knowledge and expertise regarding the legal system and substantive and procedural law which qualify them to do work of a legal nature under the supervision of an attorney.

National Federation of Paralegal Associations:

A paralegal is a person qualified through education, training or work experience to perform substantive legal work that requires knowledge of legal concepts and is customarily, but not exclusively, performed by a lawyer.

This qualified person may be retained or employed in a traditional capacity by a lawyer, law office, governmental agency, or other entity or is authorized by administrative, statutory or court authority to perform this work; OR

This qualified person may be retained or employed in a non-traditional capacity, provided that such non-traditional capacity does not violate applicable unauthorized practice of law statutes, administrative laws, court rules, or case law.

The NFPA goes on:

Traditional Paralegal—a paralegal who works with supervision by and/or accountability to a lawyer.

Contract Paralegal (Freelance Paralegal or Independent Contractor)—a paralegal who works as an independent contractor with supervision by and/or accountability to a lawyer.

Independent Paralegal (Legal Technician)—paralegals who work outside the supervision of attorneys pursuant to statute, administrative regulation or court rule, for example as

Special Advocate—a paralegal who is authorized to participate in court proceedings involving specified classes of parties or cases. The special advocate may be referred to as a "court appointed special advocate." (CASE)

Agency Representative—a paralegal who is authorized by statute or agency rules to represent clients in agency proceedings.

or who provide services to clients in regard to a process in which the law is involved and for whose work no lawyer is accountable.

These definitions have evolved over time and not without a great deal of discussion. They will be subject to further revision. As paralegals find their work environment and their professional responsibilities changing there is a continuing need to change the formal language that describes who we are. Clearly both these national groups see the responsibilities of paralegals as involved with substantive legal work that is different in nature from the clerical tasks that are also critical to the effective practice of law.

THE ABA

Paralegals are such a staple in today's law offices that the American Bar Association is actively involved in providing guidelines for the utilization of paralegals. Here is the ABA's current definition of a paralegal:

"A legal assistant or paralegal is a person, qualified by education, training or work experience who is employed or retained by a lawyer, law office, corporation, governmental agency or other entity and who performs specifically delegated substantive legal work for which a lawyer is responsible."

This definition replaces a prior version that I include below because it is helpful to see the changes.

"persons who, although not members of the legal profession, are qualified through education, training or work experience, are employed or retained by a lawyer, law office, governmental agency, or other entity in a capacity or function which involves the performance under the direction and supervision of an attorney, of specifically delegated substantive legal work, which work, for the most part, requires a sufficient knowledge of legal concepts, such that, absent that legal assistant, the attorney would perform the task."

The ABA Internet site explains that "the new definition of *legal assistant/paralegal* replaces the definition adopted by the ABA Board of Governors in 1986. It adds the term *paralegal* since the terms *legal assistant* and *paralegal* are, in practice, used interchangeably," and claims that "the term that is preferred generally depends on what part of the country one is from. The new definition, the ABA says, "streamlines the 1986 definition and more accurately reflects how legal assistants are presently being utilized in the delivery of legal services."

You should notice that part of the streamlining involves the deletion of the phrase, "although not members of the legal profession." Today there is quite a bit of cooperation between the ABA and the major national paralegal organizations. Paralegals function as, and are largely viewed as, a professional group within the larger legal profession. Certainly most of us view ourselves as professionals and that designation is not without import. It corresponds to the level of responsibility expected of paralegals by their employers and the clients they serve, and to the sophistication of the work paralegals perform. Today the offering of associate memberships to paralegals by local bar associations is more the norm than the exception. Lawyer practice groups like the American Trial Lawyers Association also provide memberships for paralegals. In addition, paralegals work with lawyers in the offering of pro bono services, another professional responsibility. To view paralegals as nonprofessionals is simply out of sync with what is happening in the legal profession.

Another significant part of the ABA's explanation of its new definition is the statement that it "more accurately reflects how legal assistants are presently being utilized in the delivery of legal services." What this statement indicates is that the definition follows, rather than regulates, the development of the ways in which paralegals function in the delivery of legal services. Currently the responsibilities of paralegals within particular practices are expanding. As those responsibilities are successfully carried out they will become yet another part of the paralegal job description and the roles of paralegals in the practice of law will continue to change.

Real-World Definitions

To be useful, definitions must bear a strong relationship to the reality they attempt to define. Many paralegals feel the degree of responsibility they shoulder in their employers' professional affairs should be the basis of a real-world definition of the word *paralegal*.

A significant and perhaps a key factor in any working definition is the fact that paralegals are not paid to simply take direction. Most real-life paralegal positions require substantive knowledge, initiative, and a willingness to undertake an ever-increasing level of responsibility. Paralegals are required to think not only of the immediate task to be done, but also about what other steps are necessary in order to meet the needs of the client or employer. If an attorney fails to tell a secretary to serve or file a document, the secretary is normally excused from blame based on the attorney's failure to direct her. Not so with paralegals. We share the blame with the attorney for such a failure. We are not free to say, "No one told me to do it." Good paralegals think about what needs to be done. Good paralegals find out what needs to be done. Good paralegals make sure it gets done.

A Million Job Descriptions

Paralegal job descriptions remain remarkably varied, and there's no real unification on the horizon. Although litigation support has historically been the classic use of paralegals, today you can find specialists in bankruptcy; litigation subspecialties like construction defect, commercial, or eminent domain litigation; malpractice, tax law, sports law, contract compliance, corporate law, entertainment, patent and copyright, immigration, personal injury, family law, personnel and employee benefits, public law, probate, antitrust, health law, elder law, collections, real estate, and more. The list just keeps growing and by the time this book hits the shelves there will be paralegals doing things no one's thought of yet.

Part of the reason for this is that the world changes quickly these days. How many of us anticipated the full impact of Internet access on information retrieval, or the impact on society of a growing population of elderly? But that isn't the only reason paralegals have increasingly complex job descriptions. It's also because the myth that those who did not go to law school were simply not up to the task and hence were strictly limited in their contribution to a law practice is fading.

BEYOND OFFICIAL JOB DESCRIPTIONS

Along with the expanding list of "official" paralegal specialties, other elements affect the job description of any particular paralegal: the abilities, intellectual tenacity, and professional maturity of the individual. This is, in fact, still a career you can create as you go along. There are paralegals writing trial briefs and there are paralegals who spend all their time putting documents in chronological order. Sometimes they work in the same office. Their job responsibilities have evolved in accordance with the skills they have demonstrated, their desire for responsibilities, and their wisdom in seeking the right employment opportunity. Today's paralegals may work longer hours or shorter hours or on interesting or less-interesting assignments based largely on their own performance and the official and unofficial agreements between them and the attorneys with whom they work.

WHY YOU COUNT

The practice of law in America is in terrific flux. The cost of legal services is often prohibitive. Currently it's too expensive for many middle-class families to take care of necessary legal matters. The courts are overtaxed and movement to trial can be agonizingly slow. There is a public perception that many lawyers are more interested in driving expensive cars than in providing legal services. Pressure is building for change in the way legal services are provided and the talk in many states of licensing or registering paralegals is only one indicator that eventually some way to provide services to lower-income people will be authorized.

It's clear that no one can say today just how legal services will be provided in the next two decades. If you're just beginning a paralegal career, chances are you will be part of some substantial changes. Paralegals are the most adaptable members of the legal team and we will be able to play a greater number of roles than either lawyers or the secretaries in the years to come. Your performance on the job will directly, and perhaps importantly, affect the development of the professional purview of paralegals.

Whether you work in a law office, in a government or corporate setting, or as an independent paralegal, the professionalism and expertise you demonstrate in the delivery of legal services will either lift or drag down the reputation of paralegals within the legal profession and with the public. Not many professions can offer you the opportunity to make such a critical difference. Welcome aboard. You can bet we'll be keeping an eye on you.

FROM BOOKBAG TO BRIEFCASE: PLANNING YOUR JOB SEARCH

The bridge from school to work may look a little daunting but it's not so difficult to cross—just don't look down. Keep your eyes trained on your future and keep your briefcase filled with the many resources that exist for today's job seekers.

And don't just fill up your briefcase. Now's the time to fill your mind with things that will help you find your spot—cheerful determination, a strong sense of purpose, and realistic optimism. Any job search presents opportunities for moodiness. You're up, you're down, you're all around. Remember that your mental state is in your control. You can choose to be positive and you can choose to be employed.

FINISH STRONG AND DOCUMENT YOUR WORK

If you're just finishing school, now's the time for you to tally up the score. Review your GPA, which should aid you both in getting a great job and in getting good assignments once you're on the job. Then look over your actual course work and think back over your instructors.

Don't throw anything out. Keep the names and phone numbers of fellow students, good teachers, and any attorneys you met while in school, as well as guest speakers from related fields. As fresh and indelible as all this information may seem today, six months or a year from now you will be glad to have a cheat sheet.

Even though you're out of school, the homework isn't over. Get out your computer and write a clear synopsis of each class you took. Think about the legal issues of each class subject. Even more importantly, think about what issues covered in each class most interested you. How does that area of law affect society? What role could a paralegal play in a practice built around that legal subject area?

This is a part of your training to work in a legal environment. It's important to learn how to think about and talk about the law. In the real world legal matters do not come nicely parsed into "contract law," "estate planning," and "eminent domain law." A particular client matter usually touches several areas of law and you need to train yourself to think about all the areas that need investigation and work.

Do not skip this step in your preparation for getting a job. Disciplining yourself to think about your classes now will increase your confidence when you interview. When the interviewing attorney says, "Tell me a little something about the classes you took," you'll be prepared to say more than, "Well, I took contracts." You can say what you liked about contract law and what you think you know about "consideration" and "a meeting of the minds." You may well end up drafting contracts yourself, because nothing impresses a good attorney more than a paralegal who is interested in talking about the legal issues and who has the knowledge to do it.

Hot Tip: Now's the time to set up a three-ring binder that travels with you for at least the first five years of your career. It will include these course summaries as well as names and phone numbers of students and teachers you liked, information about your institution, a photocopy of your certificate, a copy of your transcript, your resume(s), copies of letters of recommendation, and everything you can get your hands on about continuing education for paralegals.

MEET WITH YOUR PROGRAM DIRECTOR OR PLACEMENT OFFICER

Before you graduate, meet with your program director or placement officer to get whatever help they offer in the job search area. They probably provide resume review, and many institutions offer job bank connections and opportunities to perform mock interviews. Any job leads they provide should go right into your three-ring binder for follow-up. The follow-up should occur within five days of receiving the lead—but two days is even better. Ask the placement officer the following question:

> "What are the most critical skills and attributes to demonstrate in order to get a good job?"

Then get out a pencil. You need to pay attention and write down what these people tell you. A common and serious mistake people make is asking the right question about how to get a job and then not really listening to the answer. They daydream, think about their next question, or wonder if they remembered to take the meat out of the freezer. Pay attention to your program directors and placement officers. They deal with graduating paralegals who are hitting the pavement all the time. They know something, something you need to know.

Many institutions with paralegal education programs also have separate university career centers that will provide help with resumes, mock interviews, and job leads for free or for a small fee. Invest in yourself. Read sample resumes, cover letters, and thank-you letters and make copies when possible. Read books! Andrea Wagner's *How to Land Your First Paralegal Job* is a must-read, as are Diane Petropulos' student workshop columns in *Legal Assistant Today* magazine. Check the appendices of this book for other helpful titles.

LETTERS OF RECOMMENDATION

Opinions vary on how helpful letters of recommendation are in a job search, but in any case, they are standard equipment in a job search. Securing them is part of your preparation. Here are some ways to get them:

If you participated in a internship program while in school, good for you. You're already ahead of the pack. That experience has given you the opportunity to see what it's like to work in a legal environment and to make contacts in the local legal community.

If you did good work—especially if it was for no money—the attorney you worked for expects to pay you by way of a letter of recommendation and probably by being listed as a reference on your resume. If a letter of recommendation was not offered when you ended your internship, do not assume the attorney did not mean to write one for you. Like the rest of us, lawyers are so busy with their own practices that most simply don't get around to completing things like letters of recommendation if there's no follow-up by the people who need them. If you are no longer going to the attorney's office to work, write a cordial request for a letter of recommendation. It might look something like this:

Jessica Fisher
1020 Avenue F
Greenfield, Ohio 36574
(504) 886-3746
jfisher@rstomp.com

Karen Hamilton   May 12, 1999
Hamilton and Jones
500 Amerigo Avenue
Los Angeles, CA 94837

Dear Karen:

I enjoyed working in your office last semester. Thanks for the opportunity to see what a workers' compensation practice is all about. I liked the work and hope to get a job in this area of law.

The last week of my internship we were all so busy getting the Malcolm case ready for hearing that I failed to ask you for a letter of recommendation. Would you be willing to write one for me that I can use in my job search?

I graduate in June and will be hitting the pavement as soon as I have my certificate. SSU has given me a great paralegal education. The chance to use that training to work on a real case with experienced attorneys and paralegals in your office was a highlight of the program. I appreciated the chance to be a small part of your team.

Sincerely,

Jessica Fisher

P.S. I've been so curious about how the Malcolm case went. Was Judge Aikens impressed with our argument that the doctor totally missed Malcolm's allergy to analgesics and anti-inflammatories when he cleared him to return to work?

This letter will do the following things for you:

1. Communicate that you are grateful for the opportunity extended to you.
2. Remind the attorney of what you did while you were there.
3. Obligate the attorney to write the letter (assuming you were good).
4. Let the attorney know that you are the kind of paralegal who is truly interested in this area of law, the attorney's particular practice, and your part in it.
5. Give the attorney the idea that if she wants to hire you she should let you know soon.
6. Put your name and phone number at her fingertips so she can pick up the phone to talk about the Malcolm matter—today!

If you don't hear from attorney Hamilton in a week you should call her secretary or someone you know well at the office to get a feel for what's going on. If the work you did was useful, you will eventually get the letter. The original copy goes in a special Letters of Recommendation file. Make a few copies for your binder.

Other Sources for Letters

1.   Teachers in your paralegal education program in whose classes you did splendidly. Be realistic about this: No one clicks with everyone. If you think someone will not be comfortable writing a letter that is unqualifiedly positive, don't ask for the letter. If you haven't seen a particular teacher for some time, write a brief note asking for the letter and include copies of your best work from the class (preferably the paper with the big "A" on top). Close the note by telling the teacher that you will call next week. That will provide time for the teacher to think about what can be said on your behalf. Remember, almost everyone who teaches in paralegal programs also works professionally in the business. Their schedules are busy. Tread lightly.

2. Former employers, especially if they are in a related field or if you performed job functions that translate into paralegal skills. Think creatively here. I was a school district secretary before I became a paralegal. When I graduated from my paralegal school the superintendent of the district wrote a strong letter for me, pointing out the experience and skill I had interfacing with parents ("clients"), the fact that I was the first point of contact in most emergency situations (and that I responded appropriately and with a cool head), and finally, that I was used to tracking a large volume of active matters for which the district might have had real exposure had I not handled them well. She communicated her trust in my professional judgment and I'm sure her letter helped me get my first interview—which led to a dynamite job!

3. Other attorneys and senior paralegals where you interned. Do not forget senior paralegals as sources of help in your job search. Very often these individuals can describe your skills and performance in concrete terms that make you sound less like a diaphanous being (letters from attorneys often describe you as a "true professional" or "reliable assistant," etc.) and more like someone who can get the job done ("Ms. Jones reviewed the depositions of twenty-eight experts in litigation relating to massive flooding and produced crucial summaries including charts indicating each expert's opinion on critical matters such as 'probable greatest water height' and 'probable peak water velocity'"). Many hiring attorneys and personnel managers know that a good paralegal is often in the best position to assess another paralegal's abilities.

Do not seek letters from your pastor, rabbi, priest, old high school or college teachers (unless the subject matter is extremely relevant), or from someone your parents have known since you were six but who has no experience of you as an adult professional. These character references only underline a lack of professional references.

What Letters of Recommendation Will Do for You

Letters of recommendation are a little like high school diplomas. Almost anyone can get them, and their absence is often noted more strongly than their presence. Hopefully yours will help you, but in any case you must have them available.

No matter how your potential employers view letters of recommendation, do not underestimate the powerful effect a sincere, objective letter will have on your own confidence level as you hit the interviewing trail. Very often we fail to tell those we work with just how highly we think of them. A letter of recommendation may articulate the author's true professional appreciation of your capabilities and may let you know that you are pursuing a career for which you are suited and in which you can reasonably expect to succeed.

Remember, each original letter goes in your special Letters of Recommendation file and multiple copies go in your binder.

THANK THE GOOD GUYS

In planning your job search you will speak to many people. You'll meet with them, take their time, and ask for their best advice. If they consent to be listed as references you're imposing even further. Now's the time to thank these people formally for these kindnesses and to let them know how their input has helped you. Invest in business thank-you notes or stationery. The note cards should be beige, ivory, or some other light, neutral color and should demonstrate your client-relationship skills—they should be professionally cordial.

The color (not too cold; no gray), the quality of the paper, and your best writing skills will communicate that you are aware of how to interact professionally. The ease with which your thank-you notes allow others to reach you will communicate your professional savvy. But simple sincerity is still the most important element. Mention at least one specific thing each person told you or did for you, and say thank you for that.

If your name, address, and telephone number are not embossed or printed on the notes, be sure to use printed labels that contain all that information. If you have an E-mail address (and you should), include it. This shows that you're part of today's computer world.

Every person who helps you get ready for your job search deserves recognition, and thank-you notes will help you provide it. Thank-you letters should go out shortly after you meet with the recipient. Don't wait until you get your job. Here's how such a note might look:

Jeffrey Stoner
147 West 5th St.
Browning, PA 15344
email: jstoner @nr.net.

August 17, 1998

Sharon Jamison
Placement Director
Paralegal Education Program
Hemington University
Browning, Pennsylvania 15476

Dear Sharon,

Our visit last week was a great help to me in designing my job search. I hadn't even thought of financial institutions as potential employers. I was pleased to find out First National is looking for two paralegals right now. I'm scheduled to interview with them next Tuesday.

Your department is really crucial to the Paralegal Education program at Hemington University. Thanks for helping me think through what I need to do to get the right job. I'll stay in touch.

Best regards,

Jeffrey Stoner

This letter will do the following things:

1. Express your honest thanks.

2. Let your placement officer know who you are interviewing with; if she has additional information about the bank she will probably call you.

3. Provide your paralegal education program's placement staff with documentation that their services are needed and appreciated by graduates. Academic institutions are constantly looking for ways to cut costs, which can mean cutting what administrators think of as the "extras." Placement assistance is often considered a luxury. If you have access to placement personnel, you owe them a helping hand in their fight for survival.

CONTINUING EDUCATION

You may not think continuing education is part of a job search, but it is. Your knowledge of upcoming continuing education requirements will surface during your search and interviews, and when it does it will be an asset.

When you speak with your program director be sure to find out about what your program offers. The institution may provide CLE classes, and the program director should know about the local bar's programs as well. If you have not yet investigated the local paralegal association, do so now. The paralegals there will know everything that's going on locally with continuing education and they may also have a job bank or other job referral service you can use. Take a look at what NALA and NFPA have to offer (see the Appendix for their Web sites). Check out *Legal Assistant Today* magazine for continuing education opportunities, as well as the newsletter for your local paralegal association and your state organization.

Everything you pick up from any of these sources should go in your three-ring binder. Not in your desk, on the floor by your bed, or on the shelf beside the cookbooks, but in your binder. By now you'll need dividers, and continuing education should have a tab of its own. In fact this is such an important topic that it has a chapter of its own in this book. You should be thinking about it as soon as you have your certificate.

COMPUTER SKILLS

As you leave your formal paralegal education, assess your computer skills. I did a survey of law firms and placement firms in 1997 in order to report to a conference of paralegal educators about what skills employers sought in entry-level paralegals. I found that when it came to new hires, computer skills were number one on the wish list.

Today's computer skills go far beyond keyboard skills. You should feel comfortable with a variety of computer programs so that whatever programs are in place at your future employer's offices, you can learn them quickly and without panic. Most firms use timekeeping programs that have eliminated handwritten or dictated time sheets. Everyone has document management software of one sort or another and spreadsheet programs are commonplace. E-mail is an established way of communicating, both in-house and with clients, and the Internet has found a permanent place in the practice of law. You need to be familiar with all of these.

If you have an area of specialty already, you are probably aware of the software programs most often used in your area. Many legal departments, for example, now use software like Presentations to produce slide shows for client demonstrations or for use in the courtroom. These programs are not hard to use. Don't be intimidated by them. But if you did not have a lot of computer work during your educational process and if you are not otherwise familiar with cyberlife, get help immediately. Put down this book and check out the local colleges and libraries for computer education. Sign up for classes. It is absolutely necessary that you get up to speed with computers before you hit the interview circuit.

GIVING BACK

Even after you've reviewed your course work, your GPA, the assistance you can get from your institution as you leave, your internship, and other letters of recommendation, you are not quite ready to leave school behind. Before we move on to your actual job hunt, we need to talk about what you'll be giving back to your educational institution.

Not too long ago you knew "maybe a little something" about the legal assistant profession. You were interested enough to find out more and eventually to enroll in an educational program that has prepared you to start a whole new career. It's important to think about what you can do for the educational programs in the paralegal world, because you can help to lift the profession to an even higher level of professionalism.

Ask your program director if there are any ways alums can help with your program. Can you speak at information meetings to people who are considering enrolling? Once you are in the workplace, should you stay in touch so that you can inform the director about potential internships for students coming after you? When you have been on the job for six months can you return to the internship class and give a short talk on "What I learned in the first six months of professional paralegal work"?

You never know, the day may come when you'll be teaching in a paralegal education program. Stay in touch and be ready to help. We all stand on the shoulders of those who went before us—and we need you.

3 TIME TO GET THE JOB

There are two big job search truths:

1. You are totally in charge of your job search.
2. Everything you do related to getting a job is important.

You never know where a lead will come from, where an impression will count, where a mistake will cost you the golden ring. Think of every encounter as a "walking interview." Whoever you're talking to—a mentor, a program director, a placement officer, an internship attorney, a professional placement service employee, or an interviewing attorney—is assessing you as a potential legal professional. Their willingness to help you and their genuine enthusiasm or lack of it will result in large part from what kind of impression you make and from how good a time they have talking with you. This doesn't mean you have to make them laugh (although a little laughter is usually a good thing), but it does mean you have to persuade them that you're worth their time and that you've done your homework.

Doing your homework means coming to every meeting or interview prepared. This lets others know you truly appreciate the demands you are making on their professional or personal time. Remember, someone who recommends you puts his or her own reputation on the line. You must convince those you meet that if they recommend you, they will not be sorry later. Always be as prepared for your meeting with a potential referral source as you would be for a final job interview.

Your binder will help you to be prepared. You need to be organized. If someone asks about your grades in paralegal school or what courses you took, you should be able to locate your transcript in fifteen seconds without a lot of shuffling around. You should have several copies of all these documents in your binder so that you can offer one to the person you are talking to. Imagine how much easier it is for teachers to write letters on your behalf if your transcript is in their hands. Also, someone who can see quickly that you took and did well in three family law classes may be prompted to think of you when attorney so-and-so needs a family law paralegal.

If you're meeting with someone to get help with your resume, you should have several draft versions with you to demonstrate that you have already thought about resume formats. You are not there like a baby bird with its mouth open, waiting to be fed; you've researched resumes like a grown-up and thought about your options. You've read the books. You've asked to see samples from professionals you admire. You may have questions, but your questions are based on serious attempts to analyze what resume best communicates your abilities.

RESUMES

I'm not going to give you five sample resumes to choose from. Career centers, your educational institutional, or your local library can provide those and there are sixteen hundred books available with samples of the latest resume layouts. I will tell you that, while the resume rules about spelling errors (you can't have any) and nice paper still apply, the rest is largely up for grabs.

Some folks say, "Limit your resume to one page." Others say it's better to have two pages and communicate some solid, detailed information about your qualifications. Some say that including your references is unprofessional, and others claim that the inclusion of names and phone numbers will give you the best chance at the job. Some say computer resumes will show you are cyber-savvy. Others think a good-looking, non-folded hard copy resume that will sit on an attorney's desk crying out for attention is your best way to go. You're going to have to think about which is best for you. Here are some of my own biases.

Paper versus Cyber Resumes

During the many years I've worked in law firms I have noticed that hard copies of resumes that look good and can stand abuse (being shoved into in-boxes or marked up by several people) have the best chance of being acted on. They also have the best chance of being saved and accessed when future openings occur. Paper on desks gets looked at more than once and usually by more than one person. I wish I had a nickel for every time I've walked into an attorney's office who then picked up a resume that I'd seen lying about for a few days and tossed it to me with, "What do you think of this—think we should interview him?" My bias is toward the hard copy of a resume on good paper.

One Page versus Multiple Pages

Use the number of pages it takes to communicate what you can do. This does not mean you are not obligated to be concise. Your resume should demonstrate your ability to communicate information in a clear and economical fashion. Even so, you do not want to omit helpful information in order to meet a page limit.

I have two resumes: One is a one-paragraph version that summarizes my experience for publication and conference purposes. The other is a two-page form that lists my education and experience, my professional associations, activities and offices, all my publications, and special information that is customized in response to whatever situation prompted the resume production.

The two-page version breaks the one-page rule, but it's impressive because it details quite a lot of paralegal expertise, professional involvement, and extra-office professional activity. I include detailed information including volunteer work I've done both in the legal field and in the community. This resume communicates a lot. Someone who has done everything that's on it not only has a certain level of professional expertise, she's also learned how to make commitments, work hard, and get things done in the real world. If I have to go looking for a job I will use it without hesitation. My bias is toward a resume that reflects your skills and your accomplishments, whatever the length.

Style: Straightforward English or "Resume-eze"

There's a resume style in which professional goals, personal character traits, and general work habits take center stage. This has resulted in a tsunami of resumes that begin, "Seeking position that utilizes..." and, "Detail oriented self-starter with good communication skills who successfully masters new job tasks quickly." These claims are not persuasive because the resume itself does not demonstrate an eye for detail, communication skills, or mastery of anything even vaguely related to "new" or "job task." It demonstrates copying out of a resume book. Don't do it.

Read the resume books, but then personalize and improve on their samples. Find ways in the cataloguing of your qualifications to demonstrate that you can deal with detail (e.g., "Prepared individual forms 731 for 53 attorneys and public law clients to ensure compliance with Fair Political Practices Act"), that you can actually communicate information in your own words, and that you know something about current activity in your area of law (e.g., "Drafted detailed in-house memo to attorneys and client memo regarding implications of 1998 changes to federal drug testing requirements").

My bias: Talk substantively and don't use canned language.

How Much Honesty?

Honesty is the very best policy. Many times when people ask me for help on their resumes they are really asking, "How can I make myself look better than I am?" I tell them that most probably they can't, and even if they succeeded in fooling the interviewer, they'd still be stuck with living a lie from their first day on the job.

The people who will be reading your resume and interviewing you are smart. They are lawyers. They are trained to spot and destroy inflated claims. I don't mean that you can't use language that puts your accomplishments in the best light. You can and you should. But don't start your career off on the wrong foot by claiming to be someone you are not. Nobody likes being lied to. My bias is for telling the truth.

Hot Tip: Here is a practical tip: Never use less than 12-point type for resumes. I recommend 13 or 14 point because many of the people who look at your resume will be forty or older. Many of us who are over forty are getting farsighted, which means bigger type is much easier to read. Never use 10-point type or force information into odd layouts in order to keep to one page. Print your resume in several type sizes and get opinions from professionals you know in the forty-plus age bracket.

Remember, This Is Just the Beginning

Resume building is a lifelong process. While it's important that the document you are producing look professional and well-organized, there are many formats that will work. What's at least as important as format is that the information is substantive and honest and reflects your active involvement in the legal profession and the world.

If you are fresh out of school, and especially if you are young, you will have fewer items to list. So be it. You're an entry-level person and you're not trying to pass yourself off as an old-timer. No one will expect you to be past president of the local paralegal association if you are that new. Read Andrea Wagner's resume advice in *How to Land Your First Paralegal Job* and use what she has to tell you.

If you've been around awhile, in the legal field or in another field, build that information into your resume in whatever format will communicate your life and experience best. Perhaps you can include a brief synopsis of a case you worked on or a system you set up in another office. Maybe you have marketing or educational skills that you learned outside the law office. Perhaps you volunteered in the local library; knowledge of libraries is prized in a law office.

Whatever they are, the skills that you have developed and the person you actually are should be reflected in real terms in your resume. If you have tutored youngsters at a local school, include that at the bottom of your resume. (They'll think, "This person can work in difficult and sometimes frustrating situations.") If you have a serious interest in horticulture, find a graceful way to include that too. (They'll think, "Maybe this person has an interest in science.") You never know when something like that may serendipitously help you in a more direct way, like when you find out you're being interviewed by an avid gardener.

Doing More Solves Resume Problems

Here is my final bias. Many people have had me review their resumes and asked how they could make them better. I often tell them not to write more, but to do more. Join your local paralegal association, attend continuing education classes, volunteer at a legal clinic, research an area of law and teach a seminar or write an article on it. The best way to have an impressive resume is to be an impressive professional. Start now. Keep track of your activities and accomplishments. If your resume looks a little anemic today, that problem will eventually solve itself.

THE RESUME(S) YOU WILL USE IN THIS JOB SEARCH

Now you have a plan. You're going to review your skills and accomplishments and communicate them well and honestly. Once you have a resume you feel good about using in this job search (and you may have several), have it proofread by no fewer than three competent, trustworthy people. You cannot afford a single error on this document. Then make a master for your resume file and put at least five clean, perfect copies in your binder. (Do not punch these; house them in a plastic page saver.) Even though you have a master resume, remember that you will want and need to customize it for some interviews, slanting it toward a firm's specialty by highlighting your experience and knowledge in that area.

Hot Tip: Keep your resume close at hand on a floppy disk for quick customizations. You can pop into photocopying shops these days that have computers available so you can make changes quickly when you're away from your home base.

GETTING LEADS

You are in charge of getting job leads. Your program director, placement officer, personnel agency, best friend, spouse, or mother may all help, but the buck stops with you. It's your career.

Fortunately job leads turn up all over, and in the strangest places. Here's how you can find some.

The Informational Interview

This is a great job searching tool. An informational interview is one in which you interview an attorney or someone else in order to find out what his or her company or practice area is all about. You'll get some terrific insights into different working situations and you'll have an opportunity to impress the interviewee with your interest and enthusiasm, your preparation and interviewing skills, and your background as a legal assistant.

If you want to work in a law office you will want to interview lawyers. If you would be interested in working for in-house counsel for a company, you may want to interview someone other than the attorney in charge in order to get some insight into the company's life and goals. Then by the time you get to talk to the legal staff your investigative skills and initiative will jump out at them.

Choose some offices that you think might be interesting and write to them to ask if you can set up an informational interview. This can be fun. Remember, your job search aside, the world is an interesting place. Your letter might look like this:

Julie French
183 Madison Avenue
Washington, Illinois 33948
e-mail jfrench@nr.com

August 2, 1998

James Brown
Brown, Jones & Morrison LLP
333 South Grand Ave.
Washington, Illinois 33467

Dear Mr. Brown:

I am a paralegal student at SSU who will graduate this June. Last semester I took Joyce Bridges' class on school law. Because Brown, Jones & Morrison has been so actively involved in school district representation in the past thirty years, your firm, and you in particular, came up often in Ms. Bridges' examples.

I'd like to take twenty minutes of your time to talk with you about your experience in school district representation. I know you were a leader in the advising of school districts when Proposition 187 passed a few years ago. I'd like to hear about that and ask some other questions about this area of law. Ms. Bridges' class piqued my interest.

If you have no time during the workday, perhaps I could buy you lunch somewhere near your office. I'll give you a call next week to see if we can set something up.

Sincerely,

Julie French

This letter will do four things for you:

1. It will let Mr. Brown know that his fame has spread to the point that he is cited as an example in local legal education courses.
2. It will let him know you are detail oriented, curious, and well-informed and that you know how to gracefully take the initiative.
3. It will get you what will amount to a first interview without even showing the firm's personnel manager your resume or waiting for an opening.
4. It will give you a chance to find out something really interesting from someone who actually knows what he's talking about.

It's profitable to let your mind run with this idea. Who else uses lawyers in your community? They will most likely need paralegals. Banks, title companies, computer, biomedical, and environmental consultants and research companies, newspapers and publishers, educational institutions, and securities brokers all use paralegals.

There are even more possibilities that you may not have considered. The Episcopal Church (and others), the Humane Society, almost all environmental advocacy organizations, the armed forces, movie companies, restaurant chains, major league baseball teams, local farming cooperatives, labor unions, the Boy Scouts of America, the FBI, soccer leagues, and book stores all use attorneys and paralegals. Just today I heard about a paralegal who was hired by the new Getty Museum in Los Angeles. Be creative.

Try going through your charitable deduction receipts. Are you interested in the March of Dimes research? Call the local office to see who does their legal work. Can you run in a marathon? Someone writes the waivers you sign for every race. How about National Public Radio? Are you interested in horses? Equine law is its own specialty. Using your own interests to gather names for informational interviews is often the most profitable thing you can do. If you are interested in an organization it will show, and they will be more likely to be interested in you. Have fun. Spend an afternoon with a fellow student and generate a long list. Then invest in some stamps and turn on your computer. Be sure to include a self-addressed, stamped envelope (SASE) with each inquiry in case recipients want to reply to you via the mail.

Volunteer Work

It may seem strange to talk about volunteering when you are busy trying to find paying work, but I recommend it. Volunteering *is* working and most lawyers would rather hire someone who is working or has experience than someone fresh out of school who has not seen the inside of a law office.

Talk to your local legal clinic to find out where and how you might volunteer. Elder law is a new specialty in which there are many opportunities to gain experience. Your city may have a commission or a department that helps coordinate and administrate low-income housing. This would be a great place to get experience while you gain exposure to the city attorney's office and local politicians. More than one volunteer has landed a position that was created as a result of the demonstrated usefulness of the paralegal volunteer.

Volunteering still allows you plenty of time to read want ads, contact agencies, and pursue placement office leads. Each new person you meet in your role as a paralegal increases your chances for finding the right paralegal spot for you. Give yourself away and see what happens.

Network, Network, Network

Everybody talks a good game, but few people really network effectively. Networking is not about giving your name and phone number to speakers or legal professionals you meet. That can be a good idea, but you should also tell everyone you meet that you are trained for and looking for a paralegal position. You want to convince them that you're excited about your future in the field. How can you do that?

First of all, it's a terrific field and you should be excited about it. Who would have guessed twenty years ago that today's paralegals would be so actively involved in serious practices, sharing responsibility for work product and client contact, and enjoying real collegiality with the lawyers for whom they work? No one could have predicted the substantial salaries and bonuses earned by many paralegals today. If you are genuinely pleased that you are launching a new career, it will show. Go ahead, look a little pleased.

Second, remember that job leads come from the darnedest places. Of course you will be responding to ads in the paper, on the Net, and in your local legal newsletters, but you may find out that your dream job lead comes from your mother's tennis partner, your dentist, the person who cuts your hair, your son's clarinet teacher, the vet, your stockbroker, your choir director, or your best friend's cousin's fiancé's uncle. (Yes, there are graceful ways to bring up a job search at a wedding reception.) This means that your job may appear on the horizon any day, wherever you are—and that's exciting.

Of course you'll stay in touch with your instructors and let them know you are actively looking for work. You'll also join and become active in the local paralegal association. But don't forget other civic organizations. Investigate local chamber of commerce meetings, where you don't even have to be subtle about your networking. People will hand you their cards as you hand out yours, and it's expected that if you can help each other you will. If you are involved in other community activities, anything from coaching soccer to singing in a choir, don't forget to tell the people you share these activities with that you are ready to go to work as a paralegal.

Fitness activities also offer an opportunity to network. Do you run, or play tennis or golf or soccer or racquetball? Sports buddies are often good sources of job leads. In some towns there are YMCAs or local gyms where the legal crowd lifts weights or runs before work or at lunchtime. If you can do those things (and they are great things to do if you work in the legal field), set your alarm and meet some of the local legal community in your running shorts. Volunteer to help run a race or a tournament. If you get involved from day one you may snag the job of working with the lawyers who give advice about waivers and complying with local ordinances and so forth. It's good work on your part and another entree into the legal world.

RESPONDING TO ADS

In the midst of all this networking you will be responding to ads in the general and legal papers in your area. It's surprising how many job seekers underestimate the value of watching the papers. Newspaper ads are still the first choice for most employers seeking job applicants. Respond as quickly and intelligently as possible. Always read the ads carefully for what the employer expects by way of response. If the ad says "No calls," don't call. If an ad looks like a good opportunity and you want yours to be the first response they get, fax your resume with a brief cover letter stating that a hard copy will follow. Be smart and use initiative. You may even want to dress up, hop in the car, and deliver the resume yourself. You will get interviews.

INTERVIEWING

Interviews make us all a little nervous. That's not all bad—you want to be alert. Study these techniques to help you keep a cool head. They work.

Remember that interviewing really is a two-way street. While it's natural to be most concerned with whether you will make a good impression and get the offer, it's just as important to assess the opportunity realistically. Is this really a good career choice for you?

There are a number of excellent books on job search techniques that address interviewing. Part of your job as an interviewee is to read and assess what these books have to say. Don't follow every bit of advice like a little lamb. Analyze different approaches and pieces of advice and choose what suits you and your situation. Customize your interviewing style the same way you customize your job search. When you feel that you have developed some ideas about how you can interview successfully, do the brave thing and get someone to practice with you. It can be hard to make yourself do this because it's awkward and a little embarrassing. No one will make you do it. However, it's still your best bet. It will increase your confidence level enormously and that will show when you walk through the door.

The following article first appeared in *Legal Assistant Today* (November/December 1996, vol. 14, no 2). I wrote it after I'd served on a hiring committee for a city that was hiring its first two paralegals. I hope it will help you see the interviewing process from another angle—the employer's. Understanding that perspective will help you remain poised and optimistic when you go to that big interview.

Interviewing—Five Tips to Help You Rise to the Top

Recently I sat on an interviewing panel for an entity that was hiring to fill its first two paralegal spots. In eight hours we interviewed twelve candidates. I'm sure it was a trying day for them, but it was also a grueling day for us. Sitting on the other side of the desk, I learned some things every interviewing paralegal should think about before the big event. Arranging your interview preparation around these five "must do's" will increase your chances of coming out on top.

1. Research, Research, Research

In a good interview you'll be asked, "What do you know about our firm?" Nothing gets you off to a worse start than to answer, "Nothing, really." This translates into, "I saw the ad, I need the money, and that's how involved I am."

Well before the date of your interview, stop by the reception area of the firm. Pick up any firm literature available there and read it. Notice what's on the table. How does this firm represent itself to its clients? Read the *Martindale-Hubbell* entry on the firm.

Check with attorneys and paralegals you know to see if you can find out about prominent clients of the firm. Then you can say, "I know your firm is over a hundred years old and that you offer a wide range of services, but are especially well-known for your work in public entity representation," or "I know you and so-and-so formed the firm five years ago when you decided to leave such-and-such firm to specialize in bankruptcy." You may add, "I also know you are well-respected in the local legal community. So-and-so has told me about your work in the XYZ matter. That's exactly the kind of firm I want to work for. I have set high standards for myself."

2. Find Your Niche

Before the interview, imagine how you could fit into the firm's team and communicate that. If you have a good idea of your own skills and have researched the firm, you should be able to visualize a contribution you could make to their efforts. (For example, in the case of the development of the first two paralegal positions for a large department, we were looking for someone who wanted to be in on the ground floor and was interested in helping to structure the paralegal role in the office.)

If you find you do not know enough about the job to do this before the interview, redouble your research efforts. (For example, can you call someone in the office to talk about the opening?) If you have to go in without enough information, be sure to listen carefully for clues from the interviewer. You may be able to come up with something that illustrates the unique contribution you could make to the team during the interview. This exercise will also help you avoid interviewing for jobs you are clearly not qualified to undertake. (Such interviews not only are embarrassing, but will undermine your credibility in your legal community and damage your own confidence level.)

3. Believe You Are the One

However difficult an interviewing experience may seem to you, the people sitting on the other side of the desk are not having fun either. The interviewers are busy people in need of good help in their offices. They would love to have the perfect paralegal walk through the door. Be prepared to help them know you are just that.

- Make eye contact with every person in the room.
- Speak slowly and take time to compose answers that actually respond to the questions they ask.
- Bring writing samples and references that are brief and nicely packaged to offer at the end of the interview.
- Have someone else proofread everything you prepare connected with the interviewing process (applications, resumes, correspondence, writing samples, etc.).
- Check your appearance right before the interview.
- Smile. You're talking to people who want you to succeed.

4. Don't Say You're a "People Person"

This phrase rolls off the tongues of interviewees more often than you might think. If you are personable and reasonably comfortable answering and asking questions, the interviewers will figure out that you can get along with others of your species well. The "I'm a people person" phrase is most often given in response to the arguably unfair demand to "Tell us why you're the best person for this job." Announcing that you're a "people person" sounds too much like saying, "I have no special technical or legal skills or experience to offer you."

Not having met all the other interviewees, you may not be a position to explain why you're the best person for the job. But you can surely explain why you'd be a great addition to the staff. Be prepared with a list of specific accomplishments from your days with former employers. (For example, "I was instrumental in the development of an in-house database for the bankruptcy department that made research done by clerks and associates immediately available to all the associates and partners," or "I organized an in-house lunchtime educational series that updated all the public law paralegals and attorneys on recent legislation affecting their clients.")

Let the interviewers know you are enthused about the opportunity their position offers. If you've researched the interviewing entity and paid attention to the panel's questions, you'll be able to find a way to express enthusiasm for the job. ("I was first in my Legal Research class and can't wait to get in there and research motions," or "I've been looking for a chance to work with a number of different attorneys.") If you can't think of one thing to say along these lines, this is probably not the job for you.

5. Interviews Go Both Ways

Although the interviewer is initially in charge, you'll most likely be invited to ask questions at some point. (If you're not, take that into account before you sign on.) Be ready with intelligent queries that show you've given the job some thought. In the situation I was recently involved in, where the goal was to hire two paralegals for a large department, it would have been fair and interesting if an applicant had asked, "Do you have long-range plans to expand the paralegal staff?" or, "How did your department become interested in adding paralegals to the team?"

The initial interview is not the time to ask about medical coverage, vacation policies, or parking allowances. These questions must wait until you have received an offer of employment. However, it is fair to ask whether the firm offers opportunities for career growth and what the policy is on continuing education for paralegals. The fact that you are interested in these matters tells your future employer something important about you as a professional. Answers to these questions will also help you answer that all-important question you should always keep in mind: When they offer you the job, should you take it?

MORE ABOUT INTERVIEWING

I've spoken with many lawyers and legal headhunters about what legal employers are really looking for in their hires. Their responses are remarkably similar. Most say they look for maturity. They are not talking about age; they want candidates who can remain level headed and calm in difficult circumstances and who have their personal lives sufficiently squared away to be able to come to work each morning ready to make a real contribution. They want employees who can stand a few bad days now and then, who can roll with some punches, and who can get along with a broad range of personalities. They want people who pride themselves on doing top-quality work, meeting deadlines, and seeing a job through. While they expect certain educational credentials, character traits are the first things employers mention they want to see in job candidates. They need people who are flexible, detail oriented, disciplined, able to work under pressure, and have a sense of humor. For entry-level candidates they all say it's critical to communicate an enthusiasm for learning.

In big cities, legal employers usually say they look for candidates with a four-year degree. While the debate rages within the paralegal community about how necessary such a degree is and what it prepares you to do, if you are looking for a job in Denver, Houston, Chicago, New York, Minneapolis, San Francisco, or Los Angeles you had better be prepared to address this job requirement. Employers in smaller locales and outlying areas are more flexible, although almost everyone I've spoken with thinks a two-year degree is a minimum requirement.

A certificate from an ABA-accredited paralegal education program is mentioned too. However, the employers who mention it often do not know what "ABA approved" means. When the ABA approval process and designation are explained, many change this requirement to a "substantial" paralegal education program. Programs associated with universities are viewed favorably, as are some of the long-established programs in certain cities. Almost all the hiring lawyers were confused about the differences between "certified paralegals" and "certificated paralegals." Upon clarification most were not very interested in whether or not an applicant had passed the CLA exam. This may change as the CLA designation becomes better known.

Employers love experience, and even if an applicant is fresh out of school they like to see internship experience. References from internship supervisors were valued. Job experience in related fields was also considered important. In addition, employers loved seeing proof of skills, especially math and computer skills. Course work in accounting and in the sciences was viewed favorably and an A+ in a logic course would probably impress these employers. They also want people who can run spreadsheets, create exhibits on a computer, and otherwise demonstrate computer savvy. Speaking two or more languages was also viewed as a plus.

Think about all these things before you interview. Don't let them scare you too much. If you do not have a four-year degree you may impress a potential employer if you say, "I'm looking for a solid spot where I can train and grow. I intend to get a four-year degree along the way and any support I can get from an employer toward this goal is important to me too." You may find out the firm thinks you are good enough and forward-looking enough to hire you and pay your tuition or give you time off to attend classes.

THE OFFER

Believe it or not, it will happen. Getting a job may involve some serendipity, but it's not magic. You've done your homework and interviewed well. One of your "possible employers" will make you an offer. When the call comes inviting you aboard it's almost always a good idea to ask for 48 hours to consider it. This is normal in the business world. A job offer is a serious matter and deserves evaluation. Taking a day or two to think about it will not jeopardize your position with a good law firm or company.

Once you have the offer you can ask a series of questions that were not appropriate before, such as what benefits come with the job and which attorney(s) you would be working with. It's surprising, but many lawyers will call candidates with a salary figure and neglect to discuss medical benefits, bonus programs, educational support, and other benefits. Because these are all part of the total compensation, you will want details to make an informed assessment. If you work in a big city, paid parking can make a real difference in the money you take home at the end of the month. Think it all through.

If you think the firm is a good one and you want the job, you have to analyze your bargaining power. If you're dealing with the government in any of its guises there will be limits to the flexibility available. The job will have been authorized and advertised as a certain level position with a certain pay rating and that's that. The person making the hiring decision will have no discretion to offer money in excess of what was authorized before the job was advertised.

Private employers have more leeway, but they too may be under constraints that will force them to pass on negotiating. For example, if they have a paralegal program with career steps and a hiring committee has authorized hiring an entry-level person at a set salary, the personnel department may pass on someone who isn't willing to go along with the firm's program. Finally, if you're right out of school, you may not have much room to negotiate. Entry-level compensation is usually fairly uniform within a particular geographical area.

However, if you have special skills, you may be able to negotiate better compensation than is initially offered to you. If you have paralegal skills plus a background in journalism or nursing or statistical analysis or computers, you may well be more valuable to a given employer.

Read up on the art of negotiation and get ready before the call comes. Do some serious research into the market in your area. The number of law firms and paralegal schools in your area will affect the job pool you have to choose from, as well as the number of qualified applicants available to fill the spot. The local economy, the average partner's compensation in the particular firm you're interested in, and the amounts like-sized firms are paying will also make a difference. If you intend to negotiate, don't go in blind.

It's difficult for most of us to get salary information on our own. *Legal Assistant Today* magazine and major paralegal associations publish annual salary surveys. Read them. Remember to adjust for variables like size of firm (Generally the larger the firm, the more they will pay.); geographic location (Employers on both coasts pay more; those in small towns or sparsely populated areas pay less.); and cost of working there (dress codes that cost money, long commute, etc.). Do the best you can to get information and analyze it, but don't feel you've failed if you can't nail all the information down. Talking about money is remarkably taboo in our society and even if you have survey results, you don't know who did and didn't respond to the survey. The best source of hard information about who is paying what may well be a professional placement office.

When you assess compensation remember that in-house education and support for outside continuing education are both forms of compensation. (You will have to continue your education and someone will have to pay for it.) Paid vacations and holidays, 401K plans, and health insurance are also forms of compensation.

Hot Tip: Don't undervalue interesting work, a congenial work environment, and other non-monetary factors. You can't go out to lunch with your paycheck.

A comfortable office, a congenial crew, secretarial support, pleasant lunch quarters, free parking, and the chance for career growth may not be compensation per se, but they can compensate for quite a bit over the long haul. Don't undervalue them. Flexible hours, nonexempt or exempt status, types of duties, expected billing hours, health plan options, and retirement savings plans mean different things to all of us when we assess a job opportunity. Think it through and then think it through again. A job history of short-term employment on your resume is still something to worry about so you want to accept a job that will be a good fit for you and for the firm.

If you are at all unclear or unsure about whether to take a job or not, talk to someone whose opinion you really respect. If you know someone who is well-informed about firms in the local legal community, that's great. But don't discount the advice of a mature, experienced friend. A story comes to mind of a young college professor who was offered a prestigious job at a university a great distance from the town in which his wife was professionally well-established. When he sought advice about whether to take it he was smart enough to go to a wise friend who said, "Remember, this is not just a career decision. It's a life decision." I don't know whether he took the job or not, but he had the right perspective. When you think about whether or not to take the job, think about all the aspects you possibly can.

SMALL, MEDIUM, LARGE—FINDING THE RIGHT FIT

A fair amount of the generalizing that's done about law firms is based on their size. To some extent this is helpful, but remember that attempts at generalization all break down at some point. I have worked in a small to medium firm (8 attorneys and 6 paralegals) and a large firm (100 plus attorneys and 30 paralegals). I've read the data on the others and report here some generally accepted perceptions. Always bear in mind, though, that law firms are made up of individuals. A small firm headed up by a terrific lawyer will be quite different from one headed up by a jerk. No one really knows what a medium-sized firm is in terms of numbers, but here too personalities play a large part. When I went from a small to a larger firm, many lawyers and paralegals I knew predicted that I would not like the "big-firm" mentality. However, when I got to my "big firm" I found that it functioned much like a collection of smaller practice groups, so I had the benefits of big-firm resources and small-firm collegiality. All this is to say that when you assess a firm based on size-related factors you should proceed with caution.

Small Firms

Small firms are generally cited as being more flexible than large firms. The expectation is that, as a paralegal, you will not be held to a tightly defined role and may be allowed to extend your duties and domain to match your skills and capabilities over time. This is sometimes true. Be aware that the flexibility of a small firm may require you to take on receptionist duties, word processing, bookkeeping, and other roles not traditionally expected of paralegals at mid- to large-size firms. The perks at small firms are often negligible, but if you choose the right firm and the right attorney you may find you can function as a real "partner" in the management of cases.

Mid-Size Firms

Let's say this is a firm with twenty attorneys and twelve paralegals. (Every size and every attorney–paralegal ratio imaginable exists out there; there are even firms with two partners, no associates, and twenty paralegals.) This firm, if it is profitable, may be able to offer better pay or perks than a small firm. However, it's less likely than in a large firm that there will be a formal paralegal program or that a lot of thought will be given to how to keep "career paralegals." The lack of a formal program could result in lower pay rates, or it could result in greater flexibility in hours or job duties. It all depends on the firm!

Large Firms

Large firms start at about a hundred lawyers and go to many hundreds. These are the firms you read about a lot, the Gibson, Dunns and Pillsbury, Madisons. Most of the large firms pay more, have formal paralegal programs, have paralegal managers, provide secretarial support, etc. Most often cited on the downside are the more strictly limited parameters in which paralegals must function and the impersonality of the workplace. Many of the larger firms are also located in downtown areas where the dress code is more formal, the parking more expensive, and the pace fast.

Please investigate the particular large, mid-size, or small firm you are interested in. It may function in ways that are entirely differently from what the folk wisdom reports. I've heard of one nationally famous, very high-billing attorney with a substantial firm that makes headlines. It should be very glamorous to work for him, but he pays his associates and paralegals bottom-of-the-market salaries. They are supposed to be so happy to be working with him that they should find the disparity between their contribution and their compensation negligible. Some might. Perhaps being able to cite their experience in this prestigious office is compensation enough. Perhaps working on high-profile cases means more to them than the take-home dollars involved. The point is that there's no one formula that works for all of us.

ACCEPT OR DECLINE GRACEFULLY

Once you have the offer and have checked it out as carefully as you can, you will have to make the irrevocable choice. If you decide not to take the job, be sure you are extremely courteous in your refusal. There are very few bridges you want to burn in the business world, and the legal world is still part of the business world.

If your answer is "yes," that's great. Make the call to let your future employer know, set up a starting date, and then read the next chapter.

FIRST DAY ON THE JOB

You're standing in front of the elevator, briefcase in hand. This is your moment of triumph. You got the job. They could have chosen someone else, but they didn't—they chose you. Now you're in front of the elevator doors waiting, and waiting, and waiting. You're trying to decide whether you would rather be here with these butterflies in your stomach, having your moment of triumph, or at the blood bank making a donation, or paying your taxes, or in a dentist's chair. The elevator is slow. Pretty soon you're thinking, "Blood bank."

The woman standing next to you is eating a muffin while she shuffles through some papers. She's relaxed. She knows what she's doing. She's probably been working here for years. There's a suave-looking man in a Brooks Brothers suit. He looks calm too, even bored. You're wound up tight as a top and ready to go, but the elevator still hasn't come. You think that, if everything works out, you'll get to wait for this elevator every day for years.

Then suddenly, here it is. Big silver doors open like magic and the elevator sweeps you up to the sixth floor where your professional future is waiting. You check your watch. It's only been two minutes since you entered the building. The time gremlins have been having some fun with you.

But let's backtrack. How did you get here? Let's go over all the things you'll be glad you thought about once you hit the fast track of "Monday on the new job."

THE NIGHT BEFORE THE BIG DAY

It's Sunday night and you've set your alarm. Then you've set another alarm and had someone really responsible—like your twelve-year-old—check them both. This will help you sleep; not a lot, but it will help. You've checked to see that there's gas in the car (or you have a bus schedule, or you've double-checked your car pool schedule). Your handbag, should you carry one, is stocked with cash, a hairbrush, a toothbrush and floss, makeup (if you're male you can opt to skip this), extra deodorant, the phone numbers of your children's caregiver and school, your significant other, your best friend, and your mother. The number of your favorite teacher from paralegal school may also be included.

You also have the note you wrote to yourself about where to report on your first day. You have your driver's license and Social Security card, checks, a credit card, coins as well as bills, a small tube of hand cream, tissues, a Band-Aid, hair spray, and a magic totem. Yes, a magic totem. I don't care what it is, but you have something small and unobtrusive that will help you stay cool on this big day; something that will remind you of who you really are, what you have accomplished, and what you are able to do. It can be a religious symbol or a shell from your favorite beach or a picture of your kids as babies or the fortune from a Chinese fortune cookie. Or it can be this:

YOU CAN DO THIS

You've laid out all your clothing for your first day, down to your underwear. You have chosen conservative clothes that not only look good but are comfortable. You've listened to the weather forecast and acted on it. You have your briefcase out even if it's empty—you might even put this book in there. Okay, now you can go to sleep.

Or at least you can go to bed. Don't worry if you don't sleep much before your first day. Adrenaline will carry you through. Before your second and third days you'll need to sleep. Tonight, lie down and give yourself total permission to be nervous for five minutes. Notice I said *nervous*, not panicked or hysterical. Those are not states of mind conducive to a happy first day. Do not think bad thoughts about yourself. Do not make a mental list of all the mistakes you have ever made. Do not review your paralegal textbooks. Read something by Agatha Christie or Dave Barry. Remember, you are largely in charge of this experience. You're trained. You're smart. You're enthused. And believe it or not, you're headed straight for success.

BACK TO THE ELEVATOR

The doors are opening on your floor. Since you have the note with you that tells you where you are to report, you will remember without looking that the personnel office is to the left of the elevator. Don't go there first. Go to the receptionist's desk and introduce yourself. Tell him or her that you're the new paralegal and that you're there for your first day. Smile, but don't try to get personal. Don't admit you're nervous. The receptionist knows that. Read the name plate on the desk and try remember it. Receptionists are very important people in many law firms. They are also generally nice and they are often underappreciated. They deserve your best manners.

Tell the receptionist that you know where personnel is, and that so-and-so told you to report there first. Ask whether you should wait in the lobby or go directly in. The receptionist is in charge of the lobby and traffic into the firm's offices. Follow his or her lead.

Hot Tip: Never underestimate the efficacy of faking a calm attitude when you have the jitters. Many times your mental state is directly affected by your persona. A smile, sensible breathing, and a calm walk will all work to make you feel poised and in control.

In the best of all possible worlds the personnel staff will remember that you're coming and will have your paperwork ready and a workplace set out for you. If the law firm's small and there is no personnel department, the person who hired you may remember this is the day you start work. However, don't worry or be offended if no one remembered you were coming. It doesn't mean they don't want you, it just means they're busy. They will be apologetic. You will be gracious. It'll mean a little more waiting around, but that's okay.

Sooner of later someone will hand you employee forms to fill out. (Now aren't you glad you remembered your Social Security card?) Take your time and read them all. If you're given benefit information, read that too. The options you choose now may impact your take-home check as well as your family's health care for a whole year. If the firm has several options for you, it's perfectly acceptable to ask if you can take the papers home to read in the evening and turn in the benefit forms the next morning.

If the firm is mid-size to large there will be an employee handbook. There may be some kind of orientation program. It will seem like a lot of information, but you will absorb at least the locations of the coffee room, the Xerox machines, and the bathrooms. Many firms assign someone to take new employees around and introduce them to nearly everyone. This practice is sometimes awkward but well-meant and unavoidable. Smile a lot. Try to put a few names with a few faces. Most people will ask you the same questions, where you're from and what you do. Try to smile as you provide the same answer over and over again. If there's a real chance to talk to anyone during this first round, ask some questions yourself. How long has Marsha been at the firm? Where did Tom go to law school? Does the woman with trophies on her bookshelf still show prize horses? This will be a nice change for everyone involved in the introductions and will help you remember some of the people you meet.

If you're joining a large firm you may be given a photo directory. These are great; keep yours and use it. Put it in your briefcase for the first few weeks so you have it at the office and can also peruse it at home. In the long run nothing makes anyone feel better in an office than being recognized as an individual human being. The more folks you can greet by name, the better start you'll be off to.

Law firms differ as much as individuals. No one can tell you exactly what to expect on your first day. But you should remember to keep your knees bent and your weight on your toes (speaking figuratively). That way you'll be poised to move in any direction. Here are three scenarios describing how Day One can go:

1. Evelyn was hired by a small firm, Watson, Frank and Jones, that specializes in defending insurance claims. It's lean and mean and the opportunity to learn a lot about litigation quickly was among the reasons Evelyn took the job. As it turns out, the day Evelyn starts work a longtime paralegal with the firm gives two weeks' notice. Evelyn is summarily informed that her assignment has been changed. The attorney with whom she thought she'd be working is not in as great a need for help as the attorney who just lost her right-hand paralegal. Evelyn is introduced to her erstwhile boss (small, friendly wave followed by a shoulder shrug indicating "What's a guy to do?") and then to her new actual boss. This attorney says hello quickly: "Welcome aboard, call me Karen, and see my paralegal Jan—she just gave notice. We've been preparing the Martin case for trial for months. It looks like it's really going to go. You'll have to learn the case in the next two weeks; Jan will show you what's what." Evelyn finds herself standing in the hall. She asks a nearby secretary where Jan works and follows a pointed finger down the hall to find Jan talking on the phone to her new employer in another state.

What's a paralegal to do? Evelyn waits in the hall until Jan hangs up, then introduces herself, takes a deep breath, and waits to see what will happen next. Jan takes Evelyn down the hall to the war room for the Martin case. There are twelve banker's boxes full of documents. Fortunately, Karen and Jan have a good set of memos detailing the progress of the lawsuit from day one. Jan gives Evelyn the file, sits her down at a desk, and tells her to dig in.

Evelyn opens the file and begins at the back. She reads for an hour, every memo. She takes notes. Some of the memos lead her to the correspondence clip where she reviews what's passed between the attorneys on the two sides of the suit. She also finds status letters to the client. She reads for another hour. She keeps taking notes. At 12:30 she stands up to stretch and sees Jan in the hallway. Jan says she's grabbing a sandwich from the corner deli and asks if Evelyn wants to come. Although she can see Jan is just being polite, that she isn't dying to have lunch with her, Evelyn smiles and says, "Yes, thanks." Over lunch she asks Jan about her move, her new job, and how she liked the firm and Karen. She asks what tips Jan has for her about surviving here and what she can do to thrive as well. Jan is feeling a little loose—she's moving on—so she gives Evelyn a character sketch of the partners, the other paralegals, and the secretaries. Evelyn takes mental notes.

Most likely Jan really can show Evelyn the ropes in the following two weeks. However, Evelyn may have to work to get information from someone who's thinking about her next job. She will depend heavily on reading files and client documents and she will ask questions, lots and lots of questions, of Jan and also of Karen. At some point Karen will realize from those questions that Evelyn is getting her mind around the case. She will be relieved and start to discuss things with Evelyn in more detail. Because Evelyn is interested, alert, and on the job, Karen will begin the shift from relying on Jan to relying on Evelyn. Two weeks after Jan is gone, Karen will no longer be worried about the Martin case. She'll know she can count on Evelyn. The whole thing will work out, but it does make for an exciting first day.

2.   Theresa shows up at Forrest and Forrest ready to work. She was a top graduate in her paralegal program. She's had quite a bit of work experience in real estate. She's a little nervous, but she thinks this job will be exciting and fun. F & F has 25 attorneys and 18 paralegals. The firm does a variety of work, plaintiff tort cases, estate planning, corporate work, and a little employment law. Theresa has not decided what area she wants to focus on. At her final interview Mr. Forrest told her she should seek assignments from the various departments to see what work interested her most.

On D-day the receptionist smiles at Theresa and says the office manager is having car trouble and will be a little late. She invites Theresa to sit down. Theresa does, trying to look as natural as she can flipping through the pages of *National Geographic*. Other F & F workers arrive. As each new face graces the lobby Theresa looks up hopefully, but Mr. Office Manager is nowhere to be seen. Theresa tries to concentrate on an article about the melting ice caps.

At 9:30 Roger, the office manager, bustles in. He sees Theresa, apologizes, and asks her to wait just a minute while he takes care of a couple of urgent matters. At 10:00 he's back and leads Theresa into the bowels of the law office where she spends half an hour filling out forms. Then Roger swings her by a few desks, saying "This is Jennifer Stone. Jenny, meet Theresa, our new hire. This is David Franklin. Dave, Theresa's the new paralegal... ." Finally Roger takes Theresa to a cubicle with a desk, a phone, a computer, and three clean yellow pads all laid out. "Why don't you get settled in," Roger says, "I'll check back later." And that's it.

What does Theresa do? She sits down, breathes deeply, and opens the desk drawer to find yellow self-stick notes, a stapler, six pens, and paper clips. Then she gets out her briefcase. A picture of her ten-year-old goes on the desk first, then the penholder she got at last year's Christmas party, and finally her favorite Chinese fortune, "Never wrestle with pigs. They enjoy it and you just get dirty." Theresa carefully tapes this saying to her telephone. Okay, now this is her desk.

Next Theresa reads the firm's employee manual. It doesn't tell her too much she didn't already know ("Employees are discouraged from taking care of personal business on company time"). Then she fires up her computer and is pleased to see good old WP 6.1 for Windows staring back at her. She notices the E-mail function. Just as she's thinking about sending a message announcing her availability for work, Jennifer Stone, another paralegal, stops by. "Hey, we're stepping out for lunch in a couple of minutes. Wanna come?"

Over lunch Theresa gets to know Jenny and two other paralegals. They fill her in on the various attorneys, the way assignments are distributed, who usually works with who, who's got something hot going on right then. Theresa asks about their home lives. It turns out she and Jennifer both have ten-year-olds. On the way back to the office Jenny suggests that Theresa stick with her for the next hour. Soon Ms. Stone has introduced Theresa to five of the firm's better attorneys, three of whom have some work for Theresa. By 2:30 she's back at her desk, which now has actual files on it, reading and taking notes. When Roger stops by at 3:00 to see how things are going she looks up, smiles, and says, "Just fine, Roger. I've got work from Steve Thornton, Mary Collins, and Greg Smith." "Excellent," Roger replies and he leaves, thinking, "That was easy—looks like a good hire." Theresa's on her way.

3.   Leroy wanted to try a big firm right off the bat. He put on his best business suit and interviewed downtown where he was hired by Smith and Thompson. S & T is a nationally known firm with a large personnel department and a paralegal director. On Leroy's first day he is asked to wait in the lobby with two other new paralegals. Later they are escorted to a personnel training room where they are met by Susan Morris, the paralegal director. Susan introduces them to each other and explains that they will spend the morning in S & T's orientation program. She dispenses forms, explains the health coverage options, the 401K plan, life insurance options, vacation time, firm holidays, and the like. When they have finished their form work, Susan plays a promotional video that gives the firm's long history, talks about the various departments, and features some of the firm's major players. When the lights come on Leroy is feeling like a rather small fish in a large pond. In a way he is right. It takes more time to make your presence known and appreciated in a big firm.

Susan then takes some time to discuss the firm's paralegal program. There are nine steps in the paralegal hierarchy and, of the three paralegals starting work this day, two are entry-level and one's a lateral hire beginning at step 4. Salaries are based on the steps in the program, so if you know what step someone's on, you know his or her salary. There's also a bonus program for paralegals tied to billing hours. Susan spends quite a bit of time explaining billing procedures and showing the new hires quarterly printouts that display every timekeeper's billing to date and what it's worth in dollars to the firm.

Susan also tells them about the firm's in-house paralegal education program, as well as the firm support for outside class work. She shows them the various forms they'll need for mileage reimbursement, to request attendance at a seminar, to have copying done, and to submit tapes to the word processing pool. Finally Susan takes them on a tour of the multi-floor law firm. Leroy sees 200 new faces that day but he's smart enough to concentrate on just a few—his fellow new hires, Susan, the major attorneys in his department, and his secretary, Kathleen. Kathleen's a senior secretary who currently works for a partner and an associate. Leroy isn't naive enough to think he'll get a lot of her time, but he's happy to have a connection with someone who really knows her way around the firm.

The lunch hour is spent grabbing a sandwich and fixing up the desk Leroy's been assigned. The afternoon features two hours with the MIS department where Leroy is introduced to the firm's computer policies and various software programs. Then it's back to Susan who gives each new employee a firm "look-book" to help them identify their new coworkers. She asks if they have any questions. Leroy and his colleagues look a bit bemused. They can articulate a few of their questions, but most will have to wait until they've really settled in. Susan mentions that the litigation department is having a lunch lecture the next day ("Everything you need to know about writs"), that the probate department is having one on Friday ("Probate in a shoebox—what to do with all those receipts!"), that Weight Watchers meets in the third-floor conference room on Wednesdays, that there is a required Malpractice Prevention seminar in three weeks that takes place on a Saturday morning. She tells them that jeans and other casual clothes are appropriate for that seminar. She also explains casual Friday and Leroy is surprised to hear that blue jeans are strictly taboo but that khaki or black denim are okay. Tennis shoes or running shoes are not okay, cowboy boots are okay—go figure. Leroy is not aware of it yet, but he is already becoming acculturated to Smith and Thompson. He knows that each department has a paralegal manager through whom assignments flow and that when he comes to work tomorrow he can expect that an assignment will be on his desk. He is comfortable with the firm's timekeeping software and he intends to attend the probate class on Friday. He thinks it will take a while before he really knows anyone here, but he knew coming into this job that it was the big show. He thinks there are real career possibilities at S & T and he intends to climb the ladder.

Each of these three "first days" is a good one. The paralegals involved each found a way to take that important first step on the path to being an integral part of a professional legal team. There are a million first day stories that lead to success. Once you have your feet on the ground—and believe it or not, before long you will—you'll remember at least one aspect of your first day that will make a funny dinner party story or an exciting cautionary tale.

Hot Tip: A good goal for your first day is to find one thing you can do that is genuinely useful. Find it and you will go a long way to cementing your own awareness of your ability to make a contribution to the firm. That knowledge will help you believe that you can become part of the team.

During the course of your first day (and even after that) questions will fly in and out of your busy brain. Do not try to get each one answered as it arises. Keep a small pad at hand to write them down on. By the end of the day the questions will fall into three groups: those that were answered as the day progressed, those you don't really need to know about after all, and those you will organize into a compact list to address with the right person. The second day on the job, take your recopied, neat list to the most likely candidate (the personnel manager, the paralegal in the next cubicle, the attorney who is giving you work). Stick your head into the appropriate office, say that you have a couple of questions, and ask when would be a good time to come back and chat. Most likely you can take care of your questions then and there.

Asking the right kinds of questions indicates an alert intellect and redounds to the benefit of the asker. Do remember to write down the answers. Lawyers don't like paralegals who have to ask the same question twice.

LUNCH WITH THE BOSS

A surprising number of attorneys still hold to the tradition of taking new associates and paralegals out for lunch on their first day, or at least during the first week they're with the firm. If you are invited to such a luncheon accept the invitation. Before you go think about what you will talk about. The purpose of this lunch is to get your working relationship off to a cordial start.

It's a good idea to ask brief, friendly questions about the attorney's family or about any other interests you may have heard he or she has. You should also share a little bit about yourself. Keep in mind that offering too much personal information at a first lunch is never a good idea. Your boss is not asking to be your personal friend. If you're having trouble with your teenagers, your marriage, or your mother do not share it. Do not explain that you are usually thin, but have been having trouble with your thyroid since the birth of your last child. Do not say anything negative about your previous employers or coworkers.

If you've been a good fact-gatherer about the firm you may be able to discuss a current matter that the firm is handling. If you're really good, you will have done a little research into the latest law in the area. A new paralegal who can discuss relevant law about a legal matter an attorney is handling will make an excellent first impression.

When the lunch check comes, watch for signals. Most attorneys will authoritatively pick up the check and pay. If this happens, accept the courtesy graciously, with a brief verbal thank you. If there are a number of people from the firm there and they all reach for their wallets, reach for yours as well. If someone stops you and says he or she is picking up your tab, again, accept graciously. Make a mental note that a small return kindness down the line is in order.

ENDING THE DAY

No matter how your day started, by four o'clock you'll be tired. After all, your nervous system has been on special alert since six a.m. If you're not involved in meetings, give yourself a break, sit back, and check out the view. Whether you've been assigned four walls of fabric-covered space dividers or a window office, it will still need to be personalized. It's your space; it's your professional home. If everything goes well, you'll spend a lot of time here. Take out a pen and paper and make a list of what you should bring in tomorrow. List everything from a box of tissues to a flower vase to the pencilholder your kid made or even your classwork binders from paralegal school. Make some notes on who you met and what you learned today, and anything that occurs to you that may be helpful for tomorrow. If you have not received business cards as part of your orientation, make a note to check on that. Chapter 6 contains a lot more hints about smart things to keep in your office. Now that you've taken the big job, be sure to check that chapter.

Don't worry if you feel a little confused. It's your first day, remember? Give yourself a break. In a week you will feel at home in the building, and in two weeks you'll feel at home with at least some of the folks. Being the new person is being the new person, and getting comfortable takes time. You can't skip Go if you want to collect your $200.

Congratulations! You have just completed your first day as a paralegal. No matter what else happens, it will never be the first day again. I hope life let's you take the time to celebrate in the evening but remember, sober to bed and early to rise is still the great way to go. Before you hit the sack, think of what you need for tomorrow—what you want to wear, things you've decided to bring to the office, maybe a quick shopping list for the lunch hour. Make sure you're comfortable with the arrangements you've made for your children or for taking care of other family obligations. You're going to need to be worry-free and ready to concentrate when you hit the office tomorrow. Now, go enjoy yourself and then we'll check out your first week.

5

TUESDAY

The thrill of Day One is gone. You've worn your best suit, smiled your best smile, and met a lot of people. Beginning Tuesday you are part of the firm, a bona fide employee. You are not, however, a part of the team—not yet. That will come in time as you develop strong working relationships in which others trust you and come to depend on you. This chapter tells you how to make your first week a successful step in the journey toward team membership.

ANTHROPOLOGY: AN OFFICE SURVIVAL SKILL

People often ask me if I think a college education is helpful in a paralegal career. I always answer yes. I majored in philosophy and the philosophical training I got—learning how to make an argument—has been invaluable. I know biology majors who slipped right into environmental law practices, analyzing data and fearlessly reading reports by experts that caused lesser beings to tremble. I know journalism majors who are trained to get information that's hot and who get evidence in lawsuits that many of us didn't know was out there. We have all benefited on the job from our college educations. But the ones I have always envied, the ones in terrific positions as new legal professionals, are the anthro majors. Yes, anthropology. Here's why:

Anthropologists study cultures unlike their own to try to decipher the goings-on. Who's really important? How are disputes resolved? What are the goals that motivate behavior? How are relationships maintained, enhanced, injured, and healed? Anthropologists have to learn to set aside their own preconceptions and observe, observe, observe. They pay close and intelligent attention until they have seen enough, heard enough, and generally soaked up enough information to get a picture, however hazy, of what's going on. That's what you'll be doing this week.

The law firm you have chosen already has a culture, a set of values and ways of doing things. This culture is not a paralegal school culture or a college culture, nor is it like a church or family or a bridge club or a sports team or a group of friends who simply enjoy each other's company. Very often law firm coworkers do not enjoy each other's company all that much. But they have common interests and goals that keep them working together. They also have some conflicting interests and goals, but we'll talk more about that later. Right now your future success and your job security depend on your ability to understand and work within the law firm's culture. You won't get it all deciphered in a week, but here's how you should start.

Step one is to figure out what your real job is. What did they really hire you to do? Why did they need to fill this paralegal position? Until you can answer this question accurately you cannot perform well professionally. This may sound incredibly obvious, but I've known paralegals who were fired at the end of their probationary period "out of the blue." They had no idea people did not think they were doing their jobs. One of the reasons they did not know this critical fact was they had not worked hard enough at figuring out what the job actually was.

Hot Tip: It actually *is* your job to figure out what your job is. This may not seem fair to you. You may think it's the firm's job or the attorney's job or the personnel manager's job to tell you what they want you to do. Welcome to Real World 101. It's your responsibility. You must get clear about what is needed and learn to fill that need well, consistently, and with a willing spirit. Knowledge of what is needed is the foundation of your current employment and your future opportunities.

How do you find out what your job is? The interview process should have given you some basic parameters. The firm needed help in litigation or with corporate work, or someone to help with the probate practice. But within that broad definition there's a more important need that will probably never be articulated. Does a particular lawyer need a detail-oriented paralegal to track discovery and read, analyze, and report on the opposing side's responses? Does the corporate group need someone who can form cordial professional relationships with company clients and manage the major rainmaker's calendar? Does the will vault need total reorganization? If you can identify a job like any of these you are much closer to knowing what your job is.

Remember, there's an existing need that prompted this firm to say, "Let's hire some help." You are that help. Find out how you can really help them.

When the Shoe Doesn't Fit

"But," you may sputter, "I don't want to manage a partner's rainmaking activities or reorganize wills." That may be true, but if that's the current need within the firm, if that's why they hired another paralegal, then that's what you must do if you want to succeed with the firm. In Chapter 12 we discuss how to change your job without changing firms. You can do that later, but for now learn what your job is and do it.

Step two involves asking questions. Anthropologists ask polite, well-thought-out, nonthreatening questions. You should do that too. When you get an assignment be sure you understand the direction in which the attorney is headed. There are the basics, like when the assignment is due, but it's also helpful to understand the context that made the assignment necessary. A paralegal who knows why someone needs a particular piece of information is far better able to address the inevitable snarls and tangles that make getting that information difficult.

An important part of asking questions is remembering the answer. Again, this seems obvious but attorneys often complain about people who do not recall what they have just been told. I work on the third floor of my law firm, but many of the attorneys I work with are on the fourth floor. This means that I often travel from one attorney's office to another, back to mine, then off again to yet another attorney. I carry a pen and notebook with me on almost every trip I take. I write everything down.

While you are in the midst of a conference with Attorney Smith about an important case you may be sure that you'll remember each strategy discussed, who to call, and what to schedule, research, analyze, or recall from the archives. But if you are caught in the hallway by Attorney Jones who wants to talk to you (and this is a good thing), you can easily forget what Smith told you to do. In a field built on meeting deadlines, forgetting for even one day can make the crucial difference. Be smart. Write it down.

Step three is to watch, listen, and learn. Pay attention to what well-established employees say and do. Do they call the partners by their first names? Are there drawings by their kids push-pinned to the wall? Do they dress up, and is there a difference between the dress expected of secretaries, paralegals, and lawyers? Read the firm literature. How does the firm choose to represent itself? Observe how clients are treated. One firm's reception area may hold the *New Yorker* and *National Geographic*, another glossy firm brochures, yet another local chamber of commerce magazines. You're the new employee and like the anthropologist, it's your job to adjust. If no one else chats in the hallway, don't do it.

Check out the way people act in the lunchroom. Use your head. I remember one young man who was surprised to learn that his lunchroom boasts about taking extra time off when the firm sent him out on assignments was instrumental in his firing. He thought his fellow employees would think it was cute or cool to get away with time theft. He forgot that while he was out test-driving motorcycles (no, I am not making this up) his coworkers were back at the office helping on rush jobs. They suffered. They talked. He was history.

Step four is to be aware that within one firm, even a small firm, there may be several cultures—differing policies on how to treat clients, how to interface with lawyers, how to conduct yourself with support staff, etc. If you are working closely with one or two attorneys, pay special attention to how they do things. Are their letters formal or more conversational? Do they dress up or down? Are their deadlines hard and fast or can you talk to them about extensions? Do they mean what they say?

I once worked for an attorney who was overwhelmingly enthusiastic about his cases. When we had a case in which a man had fallen from a ladder while holding a chain saw (ouch!) this attorney closed a strategy meeting with directions for me. "Deborah!" he shouted, "I want that ladder at any cost." Well, I got him the ladder, but it cost hundreds of dollars. While it didn't break the firm, I endured ribbing about it for a year. He didn't really mean "at any cost"—that was just the way he talked. (Yes, it was my first week on the job.)

Step five is to analyze and learn from your mistakes. I learned to interpret what the attorneys I worked for meant, even when the words didn't quite match the meaning. We all do this in our personal lives, and it's a skill that transfers to professional life in an especially helpful way. A sense of humor about your own fallibility is critical, whether or not your working environment allows you to express it openly. (Here again, you must observe to find out what's acceptable.) You don't want to make many mistakes—doing a great job is still the foundation for success—but when you do, and assuming they're not catastrophic, sharing mistakes can be a way to build the bonds that humanize the work world.

People in the legal field like to be right. We didn't take up a legal career filled with right/wrong, win/lose scenarios because we are amazingly humble or noncompetitive. Still, it's important to be able to recognize, learn from, and forgive yourself the occasional blooper.

When I was a new paralegal I managed my first big document production. It involved hundreds of documents that I had a service bureau copy. Then I personally date-stamped them. Most of you will have caught the order I did that in—wrong, wrong, wrong. First you date-stamp, then you copy. Since I had to send copies to four parties I spent a Saturday, on my own time, stamping each set. This is a painfully slow practice because you have to be positive that each set matches the others perfectly. It was a stupid mistake, but I was new on the job. I took the hit. I fixed it on my own time. I've also noticed that telling this story cheers up many a new paralegal at my office.

Step six is to think long-term. I know it's your first week. It may be hard to imagine the long term. But any anthropologist will tell you that it takes awhile to figure out what's going on in a new culture. You will need to know what's going on to become a productive part of it and to be able to affect the future of that culture.

The watch-and-wait time can be hard. You will find that you have good ideas. Even after one month on a new job you will see some things your employers should change, better ways do things, to rearrange things. Even so, being able to communicate your good ideas in a positive way will take some time.

One year in a law firm is not a very long time. After two years folks begin to think you really work there. Hang in there for three years and you're a real part of the firm; at four or five years you may be a critical member of an important legal team. While all this time is passing, you will be working hard, becoming savvy about what you do and who you do it with. Make good use of the time and learn a lot. Never discount the value of what you're learning. Most real knowledge has a way of becoming useful.

THE GOOD NEWS ABOUT TIME AND STYLE

Remember, even in the same firm different people are successful behaving in different ways. This means that even though you must do a lot of initial adjusting to the firm, over time you can find your own style for success. I'm almost 50 years old. Many of the lawyers I work with went to college when I did and we share many life experiences (memories of the sixties, expanding waistlines, and college bills for our progeny). With some of these partners I have a convivial, casual relationship that we would not be able to maintain if I were 28. We also have some smart, 28-year-old paralegals who have a better rapport with other, younger lawyers, who do splendid work, and who are expected to be around producing quality work for many years. The firm has good reason to invest in their futures.

Whatever your age and experience, they will both affect your working relationships. There are advantages to being older and advantages to being younger, but it is always required that you do top-quality work. Your job as an anthropologist is to observe and then maximize how people in the firm can best notice and appreciate that good work.

UNEXPECTED ADVANTAGES

Anthropologists also know that life within a culture is not static. Not only do internal factors cause the firm to change, but economic and political climates change and practices shift in importance and viability. Some of these changes will be advantageous to you. For example, if you are bilingual you are better off in many markets these days than those of us who are not.

Some changes require quick adjustments. One of the things that attracted me to law was that it had so much to do with words and so little to do with numbers. I was surprised to learn that because clients involve their attorneys more and more in the cost management of legal services I needed to get very good, very quickly, at economic analysis.

Because I had to, I did. I've found this new skill to be invaluable in understanding and presenting evidence in lawsuits, in drafting proposals for new clients that underline cost-effectiveness, and in generally allowing me to communicate effectively with experts, attorneys, accountants, and clients. It's another professional tool and I'm grateful that changing times made me overcome my negative attitude about numbers. Train yourself to be flexible and to think of the long term—not forever but for a good, long while.

Observational skills are not taught in most paralegal programs, but they are as critical to success in a law office as good legal skills are. What you learn is also fascinating. Observe, analyze, remember, and be responsive. These skills are especially important during your first week, but once established they will become habits that continue to serve you and further your success.

THINGS TO ACCOMPLISH IN YOUR FIRST WEEK

1. *Introduce yourself to people.* There will be times when someone in charge of a meeting will take the lead and introduce you, but if the firm you have chosen is a busy one the burden of making your name known to your fellow workers will fall to you. Just be nice. When you're waiting for a meeting to begin or waiting for the elevator or waiting to get a cup of coffee, put your hand out and say, "Hello, I'm Pat Whalon. I'm the new paralegal in the probate department." You'll find other people are as relieved as you are that someone has broken the ice. Once you've made contact you can ask what they do, who they work with, or how long they've been at the firm. Getting to know new people is a great part of a new job.

Use your head in these early encounters. Don't become someone's best friend overnight just because that makes you feel more secure when you hit the coffee room in the morning. This is one time when "If you can't say anything nice, don't say anything at all" really applies. The day may come when you can tease a coworker or afford to vent your spleen when you've had a tough day, but not now, not yet. Office politics are a real part of every paralegal job and you need to practice discretion.

2. *Tour the library.* Take some time to meet the librarian if there is one, get a library map, and walk the rows of books, noting what's where. This will help you out when you have to find a statute quickly. It will also make you feel more generally at home. These are the same books you used at your last job or in your research class. The covers themselves, with all that color coding, will reassure you. Find out if the firm has library policies—which books can leave the room and which cannot. Follow the policy.

3. *By now you should have some work on your desk: If you don't you'll have to see someone.* Figure out who. It may be the attorney who hired you, the attorney who heads your department, a senior paralegal, or a manager of some sort. Don't languish at your desk, losing time and becoming discouraged, and don't take it personally. No one here knows enough about you yet to be avoiding you. They are just busy and not used to being able to give you work. Persevere.

4. *Set up your work space.* Bring what you need from home, set up files, hang pictures. Make it look like someone's at home, permanently. Be sure you are aware of what equipment you should have. Some firms hand out dictaphones, adding machines, calendars, and office plants. Others give you two pens and a stack of yellow pads and expect you to find the supply room for whatever else you need.

Create a set of files titled: Five-Year Plan, Attaboy Letters, Resumes, Continuing Education, Articles, and Possible Jobs and put them in your personal file drawer, preferably one that's in your desk and easy to reach. In Chapter 16 I'll tell you why these are so important to your success. You will need them whether you stay with this firm for a decade or move on in three years.

5. *Say hello to special people.* Please introduce yourself to the firm's support people. The person who vacuums the stairs, the one who runs the copy machine, and the people who route files from desk to desk are all part of the firm. They are also often treated as if they were chairs. They are human beings. Be cordial.

6. *Say good morning to your boss or bosses each day.* It doesn't have to be a long chat. Just stick your head in the door and say, "Good morning." You might follow this with, "I plan to go over the insurance investigator's report in the Bixfield matter, but if there's something else you need, just let me know." That way, they know you're working and they know you're available for more work.

7. *If you have a secretary, take him or her to lunch this week.* Find out who this important person is. Over the long haul it will be helpful to know if she has small children, if he's going to night school, if she has a horrendous commute, and what he thinks about the firm. You can also find out who else the secretary works for (if you've been assigned your own personal secretary, you are working in a highly unusual environment) and how you should work together. My secretary, for example likes assignments to come with a colored cover sheet that tells her it's from me, as well as what I need and when I need it. Our system works. You and your secretary will come up with one that fits you both. When you take your secretary to lunch do not forget to practice both diplomacy and discretion. News (and gossip) travel faster on the secretary grapevine than over the wires. Any comments you make about the people you have met may find their way back to the subject of the comment before five o'clock.

8. *Find out if the firm has training for its computer applications.* If it does, dedicate some time before you are too busy to get professional guidance on those programs you do not already know.

9. *Try to get to know some of the other paralegals during this first week.* They may be busy at their desks, but if you can say hello at lunch, by the elevator, or at a department meeting, do so. These are your colleagues. You may find someone who remembers what you are going through as a new player, and who may be able to give you some insights into the firm.

TIMEKEEPING

"A pin a day's a groat a year."
Henry Fielding 1707–1754

If this is your first experience with timekeeping, my condolences. It's not the most fun part of the job. It is, however, something you can master. Find out if there are firm policies with regard to billing time. Most firms bill by the tenth of an hour, so you should be recording what you do in six-minute increments. These increments show up on time sheets and sometimes on the client's bill in decimal form: .2 (12 minutes), .5 (30 minutes), or 1.5 (90 minutes). Some firms have set rates for phone calls (a minimum of .3 for instance) and for conferences. Some firms bill certain items at a set dollar value; for example, a simple will may cost $400 no matter how long it actually takes to prepare it. This is called value billing and it's touted as the latest trend, but most of us are still dealing with time increments of six minutes.

Drafting time entries is an art that must be learned. The acceptable way(s) to do it differ from firm to firm, and even for different clients within one firm. For example, client A wants to know just what's he's paying for and so asks that the bill include quite a bit of detail about who did what and when. He wants to know which paralegal called which staff member on what day about what subject. Client B is involved in serious litigation and doesn't want the other side to find out what her strategy is. Since attorney bills float from desk to desk and under some circumstances are discoverable, the bill entries must betray as little as possible about the strategy. Witnesses are not identified and conference subjects are not disclosed. Little of substance is recorded.

You will have to find out from the attorneys you work for how they want you to handle billing entries. Some attorneys want you to bill exactly by the clock and calendar. If you draft a letter one day (.3), edit it the next (.2), and then revise it a final time after the attorney's seen it (.2), you are supposed to record your time separately each day. Other attorneys want you to wait until the last day and bill, "Draft correspondence to Dr. Walford, .7." The final time billed is the same but the entry looks cleaner.

To work and bill as efficiently as possible, train yourself to organize your tasks so that you can spend more uninterrupted time on one project. It's generally more efficient. When an attorney gives you an assignment, ask for a time budget. This will give you an idea of how much time the attorney is likely to be happy about billing for the project. It will also encourage the attorney to think realistically about the project. If it's a team effort, communicate with the other people involved to avoid duplication of effort and billing. If you reach a point where you don't know what you're doing or where you should be heading, stop. Put it away until you can clarify things with the attorney in charge.

Do not cut your own time. This will be tempting, especially when you're new. It seems to take so long to get things done. You may be tempted, but don't do it. The attorneys you're working for know you're new to this line of work. If they know anything about personnel management they expect you to start out slowly and get better. They may cut your time at first, but as you improve things will get better.

Eventually you do need to know what's happening with your time. Ignorance may feel like bliss but it increases the possibility of receiving a bad surprise when you have your six-month, end of probation review. Some firms circulate computer printouts each month that tell you how many hours you've billed, what the time is worth to the firm (what they are billing your time at), and what was actually billed to the client. There is usually a variance figure recorded in percentages that tells you what percent of the time you recorded was billed to the client. For example, an 80 percent figure means that 80 percent of the time you recorded was actually billed. Eventually you want to achieve a 95 to 100 percent variance figure. That will mean you are pulling your own weight.

If you do not receive these printouts, later on you will have to approach someone about your time records. You may get the word from a paralegal manager, a senior paralegal, or a friendly data processing person. If you don't find a way to determine how much of your time is being cut, you will eventually have to ask your boss. When you've been with the firm a few months, find a relatively stress-free moment to bring the subject up. The conversation can be opened like this: " I haven't seen any information about how I'm doing on billing. Will I have the chance to? I know I'm new and some of my time may have to be cut, but I want to be sure I'm doing okay." This will allow the attorney to be up-front and let you know how you can see the billing information you need; simply say, "Oh, you're doing fine, don't worry"; or bluster and hem and haw. The second answer should worry you a little; the third answer should worry you a lot.

Many attorneys are concerned about the size of their clients' bills. They are sometimes tempted to cut time when it's not warranted. Guess whose time they cut? Often it's not their own, or their partner's time, or the associate who has been working significant hours to help the partner with a big project. It's probably not the longtime, trusted paralegal the attorney does not wish to alienate. But they may cut your time. You're new. You're in no position to defend yourself. If this happens you may actually have to live with it for awhile. But you will also have to deal with it eventually.

There are occasions when good time must be cut. The legal world is part of a competitive business environment. But when good time must be cut, the responsible attorney tells you what is happening and usually cuts everyone's time across the board.

DEALING WITH TIME CUTS

How do you deal with an attorney who is unjustly cutting your time? Like a grown-up, a smart grown-up. Do not feel hurt or get teary-eyed or angry. Find a time when you and the attorney are alone and say, "I see that you have been cutting a substantial amount of my time on the Fredericks matter. Am I working too slowly, or doing the wrong thing, or is there something else I need to know about?"

This puts the ball right where it belongs—in the attorney's court. He or she can be up front and tell you exactly why your time has been cut. Then the two of you can come up with a plan to fix the problem. The attorney can sputter that he didn't know it was being cut or she can tell you it's none of your business. No matter which response you get, it will benefit you to bring it up.

Sometimes attorneys simply stop cutting someone's time when the associate or paralegal involved politely inquires into the matter. Other attorneys use the occasion to discuss work problems they had not known how to address. Some attorneys tell people that it doesn't matter how much of their time is cut.

The first response (no more inappropriate time cutting) is great. You can smile, keep working together, and become a great team. The second response (discussing the reasons for the cuts) is also useful. There's a great deal to learn in a law practice and if you're new to the game you need to start learning. The last response (that time cuts don't matter) is untrue.

Never believe someone who tells you the percentage of your time that the firm feels it can bill is irrelevant and will not have an impact on your future success. In the legal billing world your recorded billable hours, your variance, the dollar amount billed, and the dollar amount collected are referred to as "your numbers." Your numbers tell the firm whether you are profitable. Your numbers tell the firm whether it was a good idea to hire you and whether it's a good idea to keep you. Your numbers will be reviewed before you are.

Your numbers are also circulating around the firm. Even if you do not get a copy of the report, law firms use current computer capabilities to analyze every financial aspect of the business. The profitability of employees ranks high on the list of things to watch. Lawyers who never work with you, never even talk to you, probably get these printouts. They know your numbers. Unless you plan to leave before the end of the fiscal year, never ever think your numbers don't count.

Hot Tip: All firms get involved in some matters that just aren't going to be profitable. Someone has to do the work, and you may get drafted. If someone significant is involved and also is not getting time billed out, this may be an occasion you can frame as a "gift" you are making to the firm. You're taking on a "no fun, no pay" matter because it has to be done. You're thinking of the firm's interests. You're a team player. You're making a sacrifice for the greater good. But don't do it too often, or too soon. The firm hired you to increase its profitability. Your success requires that you make them money.

DEALING WITH FEAR

Because this is your first week, we should talk a little bit about fear. How much fear makes sense? It's natural and healthy to be nervous when you take on a new job. Your whole system is a little hyped up. The adrenaline response may kick in several times a day. You may feel you can't remember things as well as you usually do. You may lose your car keys or your hairbrush or the notebook that has all your current assignments listed in it. Your attention is being stretched to include new faces, new names, new physical settings, new machines, new data, and new challenges all day long. There's no way that can feel like a day at the beach.

No one can tell you how much fear is "normal." The variables include your basic personality type, the amount of "new" in the job, and how much you have risked in taking the job. Let's take a look at the variables and then you can do the math:

1. *Personality type*—Achieving success depends in part on knowing who we are and how we operate. When you make this assessment, be kind to yourself. A lot of personality types succeed in law practices—don't count yourself out too soon. Everyone who wants to really thrive in this competitive setting must have the ability to acknowledge personal fears and deal with them effectively. If you are basically timid but have somehow found yourself in a paralegal spot, you have other compensating personality traits. Maybe you are incredibly smart or organized or determined.

You can be sure you're incredibly something, because something got you here. Identify those traits and remind yourself of those positive attributes any time the day starts getting away from you. If you are not basically timid—and most people who take up this profession are not—you may have a fear of failure. Welcome to the club. Be aware that you also have positive attributes to help you deal with this, and the ability to set your fear aside and focus on what it is you must do at the moment. This skill will serve you well.

Whatever pushes your "I'm really scared" button, identify it and then identify what other skill or character trait you have that will tame the fear lion for you. I guarantee you have one. The only warning that must be issued here is that you may not employ the "I'll pretend everything's okay even when it's not" coping mechanism. That one leads to failure and usually to firing. You must notice, acknowledge, and deal with your fears and with the realities of the workday. Remember the "totem" you brought your first day. It belongs to you. Use it.

2. *The amount of "new" in the job*—If you've been around the legal block a few times, you may find that your fitting-in skills are well-honed and that you know what to talk about in the coffee room and what to expect in meetings and what to ask your secretary to do and so forth. If this is your first paralegal job, you can expect to feel a lot of fear because you are in a totally new setting.

Everyone else will appear to know exactly what's going on and how to proceed while you, on the other hand, have to think twice about which hall you go down to find the bathroom. This is normal.

If you are fresh out of school you may suffer from what I call the "I'm a fraud" syndrome. This syndrome occurs when the bad voices that talk to you at two or three in the morning inform you that no matter how well you did in school, you really don't know what the heck you are doing or how to be a "real" paralegal and that pretty soon everyone will find out you're a fraud. Assuming you did well in school and are ready to work hard, you will simply have to ignore these voices. You won't be able to shut them up for awhile but you must turn an internal deaf ear to their carping and forge ahead.

Even if you're quite good—well-schooled, a fast learner, and ready to work hard—this may be difficult. For the first six months on my first job my fears woke me up regularly at five a.m. I could feel the column of fear standing in the room staring down at my inert body, the body that foolishly thought it could convince a bunch of terrific lawyers that it had a brain and could do this job. The only way I could get through this time of the day was to switch on the light and pick up an Agatha Christie mystery. For me these books were the perfect cure, enough plot to busy the brain cells without really having to think. I read until 6:45 every morning, which left me just enough time to spring out of bed, shower, dress, feed my kids, and make it downtown to work on time. No time to catalogue my defects and prior failures. Just time to do the chores and get to the office. After six months the fear got tired of waking me up just to be ignored.

3. *Risk of failure*—Let's face it: Any job worth moving on to has some risk involved. Even if you've been a paralegal for a decade, a move to a new office includes enough unknowns that you could have some rough going. Will you be able to fit into the new firm's culture without sacrificing your own professional style? Will you find a good team within the firm to work with? Will you like the hours, the commute, the cases, the department? Lots of stuff could get in the way of a big success. The best way to minimize these fears is to assess realistically, in advance of taking a job, whether it looks like a good fit. You have to analyze it to the best of your ability and then take a chance. You may get good advice from other folks, but in the long run you will have to make your own decision.

When I moved from a small firm that was basically a lean, mean litigation machine to my present job in a firm with over a hundred lawyers, a lot of people advised against the move. Many people told me I'd hate the big-firm mentality, the loss of tight personal working relationships, and the decreased responsibility they anticipated a big-firm job would offer a paralegal. Still, the choice was mine and I made the move.

Ten years later I'm still in the same "big firm" and have found that many of the preconceptions my former colleagues had simply were not accurate. Within this large firm there are small firms, meaning departments. Within the departments there are teams. The close working relationships that I do value are formed in these small areas of the firm. The level of responsibility given to paralegals in my firm varies with the paralegal. If you show the attorneys with whom you work that you can do the job, they are ready and willing to let you do it. These factors have made this job a good fit for me.

The fact remains that I could have failed here. If I had, the world wouldn't have ended. I would have been temporarily crushed, then I would have dusted myself off, tried to figure out what happened, and started out again. If you have not yet survived a significant failure this may be hard to believe, but it's true. Our successes teach us a great deal, but our failures teach us too. If you experience fear in a new job related to potential failure, pat yourself on the head and remind yourself that this means you're not an idiot. Then get back to work and succeed.

A final word about failure:

Failure happens to everyone. It's happened to me and it will happen to you. You may not experience failure with a capital F, but you will experience some kind of failure. You will do something just plain wrong on the job—misspeak, hurt a colleague, drop a ball, or miss a deadline. A case you thought was a probable win will go badly. A negotiation you thought was going splendidly will get out of hand. A deal you thought was solid will go south. If you use caution and care you won't have this experience often, but you need to know that mistakes happen in law just the way they happen everywhere else in this world. You need to be prepared for it.

When you make a mistake, do not give in to the very strong impulse to try to hide it. Difficult as it may be, face up to it, take the blame, apologize, and try to fix it. You'll feel terrible; we all do. We feel that way because we care about our responsibilities, our clients, our coworkers, and excellence.

In your professional life you will also see other people make mistakes. When this happens, please be generous. Try to keep the look of relief off your face. Remember that it could have been you. Nobody, not the best lawyer and not the best paralegal, gets out of this business without experiencing some failure.

For now you need to think only about this first week. It will probably feel quite long before it's over. That's natural and you shouldn't worry about it. Things will get easier as you become familiar with the place, the people, and the assignments.

Tips of the Billing Trade

1. Bill truthfully. It's not your job to cut your time.

2. Get a "time budget" for a project from the assigning attorney before you start.

3. If your project is a team effort, communicate to avoid double billing.

4. If you reach a point where you don't know what you're doing or where you should be heading, **stop**. Put it away until you can clarify things.

5. If a project balloons or slows down or is subject to client review or new direction, memorialize it. Write a letter stating that you "have requested additional research" or "have instructed the team to stop all work until redirected by you."

6. Make yourself aware of the client's billing constraints and, if it's a long-term relationship, the client's billing cycle.

7. Provide educational freebies to the client. Explain strange billing items and new personnel. Think like a client.

THE FIRST MONTH: A SOLID START

"Thank God we hired Elsa. This month would have been impossible without her." You're filled with a warm glow, feel yourself blushing, and try to fend off further compliments. Then the alarm clock rings and it's time to get up. You pour coffee, have some breakfast, find some work clothes, and hit the highway. You're in month one, a very important month. The work you do—and the impression you create—will either shoot you toward success or be a stumbling block. Let's do the success thing.

First, be sure that you are demonstrating your enthusiasm about your new job and your desire to learn and master what the firm needs you to master. This means you are not sitting quietly in your cubicle worrying about your performance or leaving early because you don't have much work on your desk yet. You may be the new kid on the block, but you are also the talented, energetic new kid. You are:

1. touching bases with the major players in your area of practice regularly to find out what new projects are available and volunteer to take them on;

2. reading the legal periodicals you will find around the office or in the library, especially those that have to do with your specialty;

3. bringing up new cases or statutes that affect your practice and discussing them with the other paralegals and attorneys;

4. checking your specialty area on the Internet for late-breaking information;

5. checking with local bar associations, your alma mater, legal periodicals, and any bulletin boards or posting places in the office for continuing education classes;

6. reading everything in every file you can find on matters you've been assigned;

7. completing each assignment given to you carefully, thoroughly, in a timely fashion, and as if your job depended upon it.

Get it? You are proactive. You seek knowledge the way you would seek work. You use what you learn in the matters you are currently working on. Don't be afraid to discuss what you're learning with the attorneys for whom you work. If you do well on an assignment, try to get some repeat performances.

Repeat performance means just that—doing the same job more than once. It's a good way to develop an area of responsibility to call your own. For instance, audit letters are law firm responses to inquiries from financial auditors that attorneys write to assist clients undergoing an audit. There are paralegals who are trained to prepare audit letters for clients. It's not all they do and it's not the most interesting thing they do, but it is something that the firm needs done. It's valuable, and they're good at it. These paralegals often prepare thirty-five or forty audit letters a year. That's repeat performance.

Those paralegals are known for their ability to perform appropriate due diligence, analyze relevant issues, and produce audit letters for review and signature by an attorney. Attorneys rely on the paralegals to do a professional job on the letters. If the paralegals were not there doing the job, the attorneys they work for would definitely notice and they would definitely not like it. As a new paralegal with the firm, you need to get something like that going for you.

YOUR AREA OF RESPONSIBILITY

During your first month with a new firm you must begin to establish an area of responsibility, something you and everyone else thinks is "your job." You'll know you have succeeded at this when people start referring to you as "Kathryn's paralegal" or "the probate paralegal" or the "contract's specialist" instead of as "the new paralegal." Assuming you have done your anthropological best to figure out why they hired you, you should be able to establish an area of responsibility within sixty days of your first day of work.

One way to develop an area of responsibility is to attack a job no one else really wants to do. Legal practices are full of them. You might organize all the expert files. Make a master list of all the experts the firm's attorneys have used (you can get names from accounts payable staff who cut the checks) and send out a survey asking what various attorneys thought about their experts' performances. Collate, organize, and distribute this information and people will begin to know who you are. They'll think you are the paralegal with all the information on experts. When they need an expert for a new case they will come to you.

Another way to establish yourself is to volunteer to help a very busy attorney. You need to do this in a concrete way, not a casual statement at lunch ("Oh, I'd like to learn that" or, "Let me know if you need help"). You need to really pitch in at the moment they need help. This means the entree to "your area of responsibility" may be something as unglamorous as taking a bunch of discovery responses down to the copy room for duplication or (here it comes) even copying them yourself.

This is the "will do what needs doing" approach. It doesn't do an attorney any good if you can research and draft a motion, but no one's available to get it finalized and out the door. Be available. Be helpful. Be willing to stay late or come in early. Later, when you have earned the respect and trust of your bosses and coworkers, you can fine-tune your regular job responsibilities. This first month is about getting someone to say, "Thank God we hired Elsa. This month would have been impossible without her."

Remember, an area of responsibility means bread and butter work. It means work that you can, at least after some reasonable amount of time, manage on your own. This kind of work not only provides you with a basic law firm identity upon which you can build, it supplies a stable flow of work that will be helpful when times are slow. Over time, if you perform well, it will become your domain, an area where your expertise is respected and your judgment is sought. It may be mundane compared to some of your assignments, but never discount the importance of being the firm "expert" on something. It might be quick Internet research or audit letters or managing the in-house education calendar. Be pleased when the attorneys you work for come to rely on you. This is step one on the ladder of success.

OUR CUBICLES, OURSELVES

In the first month you should do even more to really move into your work space. Moving in is more important than you may think. It tells your employers and coworkers that you're really here and intend to stay. This will encourage them to invest in you and to consider you for a long-term professional relationship.

Moving in means hanging pictures, diplomas, additional plants, even installing rugs and lamps. I am amazed how impoverished many legal professionals' workplaces look. They are often beige, beige, beige—and bare-walled to boot. It's enough to give a person the idea that they don't want to be there or that they don't intend to stay. This is a very bad idea for people to have about you.

Whether you are thrilled by your windowed office or dismayed by the gray cubicle that houses your professional life, invest in it. Give it a bit of yourself. Spend a little money. When I moved into my windowless, once-a-closet office the fluorescent lights drove me crazy. They made me cranky and made my bad skin look worse. But I knew I was fortunate to have a door I could close during important phone calls. I realized that if I wanted some other kind of lighting I was going to have to buy it myself.

Happily, we live in the days of affordable, sort-of-artistic lamps and a trip to Pier One Imports helped me out, but I realized I still needed plants to soften all those sharp corners. That meant a trip to the plant store for three "we can live in the dark" plants and a couple of baskets. I also decided that if Gertrude Stein could fill the walls of her Paris apartment with great paintings, I could do the same with print purchases. Most of my wall space is covered, and it's quite a contrast to the beige halls outside my door. It makes a statement. It says someone lives there, someone with, I like to think, great taste in art. Over time the decor developed. I framed T-shirts from half marathons I'd run. I hung thank-you letters from kids I'd tutored. I got a bulletin board and push-pinned my favorite family photos to it.

The Objections

But, you're thinking, I don't like that, it's too cluttered. Fine. Design your own look. Maybe you want to frame your kids' art or put up your diplomas or buy one fine painting or get a replica of the Declaration of Independence or frame the order granting the motion for summary judgment you drafted. That's great.

But, you say, my firm doesn't encourage individuality. They want total control of my environment. They love beige. If that's so, I'm sorry you had to take the job. You will not have much fun there or develop as an individual legal professional as quickly. But you can still do something good, something personalizing and inviting, with your office space. More times than we are willing to admit, the "they won't let me do it" excuse is uttered by people who simply don't want to invest the energy, the time, and the money in something they see as "the firm's office." Let me tell you where this attitude gets you.

Who Owns You

"The firm owns my office" leads right to "the firm owns my career." "The firm owes me a lamp" leads right to "the firm owes me a career." Maybe the attorneys you work for will get you a lamp, but they cannot get you a career. They may own the building, but that office, the one they own, is a workplace set up to promote the cooperative work of many individual legal professionals. Be one.

Naturally you'll use good taste. Some art doesn't belong in the office and a quick look around will tell you what is likely to offend. Within the parameters of what's acceptable, you should be able to find things that make your work space unique and identifiable, that let your bosses and coworkers know someone is really at home.

This is an opportunity to treat yourself well. Don't be cheap and mean-spirited. I know you're working to make money but this is your new job, a cause for celebration. You don't expect your children to celebrate birthdays or graduations without spending a little cash; don't treat this occasion any differently. It's a laudatory milestone and it doesn't take a lot of money to celebrate it. Wouldn't that music box your brother-in-law gave you for Christmas look great on your desk? How about your Bessie Smith poster or the art deco lamp your mother has had in the garage for seven years?

Moving into and decorating your work space may not seem like a critical career event, but it is. It says to you and the whole office, "I'm here. This is where I will be spending most of my waking hours Monday through Friday. It's my other home, where I also live." If you can't stand that thought you need to assess things carefully. What's wrong and how will you deal with it? If you are unwilling to invest time and money in your own working environment, how will you convince those who hold the law firm's purse strings that you are worth any extra investment? If you don't want to be thought of or treated as chattel, don't act like it. Be your own person even as you learn to fit in well with the firm and with your legal team. Individuality is a crucial element in your professional success.

A personal work space will also play a large part in allowing others to know you. Once an associate dropped by to tease me about all my art. I said, "I put this up so people would know I'm artsy." He glanced at the runner's T-shirts. "Tough and artsy," he commented. He was right. I meant for people to know that I could run a long distance and still show up for work on Monday. This attorney was assessing me as an individual, someone he could pick out of the crowd. Excellent skills are mandatory for success in any business, but personal human connections count for a lot in our job satisfaction and form the groundwork that underlies many a great career. Your decor should help people want to know you and want to like you.

Details

Now's the time to stock your work space with the mundane and the unusual. Bring in a desk clock that you really like and stock extra batteries. You need a first aid kit that includes not only Band-Aids and antibiotic salves but also your personal headache remedy (I keep aspirin, ibuprofen, and acetaminophen products because sometimes the nicest people I work with need different remedies), allergy pills, extras of any daily medication you take, vitamins, and antacids. Don't forget a toothbrush, toothpaste, mouthwash, and deodorant. You should also have a small hammer, several picture hanging kits, a flashlight, extra stockings, an extra box of tissues, and a pair of truly comfortable walking shoes. It's also a good idea to have a roll of paper towels, some kind of alcohol-based cleaner, and some furniture polish, but now you'll think I'm being extravagant.

No matter what you think about paper towels, you must stock thank-you notes and stamps. These are some of the most critical things you can purchase ahead of time. Over the course of the next several years, if you do things right, you will find many opportunities to use them. People in and out of the office will make some effort to help you out, to do you a good turn. At the moment you'll think, "I should drop so-and-so a note and tell her how much her support on this nomination helped." If you don't have quick and easy access to thank-you notes, right then, right there, the moment will pass and you will convince yourself that you expressed your thanks sufficiently at the board meeting and let so much time pass that a note really does seem silly. This is a grave mistake. Another important part of a successful career involves taking the time to treat human beings, especially good ones, like human beings. Apart from what it does for your career, it's the right thing to do.

You'll also need plain note cards to send when people you know deserve congratulations, or when you need to ask a special favor, or when you have a quick thought that may, if passed along today, be helpful to someone else. A note often means more to people than a phone call and almost always is more memorable.

Finally, there's your Rolodex, or whatever format you use to keep track of the many people in your business and personal life. The contacts we make over the course of our careers are assets just as surely as good skills, a professional appearance, a personable manner, and a car that doesn't break down when you need it. Cherish your contacts and keep track of the people with whom you've worked well, people who have impressed you, and people you will need again. Update your Rolodex when someone moves from one job to another (and send that congratulatory note!) and if you move, keep your contacts informed.

You should have a personal section of your Rolodex that includes your Social Security number, your driver's license number, your car license number, your insurance policy numbers, agents' telephones, numbers for your health care providers, and relevant numbers and information for each family member (including everyone's Social Security numbers), your spouse or other significant person's data, your children's school information, and anything else that you may need while at work. If you work a long day you are going to have to manage some personal things from the office. Being prepared with the right data will make these personal calls as efficient as they can be.

There's another important address book these days: your Internet address book. This book or list or file or whatever you choose to use will contain not only the E-mail addresses of important contacts, but also all the interesting and helpful sites you run into on the Internet. Yes, you can bookmark sites on-line, and you should, but excellent Web sites are also listed in books and in periodicals. *Legal Assistant Today* regularly lists helpful sites, as do the journals and newsletters of most associations. You firm may even list favorite sites in an MIS newsletter. None of us can afford to get behind in the information access revolution. Keep addresses and keep notes by the access address about what you found there. You'll be glad you did.

TAKE A PARALEGAL TO LUNCH

This is a good time to begin developing relationships with the other paralegals in the office. Getting to know your fellow paralegals can be a tricky thing. In many offices paralegals don't work together often and the lack of contact can make getting acquainted a little unnatural. If you can manage the opportunity, get to know your colleagues. If you have become active in the local paralegal group you will have met paralegals from other offices. Get together with them too.

Be smart in these first-month lunches. Get to know your fellows, but do not vent frustrations about any attorneys or paralegals or secretaries you feel have not behaved well. Do not complain about your workload, your work space, or your paycheck. Very little good is accomplished by such talk and a good deal of trouble can result. If you get a reputation as someone who complains a lot, who sees the glass as half empty, you will have a hard time living it down.

It's not all that smart to divulge negative things about your personal life either. Negativity takes a toll on the talker and the listener. If you complain about your kids, your spouse, or your landlord, you may be seen as a nag or as an energy sink. That's bad in a law office. If you must gripe, get a dog.

What should you be talking about? Since you are out in the public domain, do not talk about legal matters you're working on for clients. Most people like to be asked about their children, their hobbies, or their pasts. College stories, sports stories, and room-mother stories all make for good lunch chat starters. Talk about movies you've seen or books you've read. You're new here. Get your bearings before you bare your soul.

Share information about good courses to take and books to read. If you have recently come across an interesting legal development or a short-cut for a legal task, let your colleagues know. As you become more connected with the paralegal community and more experienced in your job, you will get calls from these people too. Paralegals share information about how to do specific legal tasks, about what's going on in the job market, about current salary trends, and about upcoming educational events. This information is extremely useful and it's fun to talk about.

TAKE PEOPLE AS YOU FIND THEM

Develop a variety of relationships and value them for what they are. One paralegal may turn out to be a friend you can talk to about anything. She may be experienced in the business and an exemplary person. If she has a good heart, can keep secrets, and is totally reliable, you've got a jewel. Treasure this friend and colleague.

Another paralegal may not be someone you click with personally, but may be a great professional who works hard, knows his stuff, and will tell you everything he knows about something. If this person will take the time to help you even though his own schedule is extremely demanding, you're lucky again. Even though the two of you may not share personal stories, value this colleague.

You may meet a paralegal who has been around for twenty-five years and is so experienced and knowledgeable that she's a source of information for paralegals and attorneys alike. Maybe she's cranky or has no sense of humor or looks pained every time you have to ask her a question. So what? This is a valuable colleague and one to whom you owe respect. Value her too.

Someday there will be a newer paralegal who looks to you for advice and help. If that paralegal is sincere, able, and willing to grow, you are again fortunate. Teaching is one of the best ways to develop and become sure of our own skills. Value this new colleague.

THE FIRST MONTH ASSESSMENT

Although there will probably not be an official one-month assessment by the firm, rest assured the informal assessment is going on. By now your employers have had a chance to see if you come up to your resume's standards—and if you can meet their needs. Try to get a real feel for how things are going. No one can tell you exactly how to do that. You need to tailor your method to the kind of firm you work in and the kind of lawyers you work for, but make a conscious effort to figure out how you think you are doing and whether your boss agrees.

Tactics that work:

1. *Time Sheet Review*: Review your time sheets and make an extra set. Then find someone who has impressed you and who has been with the firm awhile and ask if he or she will have lunch with you (your treat, of course) to go over your entries. This could be a senior paralegal or an attorney who is professional but user-friendly. Explain briefly that since you are new to the art of drafting time entries that clients can understand and live with, you'd like a quick tutoring session. The review of how you write it down should lead easily into a discussion about what and how you're doing.

2. *Project Review*: Ask if your supervising attorney can take ten minutes to go over your handling of a recent project, maybe some interrogatories you drafted, a contract you reviewed, or a summary of personnel records. Let the attorney know that you know there are several ways to do most legal tasks and that you want to be sure you're doing them the way that attorney prefers. The attorney will know what you are doing and will appreciate the politic way you are handling your need for feedback. He or she will be pleased to think that you're just as diplomatic with their clients.

3. *One-Month Review*: Some attorneys like it if you just open your mouth and say you'd like to know how you're doing. Some will take time right then and there to let you know. Others will actually set a time for a brief review.

4. *The You-Can't-Plan-This-But-Sometimes-It-Happens Review*: I can't argue for anyone doing this on purpose, but you should know that in attorney–paralegal relationships sometimes one or the other of you will blurt out something that precipitates a review of your working relationship. For example, I once worked for an attorney who really wasn't giving me enough to do. Everything seemed like busywork, nonsubstantive in the extreme, and one day it all just came to a head. I was delivering a silly assignment to this guy when I heard myself say, "Am I doing one thing for you that's actually helpful?" A hush fell over the room. I was horrified. However, the fellow looked up and asked what was wrong and whether I felt excluded from the practice.

In the next half hour I was able to explain that I was capable of much more than my current work assignments indicated. He got to say he was not used to working with paralegals and the last one he'd tried was not very smart. We got to agree that he'd try me on a couple of really tough assignments, and he did. I was careful to do splendidly on them and we became a happy (and, we liked to think, formidable) team. Sometimes things happen that way, but I was lucky—it could have backfired. I can't recommend it, but sometimes spontaneous communication works the best.

Do your own written assessment, which you will keep as a private document. List the individuals you have worked for and try to recall the projects and whether the work product you gave them was fair, good, or excellent. List individuals you would like to work with again in the future as well as what you felt was the best thing you accomplished in your first month. List other memorable events, for example a department meeting where you met more people or an in-house seminar where you learned a new skill. This is an important and private document, but you should do it and keep it.

Do not write down nasty things about people you don't like. Focus on what went well, what you can cite as accomplishments. As memorable as your first projects seem at the beginning of your work life, they fade in memory as new items take their places. Write them down; you will want to be able to refer to them later. Write down statistics like the hours you billed, the time that was cut, and why, if you know that. List what you would like to accomplish in months two, three, and four. Keep this private document in a file called Preparation for Six-Month Review. Keep the file in a drawer in your desk where you house basic, personal, non-project-related files. Do not leave it on the firm's computer system where anyone can log into it and take a look. While it's unlikely that anyone would want to do so, it's a good idea to learn now that expectations of privacy in a law office are generally inflated.

Keeping track of your own work history will also remind you that you own your career. Neither the paralegal manager, your supervising attorneys, or the personnel department are in charge of documenting your successes, noticing what you need to grow professionally, or supplying it. That's your job. Start now.

DO YOU NEED A MENTOR?

At the very least you need role models. Read about outstanding paralegals in newsletters, journals, and magazines. Attend local paralegal association meetings to see who you should get to know. Establish relationships by serving on committees and organizing events with great professionals. In my career my first mentor was my program director, Diane Petropulos. I met her in 1984 when I entered the Sonoma State University Attorney Assistant program. She'd been in the business quite awhile, first as a paralegal and then as a program director, and her energy and professional moxie knocked my socks off. She was smart and appeared fearless, and she believed in paralegals as legal professionals making a real contribution. Many of my classmates felt about Diane as I did. She was someone we could look up to, but also someone we felt we could emulate. She was the perfect mentor for us, because we too believed in the profession and wanted to be a part of its future.

I maintained a relationship with Diane over time, calling her when I had questions, when I wanted to know what she thought, when a new idea was brewing in my own head, or when my general enthusiasm needed an outlet. I took the chance that I was bugging her, and she graciously took my calls and talked me through many important career points. I sent her drafts of ideas and reactions to developments within the field so she could assess my growth from student to professional. When I knew I was sufficiently experienced as a paralegal to make some contributions to the profession outside the office, I asked her for introductions, which she also graciously provided. Whenever I worked on a talk or wrote an article for which my initial contact had come through Diane, I appreciated that she had put herself on the line by recommending me. I worked extra hard to be sure that anything I did reflected well on her professional judgment. The wisdom of my choice of mentors is best demonstrated by the fact that over time Diane was able to let our relationship shift from a student–teacher relationship to one of equal professional colleagues.

Your mentor doesn't have to be a paralegal. You may find an attorney where you work who has a gift for teaching and is mature enough to enjoy the professional growth of others in the office. I've also been fortunate in attorney mentors and still have several today. These individuals have taught me things about law office politics, about the strategic handling of a lawsuit, and about how to develop and maintain wonderful client relationships. Their pro-growth attitude was recently demonstrated when I asked for a leave from my job to write this book and they graciously consented. Seek out people in your firm who enjoy the practice of law and the professional growth of others. They will teach you things that can barely be touched on in a book. They will also be valuable comrades in your day-to-day work life and may even become good friends. Appreciate them. Support them. Be loyal to them. They are valuable people in the legal world. The future of the field depends heavily on our ability to keep them as active teachers and mentors in law offices.

If you don't find an amazing mentor right away, don't worry. You can admire and learn from lots of people, and create your own mentor from their various professional and personal strengths. Spend some time imagining the kind of paralegal you want to be. Aim high. Choose people who have similar goals to spend time with, both on work projects and during the lunch hour. True professionalism is a wonderful thing. It can lift any job to a new level.

Congratulations! You made it through your first month. You're on the way. The rest of this book is about the kind of future and professionalism that's available to you.

7

MAKING THE TEAM AND ORGANIZING YOUR WORK LIFE

MAKING THE TEAM

Being a bona fide employee of the firm is not always the same as being part of the team. In fact, it's usually not the same. Teams are special groups within law firms, subsets made up of individuals who work well, and consequently most often, together. Sometimes they're designated formally, but usually they develop spontaneously.

Attorney Jones asks the new paralegal, Frank Stevens, to help on a big closing. Frank treats the opportunity like an audition. He schedules the whole thing personally, makes sure every document is perfect, that the legal descriptions have been checked and double-checked, that every assurance required is completed, that the right numbers of copies are made, and that fresh pens are in the credenza. He makes sure all the participants have directions and parking and lunch orders. He finds out how they want incoming calls handled and makes sure the receptionist is aware of what's happening. He handles every detail including making sure that the coffee's hot. For the first time since Attorney Jones began handling closings, there are no glitches in the day. It's still a long one with lots of details to go over, but no actual problems arise and although a lot of people worked hard to make this deal go, Jones gives Frank the credit for the graceful closing. You can bet the next time Jones has a closing, Frank will get the gig. He's on his way to becoming a permanent part of Jones' team.

Jessie Parker is new to Johnson and Phelps. She mentioned during her interview that she took extra classes in eminent domain work while in paralegal school. Attorney Johnson remembers her comment when she has to turn an eminent domain case over to a senior associate and says, "If you need some help, try that new paralegal. She says she knows something about these cases." The associate is one busy fellow. He's up for partnership this year and is working 80 hours a week handling as many cases as he can get his hands on. He needs paralegal help. He gets in touch with Parker. Jessie sees this opportunity for what it is—the chance to do substantive work on a case that is actually going to trial. She digs in. Eight weeks later Parker walks into the courtroom with the senior associate. She has the exhibits, the witness list, the statement of the case, the trial brief, several critical motions, and the outline for the cross exam of the other side's expert. This case has been her main focus for eight weeks and there's not much she doesn't know about it. Mr. Senior Associate is good. He knows the case too, and the two of them get the client an excellent result. Who do you think the client will want on its next eminent domain matter? Mr. Senior Associate. And who will he want assisting? Jessie Parker's made the team.

Do you need to be on a team? Being on a team is a pretty good idea. It's the quickest way to get a strongly appreciated area of responsibility, it definitely increases job security (your six-month review will be here in no time), it gives you continuing education in a particular field that leads to an area of expertise, and it's fun. It will be a source of support for you when you want money for education or to attend a conference, and it will provide a support group if for some reason work gets slow and you need new projects to keep up your hours.

But team membership is earned. To prove yourself good team material, you'll need to demonstrate the ability to think like part of the team and to make a strong and consistent contribution to the team's efforts. You'll also need a positive, "Let's do it" attitude. Before you can prove anything you have to get a shot at being part of a great team. Here's how to accomplish that.

Identify a Team You Want to Join

Look around your firm. Who practices in an area of law that interests you? Try identifying people you think you'd work well with. Personalities count in a law practice. If you like to joke around a little, a sad sack may not be the perfect team leader for you. If you're all business from nine to five, find someone who has the same no-nonsense attitude.

When you think about a practice area, be realistic. In litigation, for example, the hours can get long—in fact before a trial they always get long—but becoming immersed in the case is fun and lots of us like the excitement level when we're face-to-face with the opposing side. When we're up against pretrial deadlines and working with experts, percipient witnesses, graphics folks, couriers, court clerks, and the rest of the pretrial crew, the workdays fly and we usually bill enough hours to justify a little break when the matter's completed. But litigation is not a good choice for someone who has to leave the office at five o'clock every day or who gets migraine headaches under stress or who never wants to work on a weekend. Think before you choose a practice area. They all have something going for them and they all have their downsides.

If a look around the office still leaves you wondering what team you'd like to join, think about your classwork. What did you like best? Try to get assignments from attorneys who do different things. Something will seem right. When it does you must notice and give that assignment and any others from the same attorney or department the special care you would give an audition. Focus.

If you need extra education to do the job well, be aggressive in getting it. Ask the attorney for texts on the subject, check for local classes, and use the law library. Whatever you do, be sure your attorney knows you're doing it. You're trying to impress the person in charge of the team. You want that person to know that you're fully engaged with the project, that you're proactive in learning what you need to know, and that you are a quick study. You must convince the attorney that you can be relied on to ask the right questions, remember the answers, and work hard to learn the ropes.

If you have identified a team you'd like to join but no assignments from that team are coming your way, try one of these approaches to get one:

1.   **The direct approach:** Speak directly to the attorney in charge of the team you like. Express your interest simply and honestly and see what response you get. If it is at all favorable, be prepared to tell the attorney what extra things you are going to do to become especially good at assisting in his or her area of law. Is there a continuing education class that would move you along in the field?

I know this approach can work. When a paralegal in my office who served as a liaison with a large city client left the firm, I immediately approached the attorney who headed that client's team and asked if I could have her spot. We set a lunch date to discuss it which resulted in my assuming the liaison role. It has been an important part of my job for the last seven years and I've been overwhelmingly rewarded for the initiative I took to get the spot. If you can handle the direct approach, it's probably your best shot.

2.   **The indirect approach:** Create your own opportunity by being in the right place at the right time. The legal business is full of what we call "rushes" (a job that needs full focus to get out the door on time). Usually if you're interested in a practice area you can hear about these in the hallway, lunch room, or library. If your day's to-do list has any flexibility in it, set one of your work items aside and volunteer, volunteer, volunteer. Don't be picky about what part of the job you help with. If a filing has to get done by two p.m., the person who unstaples six sets of documents to insert a nearly forgotten exhibit may look like support staff, but that person is invaluable and clearly a team player. Don't miss the opportunity to pitch in and contribute. Then follow up by finding out the results of the team's efforts. Did we prevail on the motion? Suddenly you have standing to ask: You were part of the effort, and the attorney involved will appreciate your help and your style.

3.   **Entertain the possibilities:** I once stopped by the office of an attorney for whom I'd done some work in the past. I liked him and his work a lot but the changing marketplace had sent me in another direction. The day I stopped by to say hello and ask what he was working on, he'd just taken on a fascinating new case. In response to his summary of the facts, I threw out a few discovery ideas and we found ourselves launched on a strategy session which ended with (you guessed it), "Hey, why don't you work on this with me?" It turned out to be a wonderful opportunity and he's kept me on his team ever since. It works for both of us.

Now you've identified a team and gotten a tryout spot. Next you must convince the other team members that their lives are better with you on the team. This is where your parents' words of wisdom about being responsible, honest, and hardworking all come into play. Learn everything you can about the area of law you are working in. Listen, read, and ask intelligent questions. Learn who the other team members are and what they do.

Associates are sometimes troubled by paralegal–partner relationships. They feel they'll get left out of the loop. Be aware of this possibility and go out of your way to communicate that you appreciate the knowledge associates gained in law school and that you are enthused about helping them too.

Get to know the secretaries who play such important roles on legal teams. Again, be gracious and express your appreciation. Do not be dictatorial and do not fail to respect the relationship between a good legal secretary and an attorney. Finally, if you have not done so, get to know the support staff (copy people, runners, word processors) who are critical to getting the team's work out the door. These people do more work for less visible appreciation than anyone else in the office. Let them know you appreciate their efforts.

Cultivate good relationships with the outside vendors the team uses. Add names and phone numbers to your Rolodex: process servers, surveyors, title officers—everyone who helps your team do its work. Keep your own files on what you are learning. Save samples. Start three-ring binders with forms. Clip cases or other news about your area of law and make copies for your boss. Act like this area of law is your specialty. It soon will be.

Now you must make the move from tangential team membership to being an essential part of your chosen legal team. You will do this by working hard and demonstrating that you are totally responsible and good at your work and that you can be trusted to perform as a true professional every day.

TRUST IN THE LEGAL WORLD

Here's how trust works in the legal world. Clients trust lawyers to work responsibly to forward their interests. Lawyers trust their staffs to help carry that burden. Within the framework of a good legal team there's room for different levels of responsibility, but if you want to be a key player be sure you are willing to take on the team's matters wholeheartedly. Key players are folks who care enough about what's going on with the team's current effort to notice dropped balls and to make sure they're picked up before harm's done. They are willing and able to assume an ownership interest in the team's work. It's not just their boss' client, their boss's work. It's theirs too, and if failure occurs they feel it is, at least in part, their failure.

If you want to become an essential team member, you will have to earn the trust of the attorneys you work with. They have to trust that you will follow through on everything you undertake for them or for their clients. They must trust your absolute obedience to the attorney–client privilege and your absolute discretion with regard to their own practice and their professional affairs. There is no room for hedging here. Clients pay money to have their interests protected. You must never violate their right to and expectation of confidentiality. Never.

Finally, the attorneys you work for must trust your judgment. They need to know that you will think things through, and that having done so you will conclude something close enough to what they would have concluded themselves to keep their clients' interest and their own practice safe. Only then can they leave a portion of their practices to your tender care. Your behavior on the job will either inspire real trust or limit your involvement in your firm's practice. It's up to you.

HOW MANY TEAMS?

How many attorneys can you develop this kind of team relationship with? Probably between one and four. The demands of a busy practice and the realities of energy and time constraints argue for two or three, with perhaps a couple more who think they can usually call on you for help, but who won't feel obligated to keep you busy. Remember, success for paralegals hinges on good—make that great—relationships with the attorneys with whom they work. You are better off convincing one or two good (and hence busy) attorneys that they need you involved in their practices than you are courting too many bosses and accepting so many assignments that you can't do a first-rate job on each one.

If you want your career to take off, to be not just good, but great, there's no room for a job half-done, or done sloppily, or too late. Most attorneys are not interested in giving "the new paralegal" a second chance to screw up. Given the number of newly trained paralegals graduating from good programs every year, they don't have to. Be sure you take care of your career.

ORGANIZING YOUR WORK LIFE

We've talked a lot about the incredible job you are going to do on every project you undertake, the education you are going to keep up, and the future of your career which you will keep happily in mind at every critical juncture. How are you going to do all this?

Managing the Work

One of the first things you will notice about paralegals is that they tend to fall into two categories—those who manage their work and those whose work manages them. You want to be among the former.

Managing your work is not natural or automatic or even easy. In the career of a top-notch paralegal, work management manifests itself as a collection of insights, attitudes, and work habits developed over time. Some of those insights and habits are the result of unfortunate events that the paralegal chooses to avoid in the future. Others are learned from using the anthropological skills discussed in Chapter 5 to discover how true professionals manage their legal careers. Here are some things all stars know:

Wherever you work, it is the home and base station for your professional existence. You will spend most of your waking hours there. You have set it up with some care. Your personal files are there—resumes, atta-boy letters, future jobs, and your five-year plan. You've moved in, artwork, first aid kit, and all. You're comfortable with your stuff and with the physical layout. You can work here.

You have to figure out how you'll manage the work flow and remember every single project and every single project deadline. When it comes to project completion you want a perfect track record. Today's offices generally have a lot of computer-based systems to help you with your calendaring. Whatever docketing system your firm uses, get acquainted with it and check it at least twice daily.

In addition, peruse all the helpful hints published by magazines like *Legal Assistant Today* and choose two or three work tracking tricks that you think suit your style. I use the good old-fashioned bright blue folder to keep copies of things that need immediate attention, a list that I update daily next to my keyboard, and a whiteboard for long-term projects. I'm also a big fan of sending E-mail to myself.

Our E-mail system allows you to send mail to anyone, including yourself, and specify a delivery date up to 30 days later. If I know on Monday that I have a client lunch on Thursday, I E-mail myself two messages—one to arrive Wednesday ("Call to confirm lunch with Carolyn Wagoner") and one to arrive Thursday ("Lunch w/ Carolyn at Fordies, 12:15").

I also use voice mail both at home and at work as a reminder system. If I have a morning meeting at a client's office I'm likely to call home the afternoon before and leave a message on my home tape. If I think of a work item while I'm brushing my teeth before bed, I'm likely to call my office and leave a message there.

Idiosyncratic? Sure, but it works for me. You'll have to find something that works for you. Maybe you're a self-stick note person or maybe you can actually make a day planner work. Whatever your method, use it and develop it. The legal business is all about deadlines. One of the best things you have to offer as a new paralegal is your ability to meet them.

Does Neatness Count?

Neatness counts for a lot. For one thing, you need to be able to find things easily. You don't want to have to go on a search and destroy mission every time you need a file. That kind of inefficiency is not for real professionals. Today's office supply stores have plenty of equipment for holding files and organizing paper. If your office doesn't supply you with the right stuff, invest in some yourself.

Remember, people really do make judgments about your ability to handle substantive work based on your ability to handle the paper it generates. You may not think this is fair or even a good idea on their part, but the fact remains that many people look at a messy office and think the person who tolerates that confusion is not the person to handle their important legal work.

You may have seen this kind of office: banker's boxes in every corner and several in the traffic path, unread legal papers and magazines in stacks both on and about the desk, and an in box that's overflowing, literally. The various cases the office's owner is working on are strewn about the chairs, piles of pale green cardboard and red pleading clips, all of which may be needed by someone else soon. Then there are the files this person was working on last month, and the books borrowed from coworkers, and very often several volumes from the library that have been needed by others for a week.

I know there are proponents of the messy office. They think it makes people think they are very creative and very busy and that they work a lot. Don't let this minority view talk you out of an organized office. This is not to say you're never allowed a paper out of place. There will be times when you will have three books and two clips open while you draft a new document, as well as four files on the credenza waiting for attention. That's fine. Just don't leave them all out for three months and bury them under a new set of files, three weeks' worth of correspondence, and the greasy paper from a take-out lunch.

Your Files

There's an ongoing dispute in law offices across the country. Should you keep your own files on a matter or should you keep everything in the files maintained by the secretary of the responsible attorney? Basically the split is that the attorneys (quite understandably) like to know they can lay hands on an entire file whenever they need to. Bits and pieces in other peoples' file cabinets don't seem like a good idea. They're right, of course.

The other side of the equation is that many younger associates and paralegals find that having easy access to particular pieces of information and particular documents is the only way to get a project done on time, and that the best way to do that is to keep copies of some things in their own desks.

Here's the rule. Never, never take a piece of a file, or the original file, and keep it if that may inconvenience anyone else, especially the attorney who's responsible for the case. Do make copies of things you need. For example, you might need copies of discovery documents in a lawsuit so you can formulate responses. Keep them where you can get them quickly. When you do need to work with the original files, and you often will, let all the people who may need the files know you have them. Don't take them home overnight or for the weekend without letting people know, and don't even leave them all in your office without letting people know. This is both good manners and smart business. Computers aside, the law is still a paper game and we need to know where our papers are.

Keep copies from your old files as forms for new work. You may choose to keep them intact; many people can find a certain deed or motion or contract by the name of the case. You may want to take them apart and reorganize them in files or three-ring binders under categories. The important thing is to build a body of work that is available to you, and later to others, that will enable you to get the work done more quickly.

Your Books

Law libraries, both the firm's and the county's, are wonderful resources, but do not neglect your own library. Invest in books. They are a part of your education and a part of your arsenal in the battle for success. It's amazing how many times I run into paralegals who complain that their bosses won't invest in classes for paralegals when those same paralegals won't spend $30 on a book that will tell them something substantive about their own area of expertise.

Every year should find you with at least eight more professional books than you had before, and that's a conservative number. Buy books in your area of law and read them. Build a library. You can underline them, turn the corners, tab them, and go back to them. You can use them and reuse them, and someday when someone is looking for the federal statutes on computer crime or the requirements for drug tests for safety drivers, you will say, "I have that right here."

Find good career books to help you think through your own situation. You will find your own special titles, and authors who speak to your unique situation. I remember the day I saw the title *Getting Things Done When You're Not in Charge*. "Finally," I thought, "a book for me!" I was right. Geoffrey Bellam's book is not directed to legal office personnel only, but it has lots of good ideas for those of us who work in law. You can build a library of your own favorite books, and if you take enough notes over the course of your own career you may even decide to write one.

Your Secretary

If you're lucky enough to need to read this section, count your blessings. Having secretarial support is still not the standard in the paralegal world. Working with and directing a secretary are learned skills. If you have not done them in the past, do not expect to be good at them right away. Proceed with care and follow these rules:

1. *Demonstrate a high standard of professionalism.* This may seem like an odd directive, but if you want professional support you must act professionally yourself, all the time. Treat your secretary with the same courtesy you would display toward a client. If you are having a bad day do not allow yourself to be harsh or short-tempered with your secretary just because you can get away with it. Apart from the fact that you may not get away with it, that kind of behavior is as small and blameworthy as any you'll ever see in a law office. Do not tolerate it in yourself.

2. *Take time to train your secretary.* If you have a particular way you want your files maintained, your phone answered, or your documents indexed, set a time when you can actually explain it. It's no more fun for your secretary to try to read your mind than it is for you to try to figure out what a vague attorney wants.

3. *Get things to your secretary in a timely fashion.* This means that you have to think ahead. If you must get a letter out by five, your secretary may well need the tape or draft by three or even two o'clock. If you need to have it reviewed by your supervising attorney and retyped, you will need to allow even more time. No one is less popular in a law firm than the person who leaves everything until the last moment, thereby creating "rushes" for three or four people down the line of command.

4. *Do not engage in power struggles with your secretary.* Keep discussions task-oriented, not personality-oriented. Approach problems that might be characterized as personality conflicts as practical problems in getting the work out. Don't say, "I can't stand it when you push my work to the bottom of your to-do pile." Instead say, "We're having a problem getting the work out. It looks like my assignments keep getting postponed while you work on Ann's stuff. Should I talk to her about it, or is there something you and I can work out?"

5. *Make eye contact when you give directions and ask if you have been clear.* Talk over how the work flow should be handled. The two of you may be able to devise task- tracking forms that help. My secretary also works for two lawyers. She's very good, and also very busy. We decided to use an orange cover sheet on all my assignments for her. These sheets record the date and time I give her the work, when I need it, and what it is I need done. She can spot my work assignments and let me know early on if there will be trouble getting them done on time.

6. *Think about how much fun it is when you get a new, interesting assignment that challenges your skills and educates you.* Remember that secretaries like a little variety and professional growth in their work too. If you have a bright, go-getter secretary, assign some work that is a little more stimulating than organizing your files and typing your letters.

7. *Don't forget to thank your secretary for all efforts and to praise a job well done.* Although it's fine to praise publicly, speak privately to your secretary about specific mistakes or general performance problems. Nothing is more humiliating than to be called on the carpet in front of half the office. It should never, never happen.

8. *Don't nitpick.* If your secretary devises a perfectly good program for handling the paper flow, maintaining the files, and getting your messages, try to live with it even if it's not what you would have devised. Encourage the right kind of initiative. You will be rewarded someday when an emergency arises and you are not around to address it. Your secretary will step forward and do something spiffy that saves the day. If it's truly spectacular, take your secretary to lunch!

9. *Take your secretary to lunch in any case.* Get to know your secretary. It takes time to develop a working program, but a good secretary–paralegal combination can be unbeatable.

DEVELOP ADDITIONAL SUPPORT SYSTEMS

When it comes to cross-training, everyone talks a good game but most law firms don't really have time to do much about it. You will need to build your own backup systems. They can take the form of something as formal as a specific request to someone to be available to help out when times get busy (for example when you are getting ready for a trial) or as informal as a friendly relationship with someone you admire and trust who will step in for you if your child is sick, your car breaks down, or the filling in your tooth falls out. There are times when each approach is appropriate, but the second one is much more congenial in the long run.

Remember that friendly backup systems work two ways. You need to be available to cover for others when they need a hand. There are so many advantages to working this way it's hard to imagine why everyone doesn't do it. You get to know terrific colleagues, you get experience in new areas of law, you get exposure to different attorneys when you help out, and you have the satisfaction of knowing you're functioning like a professional and a genuine human being.

Extend to secretaries the courtesy of understanding that they have their own lives outside the office, complete with emergencies. Like all of us they sometimes have sick children, flat tires, or loose teeth. Be understanding and do a little extra to cover for them when these hassles come up. You'll be glad you behaved well when you have to call in one morning to have someone change your voice mail message or proofread a document you forgot to finalize the night before. In the office, what goes around comes around and in the long run, managing the firm's workload is a shared responsibility. Sharing it leads to team success.

BECOME AN ARTFUL BADGER

One of the challenging things in a paralegal's life is meeting deadlines. As you will read again and again in this book, it's a critical issue. One reason this can be tricky is that just doing your part is never enough. You have to get the attorney to review, edit if needed, and usually sign the work. You may write a humdinger of a client status letter, but if it sits on the attorney's desk for three weeks the client will not be pleased. When clients are not pleased, guess who else is not pleased? The fact that the attorney is the one who sat on the letter will only make things worse. It's a situation best avoided. Even if the attorney who needs to review and sign your work is legitimately under the gun—getting ready for trial, or giving seminars, or meeting with clients, or running the firm—you have to find a way to focus enough attention on the work to get it out the door.

What do you do? Some people do nothing. This is a huge mistake. They think, or act as if they think, that their professional life is like high school. They get an assignment, they do it, they turn it in, and that's it. If the teacher doesn't grade it and return it, it's not their fault and it's not their problem. They're wrong, wrong, wrong. But how do you get a busy attorney's attention on your project?

1.   Some attorneys like to have a short meeting at the beginning or the end of the day to go over everything you have at one time. This can be useful but frustrating, because very often you will have to sit there while the attorney reads the work you need reviewed. Even so, I recommend living with it graciously because you will leave with signed, or at least edited, documents that you can get out and cross off your list.

2.   You can use E-mail or voice mail to check on assignments that are in for review. A friendly reminder that a client is waiting on a document, that the court deadline is coming up, or that you will be leaving on vacation soon will often bring your item to the top of a busy attorney's list.

3.   Don't forget to seek help when you need it. Sometimes the attorney's secretary is the best person to ask about when an attorney can get to your project. Be nice.

4.   Finally, as you become better acquainted with the attorney you work for and the attorney's overall caseload, personality, and work style, you will truly become a part of getting the final work product out. The two of you will develop a system that works for you. Attorney–paralegal teams take time to develop but when they do they are dynamic. They accommodate deadlines, court schedules, personalities, and busy law practices as well as personal lives. It's a professional pleasure to work so well with someone that the two of you figure out your own idiosyncratic ways of working cases, communicating deadlines, preparing the final product, and getting it out the door.

WHEN THE HEAT'S ON

"Everybody's talking at me, can't hear a word they're saying, only the echoes of my mind... ." Remember that old song? We all have days like that. The phone rings every four minutes, with clients who need things, attorneys who need things, children who need things. Then there's the parade past your door—paralegals who need X, your secretary who needs to know what to do with the Johnson file, three attorneys to whom you owe work, two more who need help with new projects, and someone from the copy room delivering one, two, three, four, five boxes of duplicated documents to your already overcrowded cubicle. Your own head is developing a serious headache and you haven't had time to eat all day. You succumbed to the temptation to drink too much coffee and the last time you took a vitamin you were a week younger. Is this the glamorous career you expected?

1.   Take a deep breath and get out your favorite pen and a small yellow pad. You're going to start by writing everything down—everything. The client who needs a copy of an old contract, attorney Smith who wants to see the summary of the discovery responses in the French case, the phone message from your dentist that says you've missed your cleaning appointment again, the phone call you have to make to the clerk in Dept. 7 to see if the Meyran settlement conference has been taken off the calendar, the box of documents you need to pull from dead filing—everything. Notice that you are writing all these things down, not trying to accomplish them right now.

2.   If you need it, get your hands on a headache remedy and take it. You should find it in your first aid kit. Look at the time and decide when you will eat to make up for missing lunch. Unless you have a meeting to attend, make it soon. You don't have to take an hour, just enough time to eat something that will give you strength. It should include protein and carbohydrates, so go for a tuna sandwich—not a bag of cookies. Add a glass of milk.

3.   Go over your list and prioritize it. This is a five-minute job. Shift the noncritical items to the bottom. If a project is due—or overdue—take a minute to contact the attorney in charge. Let her know what's going on and get direction. You may have to outline your workload to give her the picture. She may want you to give the project to someone else or she may be able to wait another 48 hours. Whichever way it goes your professionalism will be respected.

4.   If one job splits into two parts and the first part can be accomplished quickly, do that first. For example, if you need to retrieve documents from dead filing to search for a particular document, order the box pulled now so it will be waiting for you later when you have time to go through it. Then attack the next most critical task.

5.   If your phone has voice mail, do not take calls until you've made some actual progress on the job at hand. Constant interruptions are inefficient and will only make you crazy. If you feel funny letting the phone ring, remind yourself that if you were at the eye doctor's or at a client meeting those calls would end up on voice mail anyway.

6.   Each time you finish a task, cross it off your list. This will make you feel good and give you back your courage. Record your time for the matter also. If you have to work this hard, at least be sure you're getting paid for it!

7.   Keep a folder for information about jobs in progress close at hand. For each item you work on today that is not completed, make a note about the status in the folder. This will be more than helpful when you come in tomorrow to finish things up.

BEYOND THE CRUSH

Beyond handling the mad crush of a particularly bad time, there are other tricks of the trade to staying organized. You should have a to-do list that never truly ends. You can start new pages, whole new notebooks in fact, but you should be constantly adding and crossing off your professional chores.

Use your computer effectively. Don't just type—learn to cut and paste, to import and export text, to merge documents, create macros, perform global searches and replacements, reformat documents quickly, adjust fonts, use automatic paragraph numbering, and the host of other word processing capabilities. You should be competent with a spreadsheet program and be at home creating tables. You must be able to create footnotes, insert bullets, use signs like $\approx$ and $\neq$, convert cases, select text, print envelopes, deal with headers and footers, add watermarks, include graphics, use computational options, and perform a dozen other tasks without blinking an eye. Mastering the tools of your trade will keep crazy days to a minimum.

Use checklists. This means that when you are doing a multistep task, thinking out each step as you move through it, you should also create a checklist that will help you do it faster next time. Don't just create the checklist; create a notebook to store it in so that when the job comes around again you can find it! This is trickier to do on a busy day than you may think, but well worth doing. Think of these checklists as expanding your professional options. In time they may become resources for training you give to newer paralegals, for classes you teach, or for articles you write.

Hot Tip: Remember, as you learn to manage a crazy day you are building a foundation for a terrific career. The best people in the business are usually quite busy and they all manage hectic work schedules on a regular basis. Clear your head and buckle down. You can do it.

SOME FINAL REALITIES ABOUT HIGH STANDARDS

It's entirely possible that some in your firm will not be happy that you are setting such high standards and pursuing your professional goals with consistency and tenacity. They may think you are uppity or that you make them look bad. These are the "be good but not too good" thinkers in your firm. Sometimes they are lawyers who are so into the law school club that they refuse to recognize the abilities and expertise of nonlawyers. Sometimes they are partners who are in love with the idea of being the only professionals in the building, and sometimes they are secretaries who find the whole idea of paralegals more than they want to swallow. Sometimes they are even fellow paralegals.

If you want to be the best paralegal possible, you will just have to get over this. There will be attorneys, secretaries, and paralegals who are jealous of your success, but there will also be those who respect your professionalism and admire your work ethic. We all need approval. One of the traits of a true professional is the willingness and ability to express approval of and admiration for others who have high standards and perform at top levels. As for the approval you need, you will have to learn to seek it from yourself and from those whom you respect. This is not just professionalism, it's sensible adult behavior. Life is too short to worry about people who have no vision.

8

PROBATION ENDS

Probationary periods in the legal field are normally six months long. During those six months the firm has the option of letting you go without cause. Although there are few firms who would not accord you the courtesy of a meeting and of providing you with the reason for their decision to fire you, they are not required to even tell you why.

There are as many variations on the probationary period and its resolution as there are designs for roller coaster rides. Whether you are a connoisseur of the roller coaster ride or not, you will have to get through your probation. If your firm has a personnel manual there may be policies and rules in it that apply, but in real life here's what you need to know.

Surviving a probationary employment period is about two things:

1. Forgetting all about it and performing like the professional you are; and

2. Always remembering that you are still proving yourself.

Sound nuts? Maybe so, but if you can learn to plead alternative causes of action in a lawsuit you can learn to maintain these two seemingly inconsistent perspectives too.

During your probationary period the attorneys you work for will be assessing you every day. What you need to remember is that they will not be watching you like hawks, hoping they catch you making mistakes. They will be practicing law. They will be busy. They will be in need of assistance—yours—and nothing will make them happier than to find out that in you they have made a great hire. They want you to succeed. Your success will add to their own.

What do you do to succeed? During this period everyone expects that you will be learning your job. In addition to that, as a future star performer, you will be carving out an area of responsibility that you, your fellow paralegals, and your attorneys will come to think of as yours. Because you are smart, by the time your six-month end-of-probation review comes around you will have succeeded in identifying this responsibility and will have mastered handling it. The people around you will depend on you to handle it.

TAMING THE BILLABLE HOURS MONSTER

In the first six months you will also have mastered the firm's billing system and will have reached, or almost reached, full productivity in firm terms. This means that you know how many hours the firm expects you to bill in a year to be profitable, that you have done the math, and you know how many hours you need to bill each month and each day to meet or exceed that goal. Here's how to figure out how many hours you need to bill each day, week, or year.

Let's say you are required to bill 1500 hours per year in order to meet your firm's requirement for profitability. This is a fairly routine billing requirement for entry-level paralegals. First you divide 1500 (hours) by 12 (months) to get 125 hours (per month). In most months you have 20 to 22 workdays. Let's be conservative and use 21 working days per month. 125 (hours per month) divided by 21 (workdays per month) = 5.95 hours per day of billable time. "Well," you say, surprised, "that doesn't seem too hard."

But wait a minute. What about a vacation? That's ten working days gone. What if you get sick? That could be six more. What about the firm holidays? You may need to subtract 20 to 24 days from your original yearly calculations. This means you should figure on 19 working days per month. 125 (hours per month) divided by 19 (workdays per month) = 6.6 hours per day of billable time. This is still possible, but it's more strenuous by the better part of an hour per day. If you want to come in at 9:00 a.m. and leave at 5:00 p.m., you won't have much time for coffee room chat and lunches.

The trick to projecting and accomplishing your billing requirements is to realize that an hour a day either plus or minus quickly becomes a cushion you can rely on or a whole lot of time you need to make up in order to make your quota. Also, in order to make meeting or exceeding that quota a reality, you will need to be working steadily for the whole year.

Law firms usually generate monthly, quarterly, and annual reports of billable hours. Aim to be ahead of your goal for the year by the end of the first quarter. This will allow you to plan and enjoy a vacation and face with greater equanimity the vicissitudes of health, weather, and work schedules. It may even allow you to enjoy the holiday season with your family!

How do you do this? Keep track of what you bill on a daily basis; it's a habit that will keep you productive and honest. You should have an idea, even in January, of how many hours you'd like to bill each month of the year. This kind of planning is extremely subjective. For example, I like to start out with a heavy first quarter and a strong, solid second quarter. I usually vacation in late June or early July and that means my hours for the third quarter are lower. October's a long month and most years I plan on working long days that month so that I go into November and December with time to spend on the holidays. This yearly plan suits my work habits and usually my workload, but of course I know I need to be a little flexible. If a case I'm working on is headed for trial in late June, I will have to rearrange vacation time and work extra hours preparing for the courtroom.

The point is that I manage the year—the year doesn't manage me. If I find myself falling below my own goals, I work a Saturday or make other adjustments. I don't wait passively to see how the year comes out.

To manage your own career, you should be recording your hours on your own tally sheet on at least a monthly basis so you can get a realistic picture of how you're doing. If you get behind—and we all do sometimes—you can decide right away if you want to make the time up by coming in early for a few days or working one Saturday. I probably sound like a Girl Scout here, but believe me, it's easier to make up one Saturday in March or April than to find yourself 32 hours short in December. I can almost guarantee you won't feel like working four Saturdays in December.

OTHER PRODUCTIVITY MEASUREMENTS

If your firm does not have billable requirements, you will need to find out how they analyze your productivity. If the analysis is task based because they bill clients per task (often called value billing), then you will have to be sure you are mastering sufficiently valuable tasks to provide a profit after the firm pays your salary and benefits as well as your portion of the electric bill, malpractice insurance, support salaries, and the many other expenses required to keep the firm operational. If the firm's requirements and method of quantifying productivity are not clearly laid out by someone at the firm, you will have to find out who to talk to. This is one area in which ignorance is not bliss.

There are some jobs, mostly government jobs, for which paralegals do not record hours and no clients are billed. The legal department provides services to the rest of the organization. If you are working in this kind of situation, be sure you have a frank talk with your boss early on to get some idea of how you can find out if you are productive in the eyes of your superiors.

NONBILLABLE WORK: A DANGEROUS NECESSITY

Every law firm and every sole practitioner has work that needs to be done but that is nonbillable. Examples of this are client receptions, researching and answering billing questions, creating proposals for service for potential new clients, intake calls, and giving educational seminars. All of us who become substantively involved in the life of a law firm and who have significant relationships with clients end up doing some of this work. It's unavoidable.

It's also dangerous. Every hour of nonbillable work means an hour less of billables. You will not be surprised to hear that more established staff in law firms tend to avoid these tasks and the newer folk often find themselves bombarded with requests of the form, "Do you have time to do this one thing for me...?"

During your probationary period it's especially difficult to say no. You're trying to get to know people and to get along with them. You want them to think of you as a team player, an asset to their practice, and a good all-around Joe. Even so, if billable hours are part of the evaluation process in your firm, you will have to manage requests for nonbillable help carefully.

Here are some hints. Plan on spending some extra hours each week during your first few months at the firm so that you can make your hours and help out with some nonbillable work. Field the requests as graciously as possible. For example, if attorney X asks if you could stop by the library and research the statutes on the presentation of tort claims to a state agency for an article he's writing, you might respond that you have a full plate right now and several assignments to complete that day, but that you'd be happy to spend twenty minutes after work or before work the next morning to check those statutes. This lets attorney X know you are very busy but that you are willing to help, even if it means some inconvenience for you personally. It also lets the attorney know that you know how to take care of yourself professionally—that you are not someone to call every time a freebie is needed.

It's very tempting to ask new staff to help out with nonbillable jobs. For one thing, new people don't have a full plate of work yet. You may find that you just get too many requests for nonbillable work. If that happens, you'll have to discuss the problem with someone. If you have a paralegal manager or a particular attorney assigned to supervise you, this is one of the things that person is supposed to help you handle. Talk about it. Always let people know you are willing to do your share, but that you have real billable work you must do or that you need billable work to do if you do not.

There is another side, a positive side, to the nonbillable work issue. Although nonbillables are something you must monitor and manage, don't underestimate the significance of taking part in this aspect of the firm's life. Lawyers often feel that their employees are only interested in sucking every penny out of the firm that they can. Since getting new business and maintaining the existing client roster is so critical to the ongoing success of any law firm, it's discouraging to the firm's partners to see associates and paralegals treat the firm's clients as a smorgasbord from which they feed. Sharing the nonbillable work required to maintain a healthy firm economy is in everyone's interest. It will allow you to develop valuable relationships with clients and lawyers, enhance your understanding of the business of running a legal practice, increase your professional stature, and make you feel more a part of the firm. So participate and enjoy doing it, but use your head.

DEMONSTRATE YOUR ENTHUSIASM FOR YOUR JOB

News flash! Nobody likes a sad sack, a wet blanket, or a sour puss. Obvious as that may seem, it's surprising how many employees, new and old, feel free to wander about the halls of a law firm with a long face, a slow, somber speaking voice, and an attitude that says, "God, I wish I weren't here." They do more to slow productivity in most businesses than computer crashes.

Do what you need to do to come to work feeling fresh and ready. Sleep enough. Eat breakfast. Work out. Listen to good music on your way in. Have a second cup of coffee. Whatever you need to do, figure it out and do it. Most firms have a few people who get to stay even though they need taking care of, who are continually unhappy and unhelpful. But these employees are not the winners in the firm. They are not given terrific assignments, they are not sought after by the best attorneys, and usually they are not paid the most.

Become actively enthusiastic about your job. Allow yourself to become engaged by your work. Perhaps you are learning a new area of law. Maybe you are working on behalf of a particularly likeable client. It could be that the lawyer you are working with is an expert you can learn from or has a lively intelligence that makes a discussion of most subjects stimulating. Maybe you are on the cutting edge of an issue or you are working in a situation where almost anything can happen. There is something about your work situation that can jack your interest up a notch. Notice it and let your enthusiasm show.

How do you show it? Well, a chipper "Good morning" doesn't hurt, but substantive involvement in your work is an even more effective way to communicate your interest in the firm's practice. When you are assigned a task, whether it's interviewing a witness or organizing files, give it your full and careful attention. Do it on time and do it well, very well. Think about how your particular task relates to the overall objectives of the work the firm is doing for the client. For example, if you are asked to put a set of documents in chronological order you may think it's a particularly boring, low-level task. You can either lug that box back to your cubicle and do just what's necessary and return the files to the attorney in charge, or you can take a look at what the documents (and hence the case) are about and begin to make connections. Maybe you can produce a timeline from those documents that clarifies who knew what, when. It may be a short inference from that to critical issues in the case. By the time you next speak with the assigning attorney you will have the factual background in the case that allows you to enter into a full-fledged analysis of the client's position and the likely outcome of the matter. You may have figured out what the holes are in the story, what else you need to find out in order to understand or to prove your client's case. Maybe you'll have identified the other side's weaknesses and be ready to draft interrogatories, requests for inspection of documents, or requests for admissions. In any case you can bet the attorney who asked for your help will notice that you are enthused about the case and able to think out what's gone on and to create a plan for what needs to happen next. These are professional traits and attitudes prized by good lawyers. This is also a way to work that generates real enthusiasm in paralegals for the work they do. Real enthusiasm is a major asset to a paralegal's career.

PREPARING FOR THE SIX-MONTH EVALUATION

No one owes you an actual meeting for evaluation at the end of your probationary period. I've seen people prepare well for their six-month end-of-probation review only to find out no one intends to sit down with them to talk about it. They passed. Everyone's busy. They're glad the paralegal's around, they intend to keep him, and they just want to get on with the work at hand. If it happens to you, enjoy it. But be prepared, just in case.

The first rule of all evaluations is "There should be no surprises." Things don't always fall out that way, but in a good working relationship no one finds out for the first time that her boss is unhappy with her at the evaluation meeting. How can you ensure this? One way is to ask ahead of time, calmly and quietly, how you are doing. You need to find the right time to do this, but taking the initiative to find out if your performance is meeting your boss' expectations is often a good idea.

It's usually awkward to ask an attorney a general performance question like, "So, Lee, I've been here for four months now and I was wondering, how am I doing?" A better approach is to talk with your boss about various assignments and projects as they are completed. If you are doing first drafts of documents you will have some idea from the number of red marks on work that comes back to you, but even that can be misleading. Some attorneys routinely mark up associate and paralegal work and still think the original drafter was doing a good job.

Choose a quiet time, perhaps at the end of the day, and ask the attorney who is assigning and reviewing your work if a particular project was up to snuff. Pay close attention to the response you receive. You are not just looking for a grade on your work, you are establishing a relationship with this person that will encourage frank and friendly communication about projects from here on in. The need to seek feedback will not end when you pass probation.

If you have developed a rapport with a particular attorney you can also try this approach: "Pat, I've been here four months now and I'll be going through an end-of-probation evaluation in two months. Can you give me any ideas that might help it go more smoothly?" The attorney may have some ideas for you, but just as likely your reminder that the six-month period is coming to a close may prompt that attorney to let the personnel people know that you have become a part of the team and she or he's happy with your work. This can go a long way toward making the six-month evaluation nothing more than a formality.

What should you be prepared to say at your six-month evaluation? Not much. This is not the time to bring up complaints about your working space, lack of secretarial support, or other things you would like to see changed. There are ways to address those concerns and you should read Chapter 11 for some ideas, but for now if the firm is happy with your performance the six-month re-view should be considered a congenial event. The firm is no longer reserving a right to discharge you without cause. You are one of the team, a regular. In a case like this the six-month evaluation is a grander version of the happy day when someone shook your hand and said you'd gotten the job.

ASSESSING YOUR FUTURE WITH THE FIRM

So far we've talked about what the firm thinks of you. The six-month mark is also a good time for you to start analyzing what you think of the firm. The hon-eymoon period is over and you've had time to get to know the players, the peo-ple with whom you may be working for many years. How are they doing at im-pressing you?

There are a lot of factors to consider when deciding how satisfactory a job is. You'll need to think about the attorneys and paralegals with whom you interact on a daily basis. This is a big factor because if they are interesting, stimulating legal thinkers you are likely to find that your work with them forms a core of job satisfaction that can outweigh some negative aspects of a job. If you are lucky enough to work with such people, you may still be proving yourself a signifi-cant and trustworthy team member, but you should be able to see a willingness on the part of the assigning attorneys to extend their confidence and to provide you with increasingly important assignments.

This does not mean you can expect an attorney to be cavalier about his or her practice. It takes time and consistently outstanding performance to convince a good attorney to trust the work ethic, professional judgment, and intellectual capacity of even an outstanding paralegal. This is as it should be. Attorneys have not only their own interests but the interests of clients to protect. Clients have placed their trust in the attorney they've hired and they don't expect the work involved to be delegated to the unproven. Even so, you should have a feel for what you can expect in terms of future responsibility.

You should also be able to assess what kind of professional growth the firm will support for paralegals. What's their position on continuing education? Law is a dynamic and constantly changing field. While we work at our desks, legis-latures are in session all over the country passing laws that we need to know about. Judges are writing opinions that will impact our clients' affairs. Your firm should do something to encourage all the legal professionals in its offices to up-date their legal education, all the time.

Continuing education support may be in the form of in-house seminars, newsletters citing recent legal developments that relate to the firm's specialties, paying for all or part of the fees for outside course work, and stocking the library with the latest legal news. Be sure to petition for support for continuing legal ed-ucation during your first six months, perhaps in month four or five. You need to establish a practice of staying educated and the firm's response to your request will tell you a lot. Continuing education is such an important part of a successful career that it has its own chapter in this book (Chapter 13). Don't hesitate to think badly of a firm that will not commit any funds or energy to continuing paralegal education.

By the six-month mark you will also have had time to see how the demands of this particular job fit with the demands of your personal life. This is a real issue and deserves thought. There are plenty of good firms, and good jobs, that are not a fit for every paralegal. It doesn't mean either the paralegal or the firm has a problem—they just may have different time requirements or goals.

Litigation, still the largest practice area for paralegals, is a good example. Substantial involvement in a litigation practice requires some long hours, maybe some long weeks, and certainly some weekends. That is the nature of the beast. The court system and court calendaring create a situation with a great deal of "hurry up and wait." Since you can't control a judge's calendar, how long the case in front of you will take, or even whether your case will be bumped by a case with priority, you have to be ready to go on a moment's notice. If you have young children or have other commitments that require that you be home by 5:30 p.m. or every weekend, then you really shouldn't choose litigation as a specialty. If the firm you work for specializes in litigation, even if you love the people you work with and the location and the paycheck and the practice and even if they love you, you may not have found a good fit.

It's important to take these kinds of factors seriously. They will have a huge effect on your professional success or lack of it, and they will have perhaps a greater effect on your life outside the office. There are lots of practice areas and they each have different time requirements, different temperament requirements, and different opportunities for professional growth. Find the one that's right for you.

Another important factor is the firm's apparent plan for the paralegals it employs. I say "apparent" because it can sometimes be difficult to figure out what, if anything, the firm envisions for its paralegal corps. But you should try because this too will have an impact on your potential future there. If they have a rigid paralegal program with steps for salary increases and a capping-out limit at the top, you should know that going in. You will probably not succeed in convincing them to change their program for you.

On the other hand, if you can't see any sign of formalization of a paralegal program you may find the firm's lack of interest discouraging, or you may see it as an opportunity to become a catalyst for moving the firm in that direction, or you may be the kind of paralegal who prefers to work in a less formalized setting. As you can see, many permutations are possible. What you need to do is keep your eyes and ears open and learn about the firm you have chosen. Once it has chosen you, you need to see if the potential there is what you'd hoped. You do not want to invest your time and energy in a situation that, with a little energy and thought, you could have figured out was not going to yield the job satisfaction you require.

Dealing with Difficulties and Boosting Your Own Morale

"Difficulties are things that show what men are."

Epictetus, circa 60 AD

Epictetus said *men*, but it's true for women too. Our ability to cope with difficulties on the job shows what each of us is made of and impacts our careers in a big way. Coping is a big part of success.

I'm not talking about keeping your head when everyone around you is falling apart. That's a special topic and something you can train yourself to do. I'm talking about coping with the everyday realities of a professional life lived within the confines of a law office, an office where you will never be the lawyer, the top dog, or the boss and where (if it's well run) there is no one you can scream at when you're tired and hungry and underappreciated and behind even though you've been giving 110 percent.

This is not the usual state of affairs in a well-handled career and I don't expect it to happen to you very often, but we all have a professional weak spot and work has a way of finding it. The sooner you identify yours and decide in advance how you will handle the situations that really get your goat, the more secure your future success will be. Here are some coping mechanisms for everyday situations that may come your way.

DIFFICULT CLIENTS

Many of the people you meet as firm clients will be a pleasure to work with and serve. But (Surprise!) sometimes people who end up in legal battles really are not all that much fun, even on a good day. They will certainly not be at their best if their personal or business matters have ended up in the hands of the legal system. The fact that they are also facing hefty legal bills will most certainly test their composure and patience. Add to all of this that they may well be intimidated by the attorney involved, or at least not willing to make her angry, and you have a situation that could get stressful for you.

The first thing to deal with when interacting with difficult clients is your own expectations. Quit expecting it to be fun, or even pleasant. Face the fact that every job has a downside and working with this particular client may be your professional burden. Expect the grief.

Don't personalize it. Even if a client says he is unhappy with you in particular, don't credit the remark any more than you would take the screaming of a four-year-old as a personal affront. In 99 percent of the cases it really won't be personal, and in the remaining 1 percent it won't help to treat it as such.

Monitor your facial expressions and your speaking voice. Offer a congenial greeting every time you see or talk to the client, even if she yelled at you last time or he was unconscionably rude. Before you see or speak with a difficult client, get yourself together. Take a deep breath. Remind yourself this phone call or meeting is not your whole life, it's not even your whole day, and that giving it more weight than it merits won't help at all. Think calm thoughts, and remind yourself that this is your job and you are getting paid to do it.

Smile and don't give any indication that you expect unpleasantness. Be professional and if possible efficient, but remember some clients make efficiency impossible. If they lose documents, lie, forget appointments, or keep you waiting while they talk to their stockbrokers you will have to do the best you can and document the incidents. Keep your meetings or phone calls with difficult clients as brief as possible, but don't give the impression that you are unwilling to spend the time required.

Then reward yourself for your professional behavior with lunch out, or a stop by the bookstore on the way home, or a phone call to your best friend from college. Do some small thing that will take the curse off the day.

If the client is generally difficult you may be able to share your frustration with another member of the legal team, but be sure you don't do that until after the client has left the building. Even then it can be dangerous and frankly, the sooner you can make it a "no big deal" part of the day, the better your interactions will go in the future. Remember, it's always a little creepy seeing someone you have just spoken negatively about, even if you think the words were well-deserved and didn't really do any harm.

Guard against inappropriate familiarity with clients who try to use you as their personal therapist or their personal whipping boy. If you need help setting boundaries, talk to the attorney on the case. I've seen instances when one call from the attorney to the client outlining the paralegal's training, education, and capabilities, as well as asking that any further complaints be communicated directly to the attorney, has curtailed inappropriate client behavior quickly.

Maintain that professional attitude. A cheerful, supportive smile can help to smooth out a rough event—a custody hearing or a probate matter, for instance—but don't try to make people going through emotionally tough times happy. Be prepared for various coping mechanisms on the parts of these individuals. In an effort to feel as if they have some control over the legal processes they are unhappily involved in, they may want to double-check everything you do. They may make unjust complaints to the attorney you work with. They may call constantly or they may not return your calls at all. They may scream about the bill or promise to deliver documents they never find. After you obtain a wonderful result in their legal matter they may leave with a parting shot that cuts to the quick.

If so, you must remind yourself that clients come and clients go. Mr. or Ms. Difficult won't be around forever. However, if you usually like your job you may want to stay around a long time. Don't let a tough client put you in a position that jeopardizes your own professional future. It's a fact that there are some people you cannot make happy, and chief among them are people trying to solve their personal problems through the legal system.

Hot Tip: Think of difficult clients the way you think of other temporary challenges in your life. I think of mine as a tough hill on a mostly pleasant running trail. I just settle in and keep going, and pretty soon that hill is history and my attention's on the blue sky, the creek nearby, and the cool soda waiting at the end of the run!

DIFFICULT LAWYERS*

Your Attorney

Dealing with a difficult assigning attorney is a tougher situation. No workforce is uniformly professional in its behavior, and a law degree does not necessarily bestow a benign attitude or even a congenial personality on the recipient. Difficult lawyers can be a longer-term problem in your career than difficult clients. How you handle a problem lawyer can make a real difference in your opportunities and your success.

Rule number one is to tread softly. Once a lawyer is a partner she's pretty much a permanent fixture in the firm. There are instances when a partner can behave so badly she's asked (forced) to leave, but by and large partners are here to stay. If the lawyer in question is an associate, the behavior you find so inappropriate may well result in a solution to your problem. More than one obnoxious or inconsiderate or simply foolish associate has opened his mouth too often, displayed poor judgment and bad manners, and simple found himself out of a job. But even that you can't count on. Use your head.

Usually it's not a good idea to complain openly about the lawyer giving you trouble. Do seek advice from a trusted mentor. If the behavior is really bad, expect the firm to do something to improve the situation.

Rule number two is that managing your own career depends in large part on being able to position yourself so that you end up on a team or among coworkers who are worthwhile and with whom you feel you can develop a strong, positive working relationship. The techniques discussed in Chapter 7 are

---

* This section deals with the simply difficult attorney, not the sexual harasser or the physically, verbally, or emotionally abusive. Abusive situations are fact-specific and variable enough to require a case-by-case analysis and can't be dealt with here. If you are in a situation involving harassment or abuse, see the personnel or management team for help or consult an attorney.

very useful for helping you do this. One of the best ways to handle interactions with a lawyer who is giving you a tough time or who fails to reward your efforts with billable work is to minimize those interactions. Arrange things so that you are profitably busy on other matters that benefit the firm. Sometimes a change in working station may even solve this kind of problem. If you don't work on the same floor with this attorney, you may not even run into him.

Rule number three comes into play when you assume you cannot get out of interacting with a difficult attorney. Then, you need to decide whether you want this person to control your professional destiny. There are difficult people in every law office in America. If you leave every place you work when you run up against these un-fun people, your resume will look like you majored in hop-scotch. You can come up with alternate coping mechanisms, each tailored to your own situation and the nature of your ongoing relationship with the attorney.

For instance, maybe the woman is a pain to talk to until you get her really focused on the case at hand. If so, don't go into her office to shoot the breeze. Go in when something new has happened that may change the way you should handle the case. Go in when you are ready to work on the in-house seminar the two of you have been assigned to present. Go in when you have just read the latest cases in your area of expertise.

Even though this attorney is not one of your favorite people, you may share an interest in baseball or art or jazz or roller blading. When you meet Attorney Feelbad, take the initiative and turn the conversation to things you both find worthwhile. Just remember that you are managing a difficult working relationship. Do not look for collegiality and do not look for friendship, even professional friendship. It will probably not be forthcoming.

Rule number four states that there actually are cases when one partner in a firm can so poison the atmosphere that it really is dreadful to work there. No one can casually advise you to leave a job, but this situation may require it. If you do so, do it on your terms and in a way that benefits your future. This means you do not do it precipitously, after a shouting match in the lobby. It also means you do not just quit and leave yourself and your dependents without an income. And it means you never, *never* say the reason you left that firm was because you couldn't stand to work with Attorney So-and-So anymore.

Carefully and discreetly start a job search that results in a new and improved position for you. Upon leaving, thank all the good people at the firm for their collegiality and support and for all the things that you learned from them while you were there. Paste on a pleasant smile and go see Attorney So-and-So before you leave, shake hands cordially, and thank her for what you have learned from her too. No parting shots, no burning of bridges. That's for the playground. Take the high road.

Opposing Counsel

One of the downsides of the paralegal business is crummy lawyers on the other side: the other side of lawsuits, the other side of contract negotiations, the other side of probate disputes. Lawyers with bad characters feel entirely free to behave badly, often very badly, toward paralegals who work for their opponents. They can be rude and unkind, but much worse is their propensity for trying to use paralegals to get information unethically, to try to get paralegals to make commitments they are not authorized to make, and to embarrass paralegals and the firms they work for. Of course, some of them lie. Beware of these characters.

Always begin a relationship with opposing counsel cordially and professionally. Expect good behavior; usually you will get it. But if you find yourself face-to-face or on the phone with one of the bad lawyers out there, use caution—extreme caution.

The goal here is to stay out of the corral. What does that mean? If you have ever seen sheep being herded by a good sheepdog, you know what I mean. A good dog is canny; moves first quickly, then slowly; then crouches on the ground so the sheep think he's asleep. Just when the sheep let down their guard he's up and charging and before you can say, "Oh my gosh, I didn't mean to commit to that!" they're in the corral.

A good "bad attorney" uses similar tactics on paralegals. He may use flattery ("Frank says he relies on you heavily in his practice and I can see why...") or he may fly off the handle and start yelling. She may promise to get the information you're entitled to, and then never call back. She never intended to call back. When you call her she's "in conference." Meanwhile discovery cutoffs are nearing and when your boss asks why you don't have the information, you find yourself stammering, "But she said she'd call... ." Be careful. Follow the rules and follow procedures.

For starters, always identify yourself as a paralegal. Specify the limitations of your assignment and authority. If an opposing counsel won't let up but keeps pressuring you to reveal details about your case or make commitments, reidentify yourself as a paralegal. If that doesn't work, excuse yourself from the interaction immediately. Get in touch with your attorney and get direction.

If you must interact with a bad attorney over time, create your own paper trail by means of follow-up letters. These letters will look something like this:

Dear Attorney Blank:

This will confirm our telephone conversation today in which you agreed to provide a list of all the properties in which your client has, or has had, an interest at any time between January 30, 1968 and January 30, 1972. You have agreed on your client's behalf to produce this information without the service of formal discovery requests.

Your cooperation in this matter is appreciated.

Sincerely,

Your name
Paralegal

or

Dear Attorney Blank:

This will confirm the fact that when you called today to ask for an extension of time in which to respond to the complaint filed by James Smith against your client Sam Jones, I informed you that I was not authorized to grant an extension of time in which to respond. I further informed you that Mr. Crandall authorized only an extension of time in which to answer the complaint. I also informed you that Mr. Crandall is not in the office nor available by phone today.

You then told me you would leave a message for Mr. Crandall on his voice mail system concerning this matter. At this time no extension to respond or to answer the complaint has been granted.

Sincerely,

Your name
Paralegal

These are clearly awkward, unhappy letters to be writing and none of us wants to spend the day this way. But if the attorney on the other side of a matter is untrustworthy you are better off safe and awkward than sorry. Our job is to protect the client's interests, not to expose the client to potential controversy about the content of the telephone call.

Another client protection to keep in mind when dealing with a difficult attorney on the other side is watching the client's bill. Tricky attorneys routinely try to get their opponents to do their work, and thus generate a charge for the other client that rightfully belongs elsewhere. Here's an example. Attorney X calls to see if she can have a 15-day extension in discovery. You anticipated this request and have, in fact, discussed it with your boss in advance. You're fully authorized to grant the extension and you graciously do so.

Then Attorney X says, "Great, could you do a confirming letter?" Here you are, being amiable, being helpful—and besides that you're trained to take direction from attorneys! But the confirming letter is not for your client's convenience, nor will it advance his or her case. Attorney X is the one who needs that letter in the file. You are not authorized to spend your time and the client's money on a letter that will benefit Attorney X and her client. The correct response is to politely decline. "I'm sorry, I'm not available to do that. Why don't you have your paralegal get that out?" You have remained civil and drawn a clear boundary that you can bet Attorney X will recognize immediately. You've also let her know she's not dealing with a dodo.

When dealing with unscrupulous opposing counsel, it is a good idea to keep in mind your own vulnerabilities. If you have read much of this book you've figured out that I have quite a bit of ego invested in thinking I'm pretty smart. This can make me stupidly susceptible to flattery. If a smarter-than-me opposing counsel starts treating me like it's my case we're discussing, I'm tempted to start acting as if that's true. But it's not true. I am not entitled to make the final call on many matters. I have to watch myself and not overstep my bounds.

You may have a weak spot too. Maybe you have a temper and if someone is very rude you will start paying more attention to that behavior than to protecting the client's interests. Or maybe you're afraid of people who yell and are likely to give in to their demands. If you know yourself well enough to identify your own Achilles' heel, you're ahead of the game. Be sure to keep it under control when dealing with attorneys who are less than principled and willing to take advantage in any way they can.

Finally, don't take it too much to heart if a bad attorney ends up not liking you very much. If a bad attorney ends up not wanting to deal with you it may be a sign that you are doing your job. If you hold a deadbeat attorney to a court-ordered deadline or refuse to provide your half of an exchange to someone who is not ready to give you his, that attorney may well decide you are not someone he wants to be up against next time. He may tell your boss he thinks you are unreasonable and difficult. If you work for a smart attorney yourself, she'll understand and probably enjoy the bad attorney's discomfort—and she'll probably assign you to make most of the calls to that attorney in the future!

DIFFICULT COWORKERS

Oddly enough, difficult attorneys are often easier to work with than difficult coworkers of the secretarial or paralegal variety. One reason, of course, is that your status with regard to these individuals is less clear. Even a secretary you supervise and evaluate may also work for a partner who loves him. Of course she loves him—he does her work while yours languishes in the "to do someday" pile. How can you handle articulating your concerns about his performance without sending him running to the attorney for support?

If your difficult coworker is a secretary in this position, you will need to be smart to maintain a useful and productive working relationship, but it can be done. Try getting to know the person whose attitude is mucking up your day. Remember that when people really need understanding and a human response at work, they are often not at their best. Someone who has just failed to spell-check your motion and lost the phone number of opposing counsel is probably not going to inspire a warm, "Hey, Lee, how are you doing today?" But most of us can use a friendly hello at the office and often someone's negative attitude at work is fueled by the fact that he or she does not feel noticed.

Remember that getting to know someone and lending a friendly ear does not mean that you become intimately involved in trying to solve problems that are beyond your purview. Lee may be dealing with something as simple as a child with a cold or as difficult as a deteriorating marriage. In either case your active participation in addressing the problem is inappropriate. However, you can do the kindness of acknowledging that there are other, often larger, concerns in people's lives than your letter. You may communicate this by something as simple as asking, "How are you?" and thereby marking the fact that getting your documents out the door is not the entire focus of everyone's life.

Very little has been written about paralegal interaction. It's not a very comfortable topic. The truth is that relationships among paralegals often range from distant to competitive. This is largely because most paralegal work is done for and with attorneys, not other paralegals, and during the course of a busy workday paralegal interaction is usually limited. In addition, many lawyers do not see solidarity among the paralegal workforce as a good thing. As a lawyer once told me, "We don't want to do anything that would encourage you guys to organize!"

Strong, supportive paralegal-to-paralegal relationships are not often encouraged or fostered. There's also the fact that some paralegals see other paralegals as competition for work—work they may need to make their billable hour requirements. We have to consciously decide to see each other as valuable allies.

That said, most of us do get along well enough to back each other up as needed and to have a friendly interest in each other's work. The difficult paralegal coworker usually falls into one of three categories.

1. **The insecure paralegal.** Sometimes this is a longtime paralegal who is often low on work, but usually it's a new paralegal who is worried about success. Here, as with the difficult secretary, a tolerant attitude is the best way to go. There is usually not a great deal you can do to direct work to someone who is underutilized by the lawyers in the firm, but as your own career progresses you may find there are tasks you can delegate with your attorney's permission.

In the case of the new paralegal, give the situation some time and be as friendly as you can be. I've noticed it really cheers new paralegals up to hear about mistakes I've made, especially those I made when I was a new paralegal myself. You may find a lunch invitation is well received and that it gives you a chance to get to know the person behind the paralegal. However if you meet resistance, don't push it. This person will either come around or wash out.

2. **The superterritorial paralegal.** This paralegal hates the idea of cross-training. No one—I mean no one—except her should know her job, work with her attorney, or talk to her clients. Unless you are specifically instructed to get involved in this paralegal's caseload, give him or her a wide berth. If you are told to get involved in one of "his" projects, make sure that information is communicated to the paralegal by the attorney who wants it to happen. Then be as tactful as you can, and remember that some people are so high-strung and emotionally attached to their work that you cannot fail to get on their nerves. So be it—you won't be working together forever.

3. **The sloppy paralegal.** This paralegal presents a sticky situation. Some people just are not careful with their work. If you are assigned to work together, you should be concerned. The chances of your changing someone's work standards are very small. The chances of your ticking them off while you try are very large.

In many cases you will simply have to do more than your share of the work, checking on details, reviewing documents, etc. If the situation will be ongoing you may find you need to have a confidential chat with a trusted attorney. Otherwise, you will have to keep up the work on your own, putting the client's interests ahead of your sense of personal injustice. Remind yourself that the rest of the world isn't blind. Most people will see the situation for what it is and appreciate your professionalism.

DIFFICULT CASES

It happens to everybody in every field—the situation in which you cannot win or even do well. You don't even have to be a litigator. You can be the estate planner trying to help a client who is losing her health, a business paralegal working with a firm that is trying against impossible odds to survive in the marketplace, or a family paralegal working on a custody matter. Generally these are no-win situations and nobody, even a superstar paralegal, can change that. How do you deal with this kind of discouragement?

It helps if you can notice what's going on, that you are not quite so enthused about a particular matter as you usually are about big projects. You don't feel like picking up the phone to call the client, you don't seem to stop by the responsible attorney's desk to pick up the file, you forget to put it on your to-do list. All this is telling you that you're stuck with a bummer and you need to figure out how you will keep your head in the game, your spirits up, and your deadlines current.

1. First of all, stop and realize it's not you having the problem and it's not you causing the problem. You're one of the good guys trying to solve the problem. You may not succeed, but you are in there giving it your best. If the situation merits compassion, the compassion should be directed toward the real figures in the drama. When you take yourself out of the middle of the picture, you will take the picture out of the middle of your work life.

2. Resolve to do your best in a timely fashion all the time. Do not allow your reticence to talk with an upset client dissuade you from picking up the phone when needed. Find out exactly what your role in the case should be and fill it. Do not take on emotional matters that you cannot control. It's not easy to watch a custody battle over a four-year-old, but it won't help the four-year-old if you misplace the file or fail to telephone with a court appearance date. Face the fact that you are not in a position to make the child's parents behave any better than they are willing to. Make sure you behave well.

3. Practice professional kindness. Very often the times when, as professionals in a business setting, we are moved to extend overly personal sympathy to people we have been hired to help professionally, we are motivated more by our own needs than theirs. This does not mean you should interact in a cold and entirely unfeeling way. It means you should extend to clients the cordial, professional relationship they are seeking without projecting yourself into their private lives.

It is often helpful for people in an emotionally trying situation to be able to sit down and discuss the nonemotional aspects of the situation. They want to know what the hearing will be like procedurally, or what options they can offer their workers when they close the plant, or whether they will have to meet with an estranged relative face-to-face in the judge's chambers. They do not need to break down and cry in your office or work themselves into a state in which they shout or say things they will later regret.

Finally, try to keep this matter in perspective. It's not the only thing on your work calendar and one day it will be resolved, both for you and for the client.

DIFFICULT TRAFFIC

No, I'm not kidding. Many paralegals face both commutes and on-the-job travel that can make people want to pull their hair out. Here are some traffic tips for you.

1. Invest in a tape deck. You can use travel time to listen to educational tapes, learn a foreign language, or enjoy books on tape. I have even used that time to review audiotapes of meetings that were relevant to lawsuits I was working on. That's billable, you know.

2. If you have to drive a lot, invest in the most worry-free, comfortable car you can afford. A reliable vehicle in the "run to the courthouse, run to the client's, run to the photocopy place, then run to the law library" lives of many paralegals is a necessity, not a luxury.

3. Be sure to keep track of deductible or reimbursable mileage (it adds up very quickly) as well as any car upkeep that applies. Don't forget to keep receipts for parking!

4. Keep a pair of tennis shoes in the trunk along with all the emergency gear you think makes sense (a flashlight, jumper cables, antifreeze, paper towels, and oil) and stash an extra twenty dollars (at least) in the glove box. When you spend this twenty for gas or lunch or parking (and you will), replace it. Make sure the spare tire is functional and if you have never changed a flat tire, practice this weekend. That's right—this weekend. It can save you a lot of time, and it can save your life.

5. If you have to plan a meeting or attend a deposition in a large city, be sure you factor travel time in, including the poorly named rush hour. Check the reports of accidents or other mishaps before you go. This may not be critical where you work, but in the Los Angeles area the commuter traffic is so heavy that you must plan to leave L.A. by 2:30 p.m. if you want to be sure to miss the ordinary havoc. By three o'clock the early birds are heading home.

6. Always reconfirm meetings and other events shortly before you get in the car. Ask for details like where to park when you get there. Let someone in your office and in your family know where you're going and when you'll be back.

LEARN TO BOOST YOUR OWN MORALE

"There is such a choice of difficulties that I am at a loss...."
James Wolfe 1726–1759

It's a tough day. You have a difficult project. You really need to think but the phone will not quit ringing. Your workload is almost over the limit, but you've just been handed three rushes. You were finally able to schedule an afternoon off, but discovered you need the time for a root canal and when you arrived home, numb and fat-faced, to make dinner there was a phone message from your mom. The whole family has decided it would be great to have Christmas at your house this year.

Well, my friend, this too shall pass, but in the meantime, right now, you need something to boost your spirits. You may not get it from your firm (cutting back on raises and support staff) or your boss (whose child was up all night with an ear ache) or your paralegal crony (who just found out his car needs a new transmission) or your secretary (who will get to type all this work you are generating). So what do you do when you need a little TLC and everyone else is preoccupied with their own tales of woe? You self-regenerate. This is the opposite of self-destruct. Here's how to do it.

1. **Master yoga breathing.** Some folks call this belly breathing and it is a great way to improve your day. If you are unfamiliar with this technique, check a hatha yoga book out of the library and give it a try. This kind of slow, controlled breathing involves relaxing the diaphragm so you can fill the bottom of your lungs (extending your belly, hence the name) and then fill the upper parts of your lungs. The complete breath in is matched by the complete breath out. If you try this you may be surprised at how shallow your breath has become sitting at your computer. For quick, on-the-spot relief, it's a winner.

2. **Make that call.** Call your mother, favorite uncle, best friend from junior high, church choir director, someone from your past who made a real contribution to your life, or someone you owe. This call is not to tell them you're having a bad day, but to say thanks for something specific and wonderful they did for you. I guarantee this will improve your outlook. At the age of 44 I called the mother of a gradeschool friend to thank her for all the blueberry muffin and scrambled egg breakfasts she'd made for me during the years her daughter and I practiced baton twirling before school. She remembered me and she was glad to get the call. She was amazed to think that her efforts in 1959 were still valued in 1994. The twenty minutes you spend on your "out of the blue" thank-you call will make a difference!

3. **Don't work through lunch.** Take your secretary out for a sandwich, go to the gym, browse your favorite bookstore, but don't work through lunch. All that will get you is sponge brain and a martyr complex. Many of the rushes that make us think we haven't a spare moment for a break are things that really can wait. The hour you spend noticing what is good in the world—even if it's sitting

on a bench watching the clouds—will refresh you. Remember, if you are not taking care of yourself, somewhere deep down inside you are waiting for someone else to take care of you.

   4.   Choose one job and see it through. I know this seems like the kind of impossible advice you always get from people who write books, but give it a try. While you're working on objections to requests for production, forget the exhibits that are not yet ready for trial. If you have to jump in the car to deliver a will for signature to a sick client, do not think about the six trusts that were on the to-do list for the afternoon.

   You can discipline your mind to thinking about what you are getting done. It does no good to get into a swivet and bounce from chore to chore. When one project is as far as you can take it, cross it off today's list, move the remainder to tomorrow's list, and move on. More time is wasted in the general state of confusion "too much work" generates than in gossiping by the water cooler. You can be efficient.

   5.   Review your five-year plan. You don't have one? We all need a five-year plan. Use your commute time, tub time, or dishwashing time to let your mind ramble down the lanes of possibility. Is this your dream job? Do you want to retire from here? Or should you be making personal lists of things you intend to accomplish and places you intend to go?

   A favorite exercise of mine is to write (honestly) on a piece of paper what I want my life to be like in five years. Then I turn the paper over and write down what I am doing now to move toward my goals. You don't have to be hard on yourself, just honest. What you will probably find out is that your goals still require hard work, but you'll also notice a little wind in your sails if you set your sights on your own goals, your own life. After all, no matter how bad today may look, you are still in charge.

10 HAPPY ANNIVERSARY!

"The bell strikes one! We take no note of time... ."
Edward Young 1684–1765

Congratulations! You've been on the job for one year, a big accomplishment. This chapter covers the preparation for your review, the review itself, salary issues, how to assess your job and future with your firm, and other roles paralegals can play in a law practice. Let's start with your evaluation.

PREPARE FOR YOUR ANNUAL REVIEW

You have to prepare for your one-year evaluation, but there is every likelihood that your preparation will not play a big part in the meeting. Why? Because in many, perhaps most, working situations the evaluation of a paralegal goes on daily and by the time the actual formal event occurs both the attorney and the paralegal know how it will all come down.

This is a good situation. You want your relationship with your supervising attorney to be one in which you can expect to hear about any problems as they occur, not eight months later at a formal evaluation.

I tell the attorneys I work closely with that I prefer to be educated as I go along. I'm aiming for excellence. If I fail to meet their highest expectations I want to hear about it. There have even been instances when I have sought feedback directly after a meeting. ("Did I speak too often? Did I bring up the wrong thing?") The practice of asking to be evaluated and held accountable on a regular basis is one of the keys to developing a good relationship with the attorneys you work for and to establishing a career based in reality.

So in the best-case scenario you won't hear big news at your evaluation. You probably won't need to rely heavily on your preparation, but do it anyway. It will help you evaluate your own growth and your accomplishments and that is valuable in itself.

The first thing you'll need to do is to recheck your billable hours and your profitability against what the firm budgets for you. This information should be available in printout form from data processing or the business staff who does the firm's billing. If you are not able to determine whether you are meeting or exceeding the firm's budgeted profitability figures, make a note of that so you can discuss it at your evaluation. Law firms hire paralegals to increase their profits. You need to know if you are profitable.

Then review your calendar and time sheets and note the major projects you have worked on. Review each significant matter and note the attorney with whom you worked, as well as what kind of support you provided. If you did clearly identifiable projects, organizing data, drafting serious contracts or wills or motions, working with witnesses, serving as a contact point or liaison with an important client, make a note of that too.

Review your skill development. Make a list of courses you took, seminars you attended, and learning curve work projects such as assisting at trial. If you can, include details showing how your continuing education is making you a more valuable asset on the legal team.

If you've received any commendations, compliments, awards, or atta-boy letters from clients be sure you photocopy them for the evaluator to see prior to the actual event. If you have published any articles or taught classes, that information should be provided also.

You should also note what courses you intend to take next year and what skills you intend to develop. Give some thought to what kinds of matters you would like to work on in the next year. While it doesn't work well to demand a change of assignment, most lawyers like it if their employees indicate a special interest in a particular area. They think if you're inspired your performance will benefit—and they're right.

THE ACTUAL EVENT

Assuming that you are pretty good at reading the weather and that therefore you won't be caught by surprise with really bad news, you can expect your annual review to be an expanded version of what the attorneys you work with have been communicating to you all year. Your strengths will be noted and that's always extremely pleasant.

Do not be surprised, especially in your first few years in the business, to hear a little about areas in which your employer would like to see you grow. Maybe your writing skills are still developing or your experience with client interaction is limited. Don't panic; as long as these comments are phrased in a positive way ("We'd like to see you work on your drafting skills a little"), they indicate a willingness on the firm's part to invest in you. Take them up on it.

In response to the writing skills comment you might say, "I think I could use some work there too. Why don't I look into some legal writing courses and let you know what I find? Perhaps you could advise me on which one would be good to take." This kind of response is terrifically helpful to the evaluator, who has most likely been worried that you will take the comments as serious disapproval. It also communicates your maturity and your willingness to receive help when it's offered.

Some evaluation comments should trigger concern. If anyone notes that you come in too late, that you are often absent, or that a particular attorney has expressed an unwillingness to use you on his or her projects, take these comments as serious dissatisfaction on someone's part with your performance. These concerns merit your immediate attention. If lateness or absences are mentioned, be sure you get very clear, very quickly, about what hours they expect you to keep. Say that you intend to remedy this problem immediately and that you'd like a brief review on this particular issue in six months. Then change your work schedule to meet their expectations, right away.

WRITTEN EVALUATIONS

At some performance reviews the paralegal is handed a sheaf of written evaluations that have been filled out by a number of attorneys. If this happens to you, ask if you should read them there or later on your own. If you are asked to read them on the spot, and you usually are, sit back and do so. Read them all and read them thoroughly. You will not be in a position to work with the evaluator toward a mutually satisfactory closure on the issues addressed in the paperwork if you don't know what it says.

Evaluators often ask if there's anything you want to discuss. Proceed carefully here. Your evaluation is about evaluating you. It is not usually the best time to bring up problems you are having with coworkers, the firm, parking, secretarial support, or supplies. You may want to have the description of a course you'd like to take handy and ask the evaluator if it would be a good investment of time and money given the practice area you are involved in. You may wish to mention one project that you particularly liked working on and even say you hope you can be assigned to that kind of project again. But don't gripe at this event. There will be other opportunities to address your problems. (See Chapter 11 for tips.)

It's customary for the evaluator to close the formal event by announcing the amount of your raise. If the raise is sufficient or generous, the whole process can be closed out on a positive note of thanks from you and congratulations on a job well done. If you think negotiating a different raise is appropriate you will probably do better to thank the attorney who is evaluating you and say that you would like to discuss the raise further at some time. This leaves the evaluator the option of taking it up then and there or letting you know who you should talk to and when.

NEGOTIATING YOUR RAISE

Most firms do not expect to negotiate salaries at annual evaluations. They intend to announce your raise and receive a big thank-you in return. If you are new to the paralegal field and there are no special circumstances attached to your employment (i.e., you are not also a nurse who specializes in personal injury work) this is probably what you should expect too. A key to negotiation is being ready to walk at some point, and if you are not prepared to do that—if you like your job, are learning enough, and think you can use this as a solid resume entry for three or more years—then you may do well to live with the raise offered if it is at all reasonable.

Keep in mind that the kinds of raises based on performance that were usual in the late 1980s and early 1990s have gone away, and that many law firms do not give cost of living adjustments each year either. As I write this, the trend to freeze salaries or give very low raises seems to be easing but the days when law firms could charge whatever they thought reasonable are gone. Clients have a great deal more to say about what they pay for legal services than they once did. This has affected the bottom line for many firms and raises for firm employees as well.

If you decide to try to negotiate a higher raise than you are offered be aware of all relevant firm policies. If the firm has a cap on salaries for paralegals who are viewed as entry-level, and if you have fewer than two years of experience, then your desire to be paid as much as a journeyman paralegal will probably not be honored. But if you are ready to graciously communicate the reasons the firm should give you a better raise, do so.

Be sure to arm yourself with as much information as you can get your hands on. Your arsenal should include:

1. Your salary and benefit information in a detailed format;
2. A list of clear accomplishments during the past year—projects undertaken and completed, cases won, etc.; include special items like training newer employees;
3. Congratulatory notes or thank-you letters from clients or attorneys;
4. Hard information about the local pay rates for paralegals with your skill level and experience;
5. Information documenting any speaking engagements or other public appearances you have made that reflect well on the firm;
6. Records of classes you taught or took that will benefit the firm.

Present this material in a friendly manner. It doesn't help to appear coercive or demanding. Remember, lawyers are trained to deal with attempts to intimidate them and even if you could do it the long-term results would seriously damage your relationship with the firm. Your approach should be informational. Perhaps the decision makers are not aware of the going rates for someone with your skill level.

It really is worthwhile to rehearse your request for a raise with someone before you do it for real. Choose someone you respect and trust. Spend a few minutes going over some of the objections you expect to encounter and then sit at a table and open the meeting. You can bet the attorney you actually speak to about a raise will put the whole thing in your lap, so prepare a graceful opening.

The opening should include the fact that you appreciate the firm's (or the attorney's) willingness to meet with you on this issue. Be sure to mention what has been particularly rewarding for you in the past year ("I appreciated the chance to go to trial with Frank on the Hanson matter"). Choose something that was also positive for the firm (You and Frank won the Hanson case!). Then go ahead and state your case: "I'm here to ask for a larger raise. I was given $1,500, which I appreciate, but I think my efforts and my accomplishments this past year merit a $3,000 raise."

Be prepared to give your pitch. If your efforts and accomplishments merit a larger raise, lay them out. This is a time when you may be able to mention things that would be unsuitable in a more formal setting. For example, if there is a particular attorney who has come to rely on you, it may be worthwhile to the firm to reward you for that role. If you have developed a relationship with a good client that contributes to the client's satisfaction with the firm, this too may be compensable.

Keep in mind that there may be reasons you think a raise would be fair that will not serve as justification for one. When I transferred from a satellite office to the main office of my firm I increased my commute by forty minutes a day (minutes I could have been billing at the satellite office) and added dollars onto each week's gas bill. Although my paycheck didn't change, I was suddenly making less money. However, the move was my idea. I wanted it. The increased travel time and gas expense were entirely within my control and I would not have been justified in asking the firm to pay for it.

Likewise, if you have incurred expenses, have kids going into college, or have to buy a new car, those facts will not serve as a reason for the firm to raise your salary. Do not bring them up at a salary negotiation session. Your demeanor should be adult and professional. Do not get teary-eyed or agitated and do not make threats.

This is also not the time to complain about your workload or allude to the wonderful pay you have heard paralegals make at another firm. It's ineffective and it will certainly have a negative effect on the reviewer's image of you. If you do not get the raise you want this time, be gracious and begin to think about how you can present your case the next time or whether in fact you want to look around for a better paying job. If you are thinking along those lines, do not tell your employer about it.

OTHER COMPENSATION

Finally, if the firm is unable to give you the salary raise you desire, do not forget to consider other ways in which you can be compensated. Perhaps the firm will underwrite attendance at a conference or provide time off for you to attend college classes. Perhaps they can improve your working environment or extend some leeway in the flextime arrangement. You may need secretarial help and be able to convince them that you deserve it. If you have done an outstanding job all year, help them find a way to reward you that doesn't violate firm policy.

I know of one paralegal who moved to a new city and had to take a job that paid less than she was used to and less than she felt she was worth. In negotiations she explained that she understood they could not meet her salary demand, but that she thought things could work out well for them both if she could have one month, rather than the standard two weeks, paid vacation time each year. The lawyers at this firm were looking for a way to hire this paralegal without establishing a new salary standard. They graciously provided her with the vacation time and everyone left the table happy.

THE FIRM'S FINANCES

Don't forget to factor in the firm's current financial situation. If business is good and the partners are happy with the profits you have a better chance of negotiating your raise. If the firm leadership has just announced an austerity program or laid off other workers it is unlikely to grant you a raise, no matter how good you are. Whatever the results of your effort to get a larger raise, leave the interview with a smile on your face and a cordial handshake for the attorney. Even taking the time to listen to your request for a salary increase is an act of respect you should appreciate. Your gracious behavior now will also leave an opening for further discussions, next time.

SAY THANKS

Finally, like anyone else, attorneys are more inclined to generosity if they feel their efforts at providing you with a good work environment, interesting work, and fair pay are appreciated. Don't forget to let the powers that be know that you notice when they do well by employees. If your firm has a 401K plan or good dental benefits or paid parking, do not take it for granted. Appreciate these forms of compensation and express your appreciation. Write a note to the executive committee, stop by the managing partner's office, or see the business manager. Do something to show them their efforts have not gone unnoticed. In the long run you and the firm have the same goal—to maintain a profitable venture for you both.

NOW YOU ASSESS THE FIRM

After you have been through your performance review you will want to do some evaluating of your own. It's worth reviewing the firm every now and again and consciously evaluating the insights and judgments that have been occurring in the back of your own head.

I recommend using paper and pencil and treating the process as a formal procedure. The reason for this is that it's very tempting to think you know more about what's going on in your firm and outside it than you really do. I work in Riverside, California. I can't count how many times I've heard someone say, "Firms in Los Angeles all pay ten thousand more a year than firms out here." That may be true, but the speakers can never, I mean never, tell me just how they know that, which firms they investigated, what the results of the investigation were, or who they talked to. They have not stopped to ask, "Ten thousand more for what?" They have no job descriptions or billable hour requirement information. They don't even know if the big money-maker paralegals are paying hundreds of dollars to park their cars in downtown garages, commuting several hours a day, and have to comply with a dress code that shaves money off their paychecks on a regular basis. I don't know this either, but I know I don't know. I know I'd have to put real effort into an investigation to find out.

Blind opinions based on rumors and wishful thinking can lead to foolish action. Maybe there is a lot more money to be made at other firms in your area. Maybe other firms offer their paralegals better assignments and more support. You need to know that as in, "It's a fact I can verify" before it makes sense to act on it.

Here's the form I use to help me assess my firm, my knowledge of the facts about other firms in my area, and, consequently, my options.

JOB ANALYSIS

How my job stacks up

	Great	Good	Acceptable	Wanting	Bad
Money (add fringes)					
Intellectual stimulation					
Opportunities for professional development					
Sense of achievement					
Collegial working relationships					
Billable requirements					
Time off					
Support & office space					

Intangibles that affect my job: _____

_____

_____

I use this form to help me analyze my options.

JOB OPTIONS

Options within the firm:

    Change teams

    Develop additional expertise

    Ask for "x"
        Raise
        Better Support
        Educational Assistance
        Flex hours

Options outside the firm:

    Look for work with other firms:

Firm Name	Possible position(s)	Salary range	Openings	Source of information
_____	_____	_____	_____	_____
_____	_____	_____	_____	_____
_____	_____	_____	_____	_____

When you consider intangibles think about things like commute, window light, and location of the office. Do you like to work near bookstores and cafes? Think about family factors if they apply. Is the office close to your kids' school? Are the hours regular enough to allow you to get home and monitor homework? Is your boss the kind of person who understands if you need to go to a school play or recital? Perhaps you are finishing a degree yourself. Does your firm offer tuition reimbursement or will it allow you to take time off for day classes?

Once you have gone through this analysis you will actually be in a position to assess your options. You may find that there are more things about your current position to appreciate than you'd thought. You may think of ways to massage the situation into a closer approximation of your dream job. Alternately, you may decide it's time to go. If you decide to market yourself to other firms be sure to investigate them well. You don't want to find yourself unhappy with a new firm a year from now.

EXPLORING NEW ROLES IN THE NEXT YEAR

Now that you have established yourself as a firm fixture, a team player, a regular, it's time to think about expanding your role in particular practices. This is done not only by learning new legal skills and taking courses in subject areas, but also by entering into the thinking processes that form the kernel of a lawyer's practice in a more substantive way. I call this "thinking together."

Paralegals get a lot of jobs done in a hands-on, direct manner. Great paralegals also serve as sounding boards, attention focusers, thinking and writing partners, and cheerleaders. All of these roles are valuable—in fact over the long term they are invaluable—and often add considerably to job satisfaction. You are not just taking and carrying out orders; you're part of the thinking process that formulates what needs to get done and how best to do it.

1. Be a Sounding Board

Every day has it's nonbillable component. You can spend yours at the water cooler discussing your cats or in your favorite lawyer's office brainstorming strategies on important cases, the latest rulings that have come down in your area of practice, seminars that may benefit your current clients, or even how to attract new clients. This is an ideal time to listen carefully and give some well-thought-out feedback on what you think would be a good way to go.

What are you willing to help with? This is the perfect mechanism for involving yourself in the firm's practice. That involvement will not only increase your visibility and perceived value with the partnership, it will make it more fun to get up in the morning and get into the office. You will know that you are truly a part of what's happening at your firm.

2. Focus Attention

By now you will have observed that managing a legal practice while practicing law makes for a busy day. Phone calls, meetings, preparation of papers, training of subordinates, marketing, keeping up on the law, and doing the actual legal work on your calendar are usually all a part of the same day in the life of an active lawyer. Attention has to shift fairly often, and often quickly.

Someone has to keep in mind which of those tasks must get done today, or this week. One of your jobs should be to focus the attention of the attorneys you work with on matters that are just about to go critical. You have to respect the demands of the day enough to avoid concentrating on next month's pleadings when there are three motions ahead of them on the calendar, but you must think far enough ahead to be sure you're not reminding someone of a deadline when it's too late to get the work done.

This is where your well-developed calendaring system comes in, and the set of reminders you have put into play in your own office. There is no faster way to become an integral member of a legal team than by becoming the person who keeps an eye on what's up next.

3. Be a Thinking and Writing Partner

Here's where the real fun begins. One of the results of working for one or two attorneys closely for some time is that they become aware of your thinking and writing skills, for better or worse. If you have missed critical points in memos you have drafted or have not demonstrated careful, quick thinking in strategy sessions or good judgment in client interactions you will not be invited to join the "thinking and writing team." However, if your first year has been productive and you have made the most of opportunities to exhibit your ability to think critically and articulate the results, you will find yourself increasingly involved in substantive matters. Take this seriously and make the most of each opportunity.

You may find that the attorney you have been working with asks you to take a look at a brief to see if the statement of facts matches what you know from your review of the documents. Take the brief and get it to the top of your to-do list as quickly as possible. Then sequester yourself somewhere and give it your full attention. Check every factual allegation against every piece of information you have to be sure they are all right. Document what you checked; do not return the document with, "It's fine." You're in the process of convincing this lawyer to make you a collaborator. State exactly what documents you used to verify the facts. Saying "I checked the legal description against the title report" lets the attorney know you know where to look and what to look for, and that you are willing to spend time on the details.

When you have completed the review of the facts (i.e., what the attorney asked you to do) and formulated your succinct but informative report, read the entire brief three times. Think about it. Does it persuade you? Are there any facts you know about the case that have not been included but will support your arguments? Are there facts you know about that undermine your client's position? Bring these to the attorney's attention so he or she can decide what to do about them.

You may find typos in the brief. Mark them and mention that to the attorney. When you go back with your report, find a nonintrusive way to let the attorney know you read the whole brief. Mention the argument you found most compelling first. If you think there's a problem that needs to be addressed based on your review of the facts, bring it up tactfully. Lawyers who are any good would rather hear about it from you than from opposing counsel. Finally, ask if you can help get the brief out the door. Perhaps you can do the final proofreading or final cite checking. If it's being filed in a department (as opposed to with the clerk) you may want to check on the judge's procedures too.

All of this will allow the attorney you work with to reassess your abilities and incorporate you into the practice in a new way. The principles underlying this litigation example can be used in other practices. Are all of the client's concerns addressed in the contract you are reviewing? Does the will you are drafting include provisions for everything the client has told you about? Care, critical thinking, and craft will take you far in a lawyer's practice.

4. Cheerleader

If the idea of being a cheerleader for the other members of your legal team bothers you, get over it. We all need someone in our corner. A little background enthusiasm for someone else's goals can provide the impetus that gets a manuscript out the door or leads to a marketing seminar or gets someone to take a class that will move his career ahead.

Never underestimate the effect of a show of support. When a team member gets on the elevator to go fight the good fight based on facts you have investigated and arguments you have helped work out, wish her luck. It takes significant psychic energy to do the work lawyers do, to make arguments, negotiate deals, investigate serious matters, or deal with a sick client making a will. Be available to lend friendly support to these efforts. It's an important part of a successful practice.

Now that you have successfully completed your first year, celebrate! Go out to dinner. Buy yourself one really nice thing for your office. Remember, you will be spending quite a bit of time there next year too.

11 FAQs and Secrets of Success

1. How should I relate to clients?

For maximum success within a law firm you need to be involved in the client management team—significantly involved—because clients are the lifeblood of a law office.

> "No clients = No business"

For this and many other reasons, your contribution to maintaining and strengthening good client relations will be noticed and valued. You may not always see the appreciation when and where you want it, but rest assured that your good work with clients always counts seriously in your favor.

Likewise, if clients do not like working with you it will count heavily against you. You may not be fired, but you will be relegated to a back room somewhere, and that's not where most of the fun work gets done. It's also not where most of the promotions and raises are handed out, so make client management a real priority in your own career.

How do you relate to clients? The bottom line is that client management is not just "serving the client." It's also making the client happy with the service, and that's not always easy.

People usually hire lawyers when they are facing trouble in their lives or when they have to take care of something that involves so much paperwork it gives them a headache. Once they involve lawyers they are not only dealing with paperwork or trouble, they're facing legal bills and that doesn't put anyone in a good mood. The goal of a true professional to is make the entire engagement as pleasant as possible for the client. Remember, they are paying for your services and that includes your courtesy.

Take Your Cue from the Attorney in Charge of the Matter

The exact nature of your relationship to clients or to a particular client will depend on what the lawyer in charge of the matter wants. You will be able to get a feel for the lawyer's paralegal–client style by your assignments. If you're asked to phone the client to arrange meetings or obtain information, you should take this as an invitation to participate in the client relationship. As the matter proceeds so will your role.

Most lawyers welcome assistance in the client relations area, but there are a few who don't. Be sure you keep your eyes and ears open, especially if you are new to working with a particular attorney. If you're unclear or sense that the lawyer handling the matter is hesitant, either ask for direction politely or pull back and wait to see how things unfold.

Be sure you always identify yourself as a paralegal so you and the client remain aware of the limitations of your authority. It is common and dangerous for clients to mistake paralegals for lawyers. You will not only have to stress your title when you first meet clients, you will also need to find graceful ways to remind them that you are a paralegal along the way.

This becomes increasingly important as you become more experienced and, yes, older. I have had clients with whom I've worked for years "suddenly" forget I'm a paralegal. They then wonder why I am referring them to the attorney for legal advice. The whole thing can be handled cordially and even with a sense of humor: "You know, Bill, I'm the paralegal on this team. You need to talk to Fran on this issue."

Return Phone Calls

According to pollsters, the number one complaint of law firm clients is that their phone calls are not returned. Decide right now that you will not become one of those legal professionals who is constantly too busy to return a call. If you do not have time to speak with a client on the day the call comes in, either call briefly to apologize and say you will call the next day, or have your secretary do that. A personal call is much better and I recommend it. We are rarely too busy for forty seconds on the phone.

A more difficult phone call problem is when the client wants to hear from the attorney, but the attorney won't call. This is when your "artful badger" skills come into play. While there are limits to how much you can push, you should look for palatable ways to remind the attorney that the client is waiting for a call. As your working relationship evolves, the best ways to handle this will too. In a long-term, well-developed attorney–paralegal relationship it is not uncommon for the paralegal to handle many of the client telephone calls on fairly routine matters. However, a wise paralegal knows when to tell the attorney that the client needs to hear from her or him.

Client Meetings

Client meetings present another opportunity to cultivate good working relationships. If you are asked to attend a meeting with the attorney and client, think ahead. Is there material you should take with you? Will the attorney need the file? When you enter the room, move forward gracefully to say hello. If this is your first meeting and the attorney has not arrived, extend your hand and say, "Mr. Bellows? I'm Deborah Smith, Ms. Faulkner's paralegal. She asked me to join you all this morning. She'll be right with us. Can I get you some coffee?"

If the attorney has already arrived, he or she should introduce you. Take your seat and lean forward. Smile. Take your lead from the attorney and consider the invitation to attend the meeting as a sign that you should involve yourself in the firm's professional relationship with this client.

As you work with the attorney and the client you will get a strong feel for how that relationship should develop. Perhaps you will serve as a client liaison, someone the client can call first to check on work progress or to ask preliminary questions. Maybe you will be responsible for the client files, taking care of their special original documents. Perhaps you will learn a lot about the clients—who their employees are, what the organization's goals and budget realities are, who to call when you need a signature or a quick decision. This will make you a valuable part of the team. Pursue client relationships responsibly and your career will benefit tremendously.

Client Social Occasions

As you become better acquainted with the firm's clients you may well find yourself invited to client lunches, receptions, or parties. If you are, do go. Just be sure you behave as carefully as you would meeting your significant other's parents for the first time. Use moderation in everything, especially in alcohol consumption. Remember that although this activity is dressed up like a party it really is a business occasion for you.

Most client lunches begin with routine social small talk, ordering, and the like. Watch the attorney involved for cues on when the conversation should shift to business. This will differ from one lunch to another. If the lunch is a break from trial or serious negotiations in a big deal for the client, everyone may need some time to relax and talk trivia. If the matter you are working on is confidential and the forum is public, the actual matter may not be discussed at lunch at all. If real business is discussed, try to quietly record what goes on—a few notes so that you can write it up for the file.

Remember also that the client is not the only one you need to think about on these occasions. Your boss and maybe others in the firm who do not know you well will be there. Your performance (and in many ways it is a performance) will affect their evaluation of you as a professional representative of the firm.

2. How can I ask for money?

Getting money for projects, classes, conferences, and books is an art, an art you should learn. Disabuse yourself of the standard myth about firm money. The lawyers do not really get together every January and say, "How can we keep all the money away from the paralegals this year?" Very often they are looking for ways to reward us, to help us do our jobs better, and to keep us happy. If you want the firm to spend some of its discretionary money on you, you need to respect some realities.

• The financial condition of the firm counts. You need to be aware of the general state of the economy and of your firm's current situation. Do not submit requests for extras during periods when money concerns are in the forefronts of partners' minds. If you know they have received discouraging quarterly reports, bide your time. I have found that many lawyers are actually depressed around April 15th. They hate to think about their taxes. You may find the group that files for extensions may be in the same shape in August. Even if they're not, August is pretty late to be looking for discretionary funds. Find out how the partnership thinks it's doing before you ask for extra money.

• Investigate your firm's budget for continuing education courses. Many firms have the money socked away but do not think to advertise this fact to paralegals. This does not mean they won't assist you with course fees if you ask. The best way to find about this is to ask a partner you have gotten to know, but it is also acceptable to politely ask the business manager, personnel manager, senior paralegal, or a well-connected secretary.

• If your firm has a formal request form or procedure to get funds, follow it. Think ahead and leave plenty of time for committee review if necessary. Be sure to obtain and submit all the documentation you need for approval. Don't forget to include items like parking fees or travel costs and meals. Remember to keep all the receipts and other material the bookkeepers will need in order to prepare checks or pay bills. Be sure to keep a duplicate of everything in your own file.

• A cover memo personalizing your request is often appreciated. Include information about how the course or conference or new equipment will benefit the firm. For example, let's say you purchased your own personal laptop computer but you generously use it for work sometimes too. You have been using floppy disks to take documents from your desktop computer to your laptop for weekend use. One day you realize that if you could just call in via modem to work on your document, life would be easier and you would eliminate the chance that you will forget which version of the document contains all the latest changes. But a modem costs money you can't spend right now. What do you do?

First talk to your computer wizards and price modems at the local computer store. Then get a form to fill out that allows you to ask for the modem. Also draft a nice short memo explaining that you often work on firm business at home in the evenings and on weekends using your personal computer. You may even have a terrific current example, a case you just finished perhaps. Your work would be more efficient, you explain, if you had a modem to call in directly to your office computer. A modem costs X amount. Could you please have one? That's it. Short and sweet.

• Be sure you know who to submit the request to. In the modem case the computer person at your firm will know who has to authorize computer purchases. Submit everything with your request, including an official description and price for what you need.

• Once you get authorization, act on it quickly. No one likes giving someone a check only to find it's cashed six months later. You asked for the money. You got the money. Now move.

• Provide all the backup for the purchase (the receipt, etc.) to the appropriate department. Then—this is very important—write a thank-you note to the person or persons who are responsible for approving your purchase. This can be short, but ought to include something about how the item (or conference or course) is helping you do your job better.

Remember, you will have an easier time getting your project or purchase funded if it really benefits the firm as well as you. For instance, as we all become more computer literate, firms are more prepared to support computer-related purchases and classes. They can see that the more efficiently you use your computer, the less money they will have to spend on secretarial support for you.

In addition, if your request relates to a firm goal you have a better chance of success. Some firms see themselves as teachers in their communities. These firms are likely to be more generous with flexible schedules or billable hour credit if you want to teach than firms that have no relationship to the local educational community.

Likewise, if you have partners who support the local arts, they will be more open to doing pro bono work for a local theater group. Use your head and time your pitch. You may be surprised at the support you will get if you initiate a forward-looking program and see it through.

Finally, if you ask for money and don't get it, don't pout. You can't possibly know everything that's going on in the economy of the firm. There may be a very good reason your request is denied. Even if there isn't, it won't help if you frown and act dejected or angry. Be gracious and thank the powers that be for considering your request. If they suggest you try again at a different time of the year, take them up on it. That kind of comment generally means they will grant your request as soon as they can.

3. WHY ARE SOME ASSOCIATES SO JUMPY?

This question will make some associates I know laugh, but it's one we often feel like asking. The working relationship between paralegals and associates can be dicey. It will help you relate to associates if you remember everything that associates have on their minds.

Most young lawyers leave law school with a bushel basket of bills to pay and a sense that they have been students, and hence juveniles, too long. Add to that the fact that many take jobs before they have passed the bar and you can see how they might be a little edgy about their new roles as associates in a law firm.

Associates generally hope to be partners someday. From the first day they swing their briefcases through the elevator doors to the day they reach that goal, they are on trial. They must adjust to a work situation in which the clothes they wear, the hours they work, and the talk they talk are largely in response to directives of others. They are also suddenly supposed to join in the repartee and social life of lawyers who are the same age as their parents.

Remember, associates are supposed to work incredibly hard and be incredibly smart and do their work very quickly. While it was fine to take hours and hours to get to the right answer in law school, now they are billing clients for every six minutes of their day. The clients—and the partners—want good answers in record time. Then there's the little problem of six partners who all want their time and energy and their best work at the same time. It's very hard for an associate to say no to a partner. Even the camaraderie they feel for their colleagues is stained with competition. While all of this is complicating their twenty-six-year-old lives, many are getting married and starting families. It's a wonder they come to work at all.

Then add a legal world that is currently peppered with paralegals who have been around for more than a decade and have the expertise to prove it, and you will understand why some associates are jumpy when it comes to paralegals. Many are painfully aware that their bosses think they are wet behind the ears and that the long-established relationships between some partners and paralegals already span decades.

Go out of your way to let associates know you appreciate what they have learned in their long journey through law school. Look for ways to be helpful. A good partner–associate–paralegal team is a thing of beauty when it's in action. Be good to the associates you work with. They have a lot on their minds.

4. DO I NEED TO SPECIALIZE?

Maybe. Probably. You certainly need to answer that question. Here's how to do that.

The first rule for success is that you must be filling a need in your firm. Analyzing the firm's needs will answer many questions for you. If you work for a small firm and need to cover lots of bases, you may not have the luxury of even thinking about a specialty. Whatever the firm does, you must do. Whatever the firm needs, you do. If the firm specializes, there's your specialty. Then again if the firm you work for doesn't have a big paralegal corps and needs general help in several areas, you will need to be enough of a generalist to provide it.

If you work in a mid- to large-size firm you may have the option of specializing. However, if the firm hired you for a particular department, that will be your specialty until you have established yourself with the firm. When you are well-established, when you have proven yourself a valuable firm contributor, then you can consider switching your specialty. See Chapter 12 for tips on doing this.

Things to Think About

Specializing is usually promoted as the best way to get more money and certainly there are specialties that pay more than other areas of practice. But don't automatically discount the value of being a generalist. Generalists work with more people, are more visible, and have more opportunities to help people out. This kind of visibility and strong identification can also bring substantial monetary rewards. Being a generalist also provides flexibility and that adds to your survival potential in changing times. If one area of practice loses viability (and they do from time to time) you are poised to stay busy in other areas.

Consider a compromise, having two or even three specialties. This can be accomplished over a few years and combines the best of both worlds: You are more generally employable, but you also have proven expertise in each area so that you may be depended on to perform well there.

An often ignored aspect of the "Should I specialize?" discussion is that having several specialties will help keep your interest in your own work high. You won't get bored and you may find two areas of law that complement each other. I specialize in public entity representation and in litigation and I love them both. I also enjoy the fact that eminent domain work allows me to use what I know from both practice areas. In addition, I also consider myself a generalist in the sense that I have trained myself to have a "can do" first response to any request for help. This is opposed to the true specialist who is trained to think, "That's not my area of expertise, I'm a 'something' paralegal."

This way of working suits me, it fits me, but it's not the only choice and it's not the right choice for everyone. You need to find out what fits for you and for your firm. Give yourself some time and pay attention to how things develop. You'll figure it out.

5. Do I have to dress like a lawyer?

By way of disclaimer let me say that there are people in my office who would fall down laughing at the thought of my giving advice on how a paralegal should dress. However, I can say with certainty that if you are new to the profession or new to a particular office, you will do well to dress conservatively—and sort of "like a lawyer." The younger and more inexperienced you are, the more you will need to assert your professionalism and maturity through your appearance. Since the dress rule for lawyers is basically still suits for both genders, you should invest in some too.

As you become more experienced at your job and get to know the team of people you work with, you may find it acceptable and certainly more comfortable to dress in less formal clothing. It's not hard to tell what's appropriate for your workplace. The rule that will stay in place forever is that you should not offend clients, bosses, or your coworkers. Office clothing should not be used to get attention or to express your sexuality. See-through blouses and black fishnet stockings are not acceptable in law offices.

Your office apparel should not give the impression that you are about to go off to a social event. You want to advertise that your mind is on the job. Fair or not, younger people have to work harder to look "professionally capable." If you are twenty-six years old and you are about to meet with clients who are sixty-six, the clients will feel better if you show up "in uniform." They can't help but think of their children when they see you. The suit helps them take you seriously as someone who can handle their legal work.

Certainly, the general trend in many offices is toward less formal dress. Senior partners who would never have dreamed of coming to work without a tie a decade ago may show up in a yellow shirt and sports coat with no tie in sight. You can be sure that when that happens that partner will not be in court that day, and probably has no client meetings set. That partner also has spent twenty-five years earning the right to dress down a bit. So while the trend is toward casual, as a new paralegal you do not want to be leading the charge in that direction.

Casual day

Casual day was developed to compensate for fewer raises during the early nineties law firm financial crunch. You can dress down on casual day as long as you don't have a client meeting and don't have to be in court. However, use your head and your discretion dressing on Fridays too. Many firms have rules against blue jeans and tennis shoes. Never mind the arbitrariness or the failed logic. Unless you are prepared to jeopardize your position for your Levis, follow firm policy.

Court Clothes

Not much has changed in court. Dress up. Dress the part. I hate suits but I have two for court. In addition I keep a black blazer in my office to throw over whatever I many have on in case I am suddenly required to "run over to Judge So-and-So's court" or to attend a client meeting. On the West Coast you can wear pantsuits to court if you are a woman. If you have to carry bankers' boxes or large exhibits to court this can be a significant comfort. Check your local courthouse to get a feel for the custom there. The key to true professionalism in court dressing is that you do not want to wear anything that will jeopardize your client's position by calling the wrong kind of attention to you. Your comfort is not important in court; your client's interest is.

A final word on clothing: Why anyone wears high heels is entirely beyond me.

6. How can I get past clerical assignments?

Many paralegals complain that many of their assignments are too clerical in nature. The way to address and solve this problem is through "next step" thinking. Here's how you do it:

1. Ask yourself how much work you have done for this particular attorney. If you are just establishing a working relationship you may have to bide your time on complaining about the clerical nature of your work. The attorney may be trying you out—seeing if you can meet a deadline, do careful work, and perform like a team player. Your job, of course, is to perform perfectly, which includes maintaining a cheerful demeanor when you turn in the work.

2. To get past clerical assignments you must do the following: For any clerical task assigned to you, you find the nonclerical aspect and do that too. For instance, if you are assigned to put documents in chronological order, you should read the documents and get a feel for the story they tell. You must do this against a background understanding of the matter that you will have picked up in conversation or gotten from reviewing the file.

This substantive document review may allow you to create a timeline that makes salient the evidence that supports your client's position. You will also find gaps in the documentation that will allow you to prepare a list of items you need to request in discovery or obtain from your client or other sources.

3. Find a time to present your work (in this case the documents in perfect chronological order, indexed, and perhaps even numbered as well as the "next step" you have performed) when you and the attorney can discuss what you have discovered or figured out during your review of the documents. This will establish you as someone who knows the case and is committed to working on it. It will also encourage the attorney to talk to you as a colleague. This is the basis for a desirable ongoing work relationship.

4. When you have developed a functional working relationship with this attorney on strong professional terms, you may find yourself in a position to discuss the clerical nature of some tasks. For instance, when asked to put documents in chronological order you may be able to say, "I have to work on three other assignments today. Can I give these to your secretary to put in chron order? That way I can get right to the review tomorrow and get a timeline and list of documents we still need to you by Thursday."

This tells the attorney that you are thinking like a professional, that you can delegate, and that your services are in demand. Alternately, you may decide that many clerical tasks offer an opportunity for hands-on work with documents while providing time to think about the case. Many top-notch paralegals like to get their own hands on the paper and their own organizational plan in place. In any case, the problem should resolve itself.

7. How do I know when I should change jobs?

This is a tough question. Every job you have for a long time will have good times and bad times. There are definite downsides to jumping from one job to another, but it can also be a mistake to stay with a firm that has no vision of paralegals as real legal professionals. Without that vision you will not find support for the growth that makes a long-term commitment to the firm a good idea. Here are some things to think about:

1. It's almost never a good idea to quit a job when you are angry or upset about a particular event. Take your time. Go home. Think about it. Talk to people who can be counted on to view the situation rationally. If your desire to leave is in response to a particular individual or incident, I recommend taking several weeks to let things cool off before jumping ship.

2. Evaluate the firm as a whole. Use the format described in Chapter 10. Think about all the players. Try to envision your future with the firm. Is it possible that the situation you are finding so problematic today will resolve itself? Is there a way you can shift your work responsibilities that will allow you to reap the benefits of staying without suffering the downside that's got you thinking about leaving? Review Chapter 12, How to Change Jobs without Leaving the Firm. Can you change teams, specialties, or offices without leaving?

3. Evaluate your own situation, professionally and personally. Are you in a position to make a move? Have you put in three years getting a solid background in an area of law that will allow you to interview as a specialist? What's your financial situation? Are your kids on their own or have you just committed to paying for college? Is there a train that will allow you to commute to another work world or is there a valuable benefit in being just down the road from the office? Are there professional relationships at your current job that are necessary to your future plans or have you topped out in responsibilities? All of these factors will count in your decision making.

4. Evaluate the potential in other firms. This is hard but you have to try. Read ads. It may help to make some confidential inquiries. If you feel quite serious, see a placement professional in a good agency. These people will be able to tell you what kind of opportunities you can expect if you leave your current position. They will have hard data about salaries, educational requirements, etc. Talk to other paralegals and try to get them to tell you the truth. Read trade journals, review court decisions involving cases argued by a firm in which you are interested, and ask around.

5. All of these steps will take some time. If you're still feeling serious about leaving after going through them all, you probably are ripe to move on. Plan ahead. See placement counselors. Review and rewrite your resume. Apply confidentially for other jobs before giving your notice. Do not allow yourself displays of temper and never, ever write down anything negative about your current firm: no memos, no notes, no letters. If you cannot find anything cordial to

say in your letter of resignation, write a one-line tender of resignation. It is never wise to say or do something when leaving that you would not have said or done if you were staying.

6. If you decide to move, remember this interviewing maxim: Never denigrate your current employer. You will probably be asked why you are leaving the firm. Be prepared to say something positive about why you are ready for a change and new responsibilities. Leave behind your gripes and train your eyes on the future. You want to be moving toward something, not running away.

Thirteen Bona Fide Secrets of Success

1. **Develop your own intellectual curiosity.** It's hard work to be curious. You have to stay awake and notice the weird little idiosyncratic details in the world. Then you have to pay enough attention to wonder why it's like that. After you've put out all that mental effort you have to figure out where you will learn about whatever it is that you want to understand. Finally you have to chase the information down, think the whole thing through, and try to remember it. No wonder so many people are asleep on their feet. But top performers are curious folks. Their wheels are always turning. If you're like me and have a lazy streak that makes you think of hammocks more often than research books, train yourself now to pay attention, wonder, and follow through. It will contribute enormously to your future success, and it will change your life.

2. **Say "yes" when you can.** A positive attitude and a readiness (not just willingness but an educated and prepared readiness) are still core attributes required to succeed as a paralegal. Opportunity's a tricky beast—it comes when it will. Hone your skills. Enjoy the spirit of team play. Master your calendar and achieve enough flexibility to catch the next wave of opportunity. Say "yes" when you can.

3. **Learn to see the firm's point of view and set goals that are consistent with your firm's goals.** In most firms there are several competing points of view and accompanying goals, and you will need to become familiar with them all. Ask partners with whom you work what they see for the firm in five years or ten. Be interested in these points of view. If making more money is the main goal, show them that advanced training for you will make money for them. If you want support for doing pro bono work, see if some partners think the firm's image needs enhancement in the community. Keep your eyes and ears open and look for umbrella goals under which your desire to attend local college classes or a national convention fit perfectly.

4. **Take your time.** You can't build a career overnight. Settle down to the hard work of making your way. Accept that building a reputation as a strong performer requires time and remember that there is no substitute for performance. If you need education, get it. If you need experience, get it. Remember, one year on the job means almost nothing in the professional world. If you're good, five will count for a lot. But like everyone else, you will need to prove yourself over the long haul. You cannot expect people to recognize a commitment to excellence that you have not made demonstrably clear.

5. Learn to support the successes of others. Build strong working relationships with other paralegals. If you are competitive, face up to it and do not let your desire to be number one control your attitude when others perform splendidly. If your gut is not inclined to rejoice over the success of others, listen to your head. It will tell you that your success cannot be based on the failure of others.

"Few men have the natural strength to honor a friend's success without envy."
Aeschylus

Supporting the success of others will forward your career in many ways. As your colleagues and friends move into enviable positions they may be able to offer you an opportunity to prove yourself as well. If others feel they can count on you to support their efforts, they will be more willing to include you in their plans.

Most of all, developing an attitude of support for the success of others will provide you with a reliable base from which to plan and execute your own plans and dreams. You will move forward not as a desperate or mean-spirited competitor, but as an individual who is not afraid of the rest of the field and who is interested in growth for all. In short, you will be a better person, and as such you will like yourself more. That will improve your own performance and your own career. It's a win-win situation.

6. Treat individuals as individuals. Build strong working relationships with supportive attorneys. Be interested in what they hope to accomplish in their own careers and what they have to teach you. Earn their confidence and trust by supporting their practices, respecting their expertise, and watching their backs. Be loyal. If someone has been good to you, has provided you with great work and congenial circumstances, allow them the luxury of not being perfect. Remember, even terrific people behave badly once in awhile.

Do not think of attorneys as one big homogeneous power structure. When individuals do well by and for you, appreciate and acknowledge it. Recognize them as superior individuals, not as members of a ruling class.

7. Treat clients as if they are the most important part of the business of practicing law. They are. We all say that but we do not always stop to think of what that entails. No one can tell the client, "We meant to do it right." This is the client's important legal matter. The client will live with the outcome. Great paralegals, like great lawyers, go the extra mile with and for the client. They investigate and learn to understand the client's goals and priorities, including respecting financial realities and psychological needs. Remember, there are no routine legal matters to the client who is paying for them.

8. Beware of depending on the praise of others. In his wonderful book, *Getting Things Done When You're Not in Charge*, Geoffrey Bellam warns against developing a need for praise from others. Oh, praise is grand and we all enjoy it, but coming to depend on the praise of others is a surefire way to lose control of a self-directed career.

Learn to set your own standards for excellence and then meet them. Just as you are able to evaluate others, analyze your own performances and assess your accomplishments. Do something concrete to memorialize that assessment: Write a memo for your resume file, make photocopies of good work for your form file, and give yourself a reward to go with it.

9. Learn to reward yourself. Speaking of self-reliance, when you judge your performance worthy of reward, provide some of your own. Take half an hour off to read some poetry, stop on the way home to get a CD you've been wanting, go work out, call an old friend, call your significant other with a dinner invitation. You don't have to buy yourself a new car, but do something.

If you are not taking the time and investing the energy to make your professional life fun, you are really waiting for someone else to do it. Make your own rewards and your own fun. It will make a difference in your success.

10. Maintain your personal life. Almost everyone in the legal field has at some time suffered a nagging fear that if they leave the office for two weeks they will return to a desk devoid of work—or even no desk at all. If that's the case, better to find out now.

Take needed breaks. You will find that you will return refreshed and ready for new challenges. No one needs a paralegal who is always overworked and overtired and who never goes home. Go home and take care of yourself and the people you love. Live your whole life. You owe it to your family, your friends, yourself, and even your employer.

11. Master the art of creative waiting. If you are energetic, ambitious, intelligent, and creative you possess many of the attributes for success in a law firm. But all the energy and creativity in the world, all that ambition and intelligence, may come to naught if you haven't mastered creative waiting and learned the patience that working within the structure and culture of the firm requires.

Simply put, things take time. Sometimes things take a lot of time. There is the obvious time factor involved in calendaring things for committee review, but even more importantly there is the "time is right" element that cannot be calendared at all. General mind-sets and attitudes are just as important to making an idea work as a particular plan, no matter how well the plan is laid out.

Patience has been one of the hardest qualities for me to develop. Here are some "creative waiting tools" that helped.

- Don't sit around and think about your latest idea waiting anxiously for the firm to adopt it. Move on. If you come up with a plan to revamp the paralegal evaluation program, it may be a good idea to talk it up a bit, to write it up and submit it to the paralegal committee. Then let it go for awhile. If you're so smitten with your plan that you think it really must be assessed soon, write an article for a local bar association newsletter or other forum, laying out your idea and arguing the benefits it will provide. Do not bother the paralegal committee members constantly to see if they have thought about or better yet fully embraced your proposal.

- Don't put all your eggs in one basket. One or two good ideas are swell, but you want to train your brain to produce a constant stream of pretty good ideas. Once you have submitted one idea for review, turn your thoughts to solving other problems. They don't all have to involve changing firm policies. Maybe you should just figure out how to organize your books or work more efficiently with your secretary or make it to your daughter's soccer games.

- Keep one eye turned to the outside world. A real secret to success in a law firm is staying in touch with the world outside the office. If your firm announces a salary freeze, think about how you can earn your "raise" for the year outside the office. Maybe you can teach a course or write some articles for magazines. That way you can act on the idea of raising your income while you increase your visibility and credibility in the legal world outside the law firm's door.

12. Develop your own professional intuition. We are all getting signals from others all the time. Some people are better than others at noticing and registering those signals. We often look at those people and say they are intuitive. We say, "Boy, Jones really knows when to put on the pressure" or, "Barbara had an idea I shouldn't return that call this afternoon and I'm sure glad I listened to her!" Neither Jones nor Barbara is psychic; they are observant folks who have developed the skill of listening to what the world is telling them.

You can get good at that too. How? Try asking yourself questions before you act.

"What will happen if I try to talk to John about this today?"

"Why on earth is Katherine so negative about this idea?"

"What problems will I face if I do X?"

"How can I make this happen?"

Then listen to the answers you get. Just listen. Don't judge them, don't act on them. Just notice them and give yourself some time to sift through the information that really is available to you.

Learning to listen to others, and to the situations that arise with others, is very smart professionally. It's also very therapeutic and very fun. Suddenly the focus is off you and your problems, limitations, frustrations, etc. You're taking a look at the world, letting things come into focus. You can relax and notice things. This will allow you to choose your response. You will see options and possibilities. Develop this pattern of action in your career and you will cut in half the time it takes you to reach that all-important goal, or you may find out it's not the goal you want to reach. Veering off the well-trod path is sometimes the best way to go.

13. Define Your Own Success. One of the true secrets in life is to recognize your own success when it's right in front of you. It comes dressed up in lots of ways, and in the best case it is customized to fit you, your personality, your life, your talents, your desires, and the needs and desires of those with whom you share your life.

It's not always the most money, the biggest office, the most prestige, the most glamour, or even the most interesting work. It can be some or all of those things, or a unique combination of factors that is available to, and right for, you.

Do not feel apologetic if you define success differently from all the self-help career books or the latest article in a professional magazine. At the end of the day we all go home to our own worlds. You can define the success you value, and you can achieve it.

12 Effecting Change and Promoting Your Goals within the Firm

"There is in the worst of fortune the best of chances for a happy change."
Euripedes 484–406 BC

The first step in learning to effect change and promote your goals within the firm is to understand the firm's point of view. Talking about a "firm" point of view is somewhat simplistic. Every firm is made up of individuals who, no matter how well aligned for mutual gain, still have individual points of view, individual agendas, and individual life goals. Even so, a key to succeeding in any firm is recognizing and to some extent adopting the "firm point of view."

Remember when you were researching the firm for your interview? You read the brochures, asked around town, found out how the firm viewed itself. It may have a "lean and mean legal machine" self-image, or it may see itself as a grand old firm and longtime supporter of and leader in community events. It may have a reputation for being on the cutting edge, or for supporting cultural events, or for maintaining the highest levels of professionalism. You need to identify and support the goals and image of the firm. If you can do that willingly and if the firm is not a total disaster, it will find ways to support your goals too.

Think of where the firm is spending money. For example, if your firm is updating its computer system, your desire to update your computer skills may fit right into the year's game plan. You may be able to get tuition reimbursement for computer classes or requisition additional software programs that will increase your own efficiency.

If your firm has been hiring additional entry-level paralegal personnel to take on new matters, the time may be ripe for you to ask for support help on an onerous job of your own. If your firm sees itself as one of the legal education resources for the local college, you may be able to get hourly credit for teaching a class in a paralegal program.

Don't be limited to "legal" in your thinking. My firm has a commitment to public service in our city. We have a relationship with a middle school in which we supply tutors to seventh and eighth graders. The firm not only encourages participation, it pays for lunches for students and sponsors a year-end trip to a professional baseball team for the students and the tutors. Because I'm interested in writing I teach a creative writing workshop to the students at the school, and my firm graciously buys them terrific hardbound notebooks for their writing. The attorneys I work with are understanding about the fact that, barring emergencies, I am committed to meeting "my kids" at three o'clock every Monday afternoon. Recently the personnel department made special arrangements to allow a secretary to participate in the program. All this works because the goal—helping children—fits into the firm's long-standing commitment to serve the community.

Another part of understanding the firm's point of view, and forwarding your goals too, is making peace with the realities of its long-term practices. If you work for a firm that uses associates, not paralegals, to write motions, you will have to work long and hard to convince the partnership to change its policy. You may get a particular partner to let you draft things on the sly, but effecting a real policy change will be tough. If research and writing are what make your paralegal day worthwhile, you should look for a firm who uses paralegals in the library more.

Likewise, if your firm has a well-established committee review procedure for requests for educational support or time off or changes in assignment, you will probably not be able to bypass those channels. You will need to do all the paperwork and double check your backup material. Plan ahead so you can give the committee time to do its work.

The most critical part of a firm's point of view for you will be the firm's view of paralegals. This is one aspect that you can have an impact on over time—and you should. If the firm you work for does not see paralegals as an important part of its practice, you need to be one of the standout professionals who shakes up their world view.

I don't mean you have to be offensive in any way; in fact that would be counterproductive. But you can make a practice of behaving professionally, completing excellent work on time, thinking ahead, speaking up, and taking appropriate initiative to move cases and other legal matters forward. This kind of performance will advance your career and the firm's interests and will further the paralegal profession as a whole. That's a potent combination of effects. If you are serious about working toward this kind of professionalism you can expect some fairly exciting results. It may not happen just when you expect it, but good things will come your way.

IDENTIFY YOUR CLIENTS

One of the demarcations between lawyer and paralegal is the client relationship. According to the rules, lawyers have clients; paralegals don't. This distinction comes from the fact that paralegals are not authorized to enter into representation agreements, set fees, give advice, represent people in courts, and so on. Therefore they do not have clients.

In fact, as paralegals are assigned greater responsibility for account management, and as they become integrally involved in serving particular clients, this distinction is fast becoming an illusion. Neither the lawyers or the clients or the paralegals are very clear about what to do about it. For now I think nothing needs to be done except to realize that in a great many situations clients rely heavily on their relationships with particular paralegals to help them.

Attorneys also rely heavily on paralegals, to help them maintain their client base and to keep particular client relationships on track. Undertaking responsibility for maintaining a good relationship with a client is an effective way to increase your involvement in the firm's practice and in the practice of a particular attorney, and I recommend that paralegals seek opportunities to serve in this way.

However, lawyers themselves remain the true client base for paralegals. Your various lawyer bosses, your potential bosses, and hopefully your potential professional colleagues are still the most important clients you need to think about, serve, and maintain. In essence, they buy your product. If they are not sold on the wisdom of making that investment, all the client contact in the world will not help you at the office—or in your career as a paralegal.

The paralegal role is essentially a support position. It was created and has evolved to support lawyers in their practice of law. As the needs of the nation for affordable access to the legal system continue to grow and gain attention among lawmakers the parameters of paralegal practices may change, but for now it remains a support position. One of the keys to success is realizing that fact and acting on it. While many paralegals are held back in their careers because they fail to take initiative and act like self-starting professionals, just as many careers are retarded by a deep-seated resentment of the fact that the lawyers they work for are the bosses.

Look around your firm. You will see this resentment demonstrated in the attitudes of paralegals (and secretaries and associates) every day. They drag their feet on assignments, they grumble (literally) in the halls. Often they produce sloppy work products. They wear dour faces and complain that they have too much to do at the same time that they complain they don't have enough work. The fact is, they often do not have enough work because no energetic, enthusiastic lawyer wants to have them on the team.

These paralegals have completely lost track of reality. They have forgotten that they are not out there in the world drumming up business for the firm, nor are they willing to let their compensation be directly tied to this month's receipts. Without assuming the responsibility for keeping the firm afloat they want to have the power to make critical firm decisions and give direction. They have forgotten who hired who—and they have also forgotten what they agreed to when they took the job.

Hot Tip: You must serve your in-house clients faithfully and fully, and with a willing spirit. Within six months of starting any job you should be able to sit down and write a list of your lawyer clients. You shouldn't have to hem and haw about it; it should be as natural as writing down the names of your children.

Because the lawyers you work for are your principal clients, you must treat them as such. Worry about whether you understand what your client wants and needs from you. Seek feedback about particular service opportunities. Did the whole thing go the way they had hoped? Keep them informed about the progress you are making on their work, and get it done on time. Very often late work is not only annoying, it's depressing. Remember that when you come in with your great idea, your on-point case, your big play after the game's over: It's worthless to the attorney. It's futile. It's embarrassing. It's money down the drain.

Remember also that if you lose the respect and support of lawyers who value your work product and admire your work ethic, you have lost the opportunity to increase your involvement in the firm's practice, to develop your own expertise, and to expand your own role in the matters you take on. You have, in fact, lost everything but the job itself, and if the firm's on the ball you may be well on your way to losing that.

A final word on managing your attorney client base: Let them know what you appreciate about working with and for them. Much of an attorney's day is spent in adversarial situations. If they are not in court fighting for a position, they are drafting their client's side of a contract or handling a meeting at which they have to represent a particular point of view.

Even when they do a terrific job, they do not get a lot of strokes from their partners or their clients. The paralegal and the attorney are supposed to be on the same team, not in an adversarial relationship. Like good team members they are supposed to support each other. When your attorney does something supportive—something helpful, kind, encouraging, friendly—find a way to communicate that you noticed and that you appreciate it. No matter what you think, raises are not mandatory. Financial support for continuing education is not mandatory. Allowing you a family leave may be mandatory, but doing so with a show of understanding and support is not. If you want a mutually satisfying relationship with your attorney-boss-clients, treat them like valued professional colleagues and the most important clients in your professional life.

Hot Tip: Paralegals often cite lack of respect as a source of job dissatisfaction. After spending real time working hard to support your lawyers and after proving yourself a true professional, if you find yourself badly treated or maligned or ignored, you need to find a new workplace. In a good firm a track record of stellar performance results in real respect for the kind of legal professional you are and the work you do. This kind of respect is critical not only for job satisfaction, but for ongoing professional success.

BECOME A CONSULTANT TO YOUR FIRM

One of the ways to expand your role within the professional life of the firm and to create change is to become an in-house consultant for your firm. This is both difficult and fun. It requires a commitment of time and an expenditure of energy for which you may never be paid. Then again, if you're good, you may be paid, and quite handsomely.

In any case, if you're bright and insightful you're bound to think of things that will make the firm a better place to work, better able to serve its clients, and more profitable. Finding a way to helpfully communicate those ideas to the firm's decision makers will certainly be more satisfying than just sitting on them.

One of the first things to realize in becoming an in-house consultant is that some of your ideas will be welcomed, some will be ignored, and a number of them will just hang around for a year or two and then emerge as an announcement from a committee or a directive from a senior manager. In that case you will most likely not get credit. Don't let that dissuade you. Good ideas come to those who are alert and open and who act on their ideas. You want to be the kind of person who has the good ideas, and you must cultivate this capacity in yourself.

Second, even if public announcements about a good idea do not single you out as author, people do notice who is coming up with winning suggestions. Don't underestimate others; most people aren't stupid. If you submit even three good ideas to a partner or a committee, you will be identified as someone who's a thinker. If you can submit those ideas in a friendly, nondemanding way you will be thought of as someone they're glad to hear from, a team player, not just a self-promoter. If you can respond in a reasonable way to the natural hesitation law firms have about changing policy—and appreciate the fact that most law firms are procedure-oriented and do not have a procedure for receiving and evaluating ideas from paralegals—you will have a chance of working within the firm to get your ideas to the people who are open to input and have authority to act. It's an art.

You may ask, "Why should I do this? Won't this mean hours I work for which I am not getting credit? Doesn't this kind of 'giving away' ideas mean I'm a sap who doesn't know how to protect myself in the big bad corporate world of law?"

Yes, Virginia, you will definitely put in nonbillable hours if you allow yourself to think about things beyond your next billable project. You will definitely end up "giving away" some good ideas. But giving away good ideas is not the same as getting nothing for them. Building this kind of relationship with your firm is one of the best, most savvy things you can do for your career. It will identify you as an individual with capacities and attributes that make you valuable beyond your normal contribution of good, solid legal work. It will flag you as someone who is smart and capable. It will encourage decision makers to think of you when a new program needs to be implemented or when input from the firm's paralegal corps is needed.

Contributing helpful ideas in a nonconfrontational manner will also put you in contact with individuals in the firm who you might not otherwise meet and who are on the cutting edge in their own thinking. They will be encouraged (and may even be surprised) that anyone from the rank and file is thinking about how to produce a better work product, manage resources more effectively, and improve the firm's finances.

It takes patience and an attitude that "que sera, sera" to keep coming up with good ideas and sending them out into the world of policy makers where they may or may not receive a warm welcome. I was terrible at it for years. Every idea I came up with seemed like a good idea to me, an obviously splendid idea that ought to be immediately and heartily embraced and of course implemented at once. I was so focused on me and my idea that I failed to take in the corporate structure that was the unsuspecting recipient of my unsought insight. More than once I paid an ego price for my fixation on "my idea."

Over time I developed a different attitude toward my ideas, seeing them as basically worthwhile but perhaps not right for the time or the current power brokers. I learned to send them off in little memo boats to sink or float on the ocean of committee and partnership review. Once they were out there I learned to turn my attention to other matters in other spheres, which leads to the next step for effecting change and shaping your own future within the firm and in the greater legal community.

A Prophet Is Not without Honor Save...

Establish yourself as a legal professional outside the firm, out in the world. Make contributions, forge alliances, and gain recognition in a larger forum. You will be surprised how much it will do for you at home.

Are you a good writer? Research an interesting legal topic and write an article for a magazine. Do you feel called upon to do good works? Volunteer at the local legal aid clinic or organize a pro bono project. Call the local high schools and colleges and ask if they need speakers on your career for informational days. Get involved with the local bar association and your local paralegal association. Attend NALA, NFPA, and AAfPE conferences. Read up on the status of current activities of the ABA Standing Committee on Legal Assistants and write a summary for the local legal newsletter. Get visible.

All your activities don't have to be law oriented. Maybe you feel strongly about raising funds to support cancer research. Do it. You'll help where it's needed and meet other worthwhile people in the community. I once tutored a junior high school student who worked very hard to improve his grades. He worked so hard he won a prize. I did not associate the tutoring with establishing myself in the legal community. Even so, a partner in my firm reported to me that a local judge had singled me out in a speech he made at a large legal event. He was talking about being involved with the community and someone had told him about my hardworking student. Get out there and do things. You never know where it will lead. Nothing impresses the lawyers you work with like someone outside the firm being impressed by you.

MAKE MEETINGS WORK IN YOUR FAVOR

On a busy day in most law firms people in offices and cubicles are bent over files reading, dictating, or clicking away at the keyboards. Those not so engaged will be found in the library with a stack of books and a small mountain of yellow pads, chewing on the ends of pencils and trying to figure out the best way to make the argument. Occasionally you see a few folks gathered in an office or around a secretarial station chatting, but for the most part the focus is on meeting the current deadlines and getting the work out. It's a series of individual pieces of work, and people can go all morning without talking to another soul.

Beyond the lunch hour, the main social interaction of legal professionals occurs at meetings, and even many of these are scheduled from noon to one o'-clock! Meetings are the mechanism for in-house education, for orientation to the firm and it's culture, and for making the firm's organizational system work. They are also opportunities for you to get to know people who you might not otherwise meet and to participate in the life processes of this legal organism. Your behavior at meetings will have an impact on whether the lawyers of the firm see you as a potential colleague or whether they lump you into what for many lawyers is still an indistinguishable mass of support players called "the paralegals."

Prepare for firm meetings the way you would prepare for any important professional event. Even in-house educational meetings require preparation. If there is written material, make sure that you have read it and thought about it before you get to the meeting. Bring pen and paper to all meetings.

Show up on time. No speaker likes to compete with the spectacle of someone filling up a lunch plate and trying to find a seat in an already crowded room. Flying in breathless at the last minute because you had a telephone call you couldn't wind up may have to happen once in awhile, but it should not be a way of life.

Arrange your morning so that you have time to wind up your current project, stop in the rest room, and then arrive ready to chat with other firm professionals as you get lunch. This small talk can go a long way toward establishing you as a friendly presence and as someone who isn't scared to death to act like a grown-up human being in a room filled with attorneys.

Do not skulk by the door with another paralegal and whisper. This is adolescent and unkind. As you find your seat, introduce yourself to anyone in your vicinity whom you may not know. Just look them in the eye, smile, and say "Hi, I'm Janet Singer. I work in litigation." You may be surprised how many attorneys will be relieved that someone said hello to them!

Keep your mind on the meeting. Be clear on the subject matter and focus on it. Do not use an educational meeting to address departmental concerns or bring up issues that the congregated group is not set up to address. This is where the research you've done about the firm comes into play. If there is a paralegal committee that reviews salary issues for paralegals, do not bring up salary questions at a departmental meeting.

There are meetings at which speaking out is inappropriate. If the meeting is clearly designed for announcements from on high, think twice before you say anything in response. You should think it over and if it's something you need to speak up about, choose your method and control the timing. It may be more effective to have a chat on the side with a partner who is sympathetic to hearing your views. Never blurt out a quick response to bad news at a meeting.

The key to knowing what to do at meetings is careful listening. If the meeting is an educational one, participate fully. Do not assume that the attorneys are the only ones who are supposed to talk. Listen to the presenter, ask relevant questions, and treat the in-house class as you would a class at the local university. Many in-house sessions are as good as university classes so be sure to read the material and keep the handouts. If you find a particular class especially helpful, let the presenter know. People often put a lot of work into these classes. An E-mail message or short note letting the presenter know you learned a lot will be appreciated.

Take notes on anything that comes up at a meeting that requires follow-up and then follow up. Often at an educational meeting a point will emerge that no one is completely clear on. Research is needed. Do the research yourself, as soon after the meeting as possible. When you're clear about the answer, write it up and circulate a memo.

A classy way to do this is to address the memo to the presenter. That way she or he can check over the research, and most likely will send copies of the memo to all the people who attended the class. In one fell swoop you have increased your own understanding of the subject matter, helped your department, and advertised your research skills, your follow-through, and your team spirit.

In a world that's built on billable hours it can be tempting to skip departmental meetings or to pass up in-house classes. Don't do it. Although you cannot bill for meeting time, it is necessary to be involved in these events if you want to be a real member of the professional staff at your law firm. It's another investment in yourself and in your career. Failure to attend and failure to participate simply says, "I'm not interested" or "I'm not committed" or "I'm lazy" or "I'm dumb." Which of these messages do you want to send to the attorneys you work for?

DEVELOPING YOUR OWN STYLE

If you take a look at the really successful paralegals you know, it will hit you: They have style. Each one has a personal style. The kind of style I'm talking about is multifaceted. It's personal and can incorporate a lot of different things. It might be the way one paralegal thinks, talks, gets enthused, maintains a cool head, jokes around, or works long hours. You might notice another with a serious demeanor, attention to detail, classic business suits, old-fashioned high heels, fast repartee, and drop-dead writing skills. There are a lot of ways to be a superstar paralegal, but superstars all share two traits:

1. *Totality*—Superstars are totally committed to their careers and to excellence. People talk about how they never drop the ball, about how they take responsibility for their own actions and demonstrate good judgment. That's what comes of commitment and you've already read a lot about it in this book.

2. *Comfort*—All superstars share a sense of comfort about who they are professionally. They're comfortable because they're smart enough to know themselves. They've been around awhile and learned a lot about the legal world. Of course, what they learned led them to change some aspects of their office performance. But they have also identified some things about themselves that they didn't change—core traits, personality traits. They've been able to fit those personal traits into their working style and working environment in ways that don't hurt their professional standing. In some cases they may even enhance it.

Let me give you some examples. If you have an active sense of humor, even an irreverent one, you're going to have a hard time keeping a lid on it all the time at work. You need and deserve an outlet for your humor. I don't mean you can be irrepressible or that you can be hurtful or thoughtless. You must be civilized and kind and everyone in this business has to be able to maintain a sober sense of decorum when needed. But if you find the funny side of things appealing you will do well to find folks to work with who get the joke.

On the other hand, if you want to be all business at work and don't want to take time to chat about your coworker's daughter's cheerleading tryouts, you need to find a team that won't think you're a cold, heartless meanie. There are teams that know a lot about each other's families and there are teams that focus on their joint legal projects. Both can be exceptional and both can provide rewarding work experiences. The secret's in the right team makeup.

Developing your own work style takes time. If you're new to the profession you will probably do well to dress like a professional, and you should act like one too. It will make everyone (you included) feel more comfortable and you can all get on with the work at hand. As time goes by and you gain more experience with your area of practice and with the firm, you will notice that you are developing a personal work style. It won't be set in stone but you'll notice that you'd rather work four long days and leave early Friday, or that you like to stay after five and talk through the cases with your attorneys, or that you'd rather be at your desk by 7:30 a.m. to get a jump on the day.

Pay attention to the ways of working that work for you. Having a style that allows you to enjoy being a paralegal is key to avoiding the much-dreaded paralegal burnout that can set in after a few years in the business. You'll also notice that some people are much more attractive as work partners to you than others.

(We're not talking romance here, we're talking work.) Maybe they're intense about analyzing cases, maybe they never miss a detail, or maybe they maintain their cool even in a crisis and you really like that. Perhaps they have a habit of working on a matter for half an hour and then stopping to tell a funny story, or perhaps they can work for three hours straight going through detailed documents. Whatever their style is, it feels like a fit. You will benefit from using your skills at arranging your own assignments to continue to work with people whose styles fit yours.

If you are able to maintain a rigorous work schedule, if you produce a good work product, and if the firm is able to bill and collect most of your time, you may be surprised how little the powers that be care about your harmless, idiosyncratic personal behaviors. I wouldn't try sliding down the banisters or dropping in to discuss the front page of the *New York Times* with the senior partner, but you probably don't have to wear a dark suit every day either. Work hard but enjoy yourself and discover your personal style.

How to Change Jobs without Leaving the Firm

Consider this scenario: Basically you like the firm you work for. You like the commute and enough of the players to want to stay. But you've been there a long time. You've been doing the same thing for a long time. You find yourself thumbing through the *Journal* job ads on your lunch hour. You're restless.

Perhaps you like the firm but somehow your department has acquired new leadership. This guy is not paralegal friendly. He doesn't want you working on anything substantive and he doesn't want you talking at departmental meetings.

Maybe you've always been in litigation, but you just had baby number two and you really can't work weekends any more. You need to leave the office in time to get to the day care center by 5 p.m. You need to be able to predict when your busy time of the year will be. You need to switch to corporate work.

Whatever the reason, it is often worthwhile to consider staying with the firm and changing your job description enough to get the benefits of a larger move. There are still advantages to employment longevity. If you are new to the paralegal profession you should realize that employers are still suspicious of one- or two-year job stints. If you've been around a while then you've proven yourself a team player, top producer, and general all-around good fellow. You enjoy a certain seniority even if it's not laid out in the personnel manual and you may not like the idea of starting all over with a new firm if you can change jobs without leaving the firm.

Maybe you just don't want to have to spend years identifying the forward-thinkers, establishing strong backup systems, and finding allies among the powerful. You have done those things where you currently work. And frankly, if you're well compensated you may not find changing firms all that financially rewarding. At your current firm they know you're good; they may know you're worth generous compensation. A new firm is entitled to ignore professional attributes that don't show up on a resume and pay you on a skill-level basis. They do not know you have exceptional judgment, can be relied on to protect firm interests, and are genuinely interested in a cooperative working venture. They don't have to pay for those "worth their weight in gold" character traits until you've been around long enough to demonstrate them.

How can you change jobs without leaving the firm? One of the first things to realize is that even small firms may have options that allow you to change job duties. Mid-size and larger firms and firms with several practice areas or departments offer even more chances to make a switch.

The first step is to think things through. Are you currently integral to someone's practice? If so, you need to be careful about moving on too abruptly. To do so would be unprofessional, unkind, and stupid. If someone has taken you on as a team member you owe that person loyalty and gratitude. Any move you make to change your position without the support of your team leader will probably be viewed negatively by the powers that be. That won't help your career at all.

If you intend to make a change, the first thing you need to think about is your current spot. Is there a way to move out without damaging the team? One thing to consider is training someone to take your spot. This can work if someone new is on the scene and if you are on such good terms with your team leader that you can broach the subject.

You need to do this carefully. It won't work to just announce you're jumping ship, but you may be able to be frank about wanting to learn new things. If you're known as a fast study and there are a lot of routine aspects to your current duties, you may find more understanding than you expected. Ask if you can train the new person on some of the easier parts of the job, making it clear that you will still be responsible for the final work product. This is a fair way to go and it will assure the attorney that you are still the same fine person. It will also give you experience training a newer paralegal, and that is a valuable job change in itself.

The second thing to do is to approach the team you'd like to join. If you review Chapter 7 you'll find a lot of ways to do that. Planning your approach is actually fun, and in doing it you will develop more career skills. Remember that learning a new job or a new specialty takes time and energy.

Hot Tip: All changes have an element of risk; you don't want to blow it. Plan your move for a time when you can invest enough time and energy in the change to be successful.

As you move into your new job responsibilities, remember your promise to train your replacement. Budget time to work with this person each day at first. Remember that what is now easy and routine was once a challenge for you too. Remember also that you are still responsible for that work product. At some point you will need to touch bases with the attorney who is the team leader to see how your replacement is doing. Take this seriously. Letting down the side or leaving people in the lurch is the kiss of death in a law firm. At some point you will hear lawyers say these words: "I'll never use so-and-so again. She was supposed to help me with the Francis case and the next thing I knew she was off helping Jack. She left me holding the bag." You never want someone to say this about you. You never want someone to think this thought, never.

Another way to change jobs is to maintain your current workload and add one new project in another department. As time goes on you will be able to shift the total workload to include more work in the new area and less in the old. Since a lot of legal work is project-sized (e.g., a will, a piece of litigation, a contract) this is a realistic way to add new skills and change your overall workload.

Remember, changing teams in the same firm takes time. Don't get impatient. If you were retooling your resume, combing the ads, mailing letters, and interviewing it would take time too. In that situation you'd then have to learn a roster of new personalities, new clients, and new office procedures and convince a new set of attorneys that you're a standout. If you work for a good firm, consider staying. Maybe you can maximize your position there.

13

Back to School:
Continuing Education

"...where I will point ye out the light path of a virtuous and noble education, laborious indeed at the first ascent but else is so smooth, so green."
John Milton 1608–1674

This article originally appeared in *Legal Assistant Today* (Jan/Feb 97, vol. 48).

You've worked hard to get here: not an aspiring paralegal, but a for-real, honest-to-God, working paralegal. School's out, right?

Wrong!

It's time to take on your continuing education. Is it tough to fit into your paralegal work life? Absolutely. Should you do it anyway? You bet.

Each year, changes in the local court rules, state legislation, Supreme Court rulings and "generally accepted methodology" affect the way lawyers and paralegals serve clients. Unless your professional responsibilities stop at putting documents in chronological order, you need to stay on top of the law. If you get behind, you're headed for failure.

Even if the law in your area of practice hasn't changed lately, you may be in need of a thinking fresher-upper. Continuing education can address both your need to keep up with the law and your need to keep mentally alert, but the choices and time constraints are serious and you must make informed decisions about the continuing education avenues you pursue. So, you wonder, how do I find and assess continuing education?

Continuing education has become a significant part of the paralegal studies program at many colleges. The program administrators know they are targeting "students" who work full-time so courses are offered at night and on weekends at reasonable fees. Most institutions accept major credit cards and many will register you by fax.

These classes cover recent developments in specific areas of law as well as computer-related courses. If you need to learn about a new area of law, you will probably be able to find an appropriate course at a nearby institution. Bankruptcy, real estate, medical malpractice, administrative law, ERISA, environmental law, and computer-assisted research are all common continuing education course subjects. Most of these courses are taught by local attorneys and paralegals. So, not only is this a learning experience but also a great networking opportunity. Many local legal professionals who teach are on the lookout for students who would make good hires. If you can submit work to a teacher that he or she would like to see in the office you may turn your continuing education into a real career advancement move.

Another advantage to taking college courses is that you can choose from a variety of courses and instructors. This will expose you to both practicing professionals and professors who teach on a full-time basis. Also, if there are two classes on this semester's schedule that you are really interested in you can take one class this semester and take the other class another semester, because colleges tend to offer the same classes regularly.

If you are not wild about the idea of literally going back to school or just don't like those ivy-covered halls, consider seminars, independent trainers, in-house programs, or teaching yourself. Continuing education doesn't have to mean going back to school.

If you're a member of a local or national paralegal association, you are probably aware of countless opportunities to take classes, attend conferences and workshops, and purchase other educational information directly from the association. This is one of the advantages to belonging to local, state, or national associations. For instance, many local associations invite an experienced paralegal or attorney to speak on a substantive or procedural issue particular to the area during a brown-bag lunch session.

These gatherings are often of special interest because they involve real-life, getting it done in our town issues. Local groups are often the most responsive to requests from the membership for specialized seminars. These seminars are convenient and usually inexpensive ways to educate yourself. They are usually held at a local firm or bar association meeting room, and should be announced in your paralegal newsletter. The only downside is that they occur in the middle of the day at a set time and are not usually repeated. You just have to plan that time, usually an hour or an hour and a half, into your schedule and make time for the program.

You may also have to check with your national association (if you are taking the class to meet the requirements to maintain accreditation from your national association) to determine whether the program will count toward their requirements. Even if it doesn't, if the program interests you or will help you on the job, take it!

Your state and local bar association many also offer seminars that you can attend. Although some of these programs are designed solely for attorneys and may not be open to the public, many courses will be helpful to both lawyers and paralegals. In addition to being a good learning experience (you're learning what your boss is learning) these are also good networking opportunities.

The downside is that the prices for bar association seminars can range from inexpensive to hundreds of dollars. This may not be an expense your firm will pay. If you have to pay the fees yourself, don't let that scare you away from these courses. Call the local, state, and American Bar Association (ABA) and find out what's offered in your area, the cost of the program, the time constraints (it could be a daylong program that costs you a personal day, depending on your firm) and who's speaking. It might be worth the money and the personal day if someone you really respect is teaching.

If you are a Certified Legal Assistant (CLA) you probably already know that the National Association of Legal Assistants, Inc. (NALA) has requirements for continuing education for legal assistants with the CLA designation. According to NALA, most CLAs fulfill those requirements by taking classes already approved by NALA, or by submitting data about classes they have taken and seeking approval after the fact. Like continuing education for attorneys, CLA requirements address both substantive and law office management issues.

The National Federation of Paralegal Association's (NFPA) Model Code of Ethics addresses continuing education as a means to maintaining your professionalism, and NFPA certifies certain courses as meeting their standards. According to Susan Kaiser, NFPA's president, continuing education is considered so necessary to a professional career as a paralegal that it has never been a controversial issue at NFPA. In addition to offering educational programs and workshops at their annual and mid-year conferences, NFPA has also established the Paralegal Advanced Competency Examination (PACE) and the Paralegal Accreditation (PA).

Many of the national and state associations such as the American Association for Paralegal Education (AAfPE), National Black American Paralegal Association (NAPA), Legal Assistant Management Association (LAMA), Association of Trial Lawyers of America (ATLA), and the National Notary Association (N.A.) also offer educational programs. In addition a lot of these associations have annual and mid-year conferences (held in different cities each year), and offer educational programs at those conferences.

The association opportunities are limitless. The ABA alone sponsors or cosponsors a variety of programs dealing with every practice area imaginable. Between your local, state, and national associations, there is bound to be something of interest to you and within your (or your firm's) price range.

Legal vendors are also a great source of further education. For example, both West Publishing and Lexis provide free training sessions to their subscribers. Even your local imaging provider may hold occasional seminars. You just have to be on the lookout for these types of opportunities. You can start by asking your vendors what programs they offer.

West will train on-site and will even customize a training session to fit your firm's needs. But West not only sends trainers to job sites, they also have permanent facilities in many locations where classes are offered. For instance, West has a permanent training center in the Los Angeles area as well as in all major metropolitan areas. Paralegals and attorneys can go to these centers for additional training. West also sets up temporary Learning Centers in many locations to offer a limited set of courses.

West's current Los Angeles listings include seminars on Intellectual Property Law, SEC filings, Public Records Access, Statutes and Legislative History, Corporate Information, and the ever-popular Citation Checking. Don't count on the courses remaining the same throughout the year. West changes them to meet the needs, requests, and interests of attendees.

West also has a certification program. If you're unemployed, West offers a job searching seminar that will teach you to access West's job search databases, including the National Association for Law Placement (NALP). Finally, West offers telephone classes for those customers located in outlying regions.

Lexis also offers education to legal assistants and you can receive on-site training if your firm subscribes to their services. In addition, Lexis assigns account professionals to be available to answer questions and provide customized one-on-one training and general support.

Like most fields, paralegal continuing education has its entrepreneurs—people or training centers that offer continuing education courses, seminars, and workshops to individuals, groups, and the public at large. For example, consider Cheryl Evans, a former paralegal turned consultant. Evans is just one of many independent trainers. She teaches a hands-on document organization seminar called "From Soup to Nuts" that is designed to get you out of the conceptual and into the actual. Evans describes her program as three hours of myth-debunking in which attorneys and paralegals learn the truth about new document management computer programs and related technology such as scanning.

Participants get to ask Evans lots of questions like, "How do you get data into the system?" "Who has to do it?" "How long does it take and how much might it cost?" And of course she addresses the really big question that often stymies paralegals faced with a rush assignment: "Once it's in there, how do I get it out?"

Evans' course will tell you how to set up database fields that will give you responsive information when you need it, as well as alert you to the pitfalls of bad typing and bad spelling or of thinking your system will do all the work for you.

One of the advantages of taking courses from an independent trainer is that they will often customize a program just for your firm, or for you individually. Of course you should expect a solo training class to cost more than one that is open to the public or at least to the paralegal or legal profession. Remember, though, before you run out there and hire a professional trainer to customize a training program for you, to ask what courses they offer. Maybe they already have one that's right for you.

Some trainers or training programs may be just what you need, even if they are not geared to the legal profession. For example, you may wish to take an accounting course if you do a lot of estate, family, corporate, or bankruptcy law and you review financial records on a regular basis. Maybe you've already gone to the bar association sponsored seminar, but you still want to learn more. You may have to take a class outside what the legal professional provides. Likewise, if you're looking for a course on stress reduction, time management, or assertiveness, these workshops may be more readily available outside the legal arena.

Most law firms have a lot of lawyers who are already experts in their fields (such as the tax lawyer who does corporate taxes, the bankruptcy lawyer, and the litigator who tries family law disputes). You can help your firm tap that resource for in-house seminars. Why not organize a program for you and other paralegals and lawyers? Practice groups often find that these seminars increase their sense of community and provide greater consistency in the way certain matters are handled. You can brown-bag it, order pizza, or if the partnership is willing, buy the attendees lunch. Then someone begins a class by presenting material. A discussion will ensue and you may find yourself amazed at the aggregate knowledge in the room. In my office these seminars provide substantive, helpful knowledge and also acquaint us with each other's strengths so we know who to go to when a specialty issue arises. Sometimes this kind of seminar program can be sold to the partnership as a component of a malpractice prevention program. If your firm is authorized as a MCLE provider you should find help from the firm's MCLE coordinator.

If you commute to work, you can use that drive time to develop career advancing expertise by listening to MCLE or general education tapes. Many continuing education courses are available on audiotape as an alternative to or in addition to attending the seminar. Most of those tapes end up in law firm libraries or tucked in the back of a boss' desk drawer. Ask around. There may be tapes detailing new legislation affecting the firm's clients or reviewing methods for protecting assets that will add to your legal knowledge. This is a fairly painless way to pick up a bit more knowledge and it can lead to new areas of practice for you.

Don't forget to talk to individuals in a particular practice area to see if the source you are planning to listen to is current and interesting. If so, be sure to go back after you have listened once or twice to the tape for a short discussion of what you learned. You may find yourself involved in a lively conversation and you may convince someone you would be a good person to involve in that type of work.

Don't forget your own areas of expertise. You may be ready to provide continuing education yourself. Contact local paralegal studies programs to find out about their policy on accepting proposals for classes. As most teachers will admit, one of the real benefits of teaching is that it forces you to master a subject. Volunteer to present material in your practice group. If paralegals are not included in your firm's in-house educational seminars, approach a sensible partner to find out why. (You will be amazed at how often they'll say, "I had no idea you would be interested.")

Choose a topic with reasonable parameters (like the Public Records Act, pitfalls in serving subpoenas or verifying discovery, local rules for courts in your county, etc.) and draft an outline. Add handouts that provide examples of how the task is done—or how it is often mismanaged—and voila! You are ready to lead a seminar. Be scared, be nervous, be a little pushy, but do it. You will educate folks, not only about the subject matter but about what paralegals can do as colleagues and educators.

As a hardworking paralegal you're juggling job responsibilities, family concerns, and the desire to have a little time to yourself, and you're probably thinking the last thing you need is a course or two on the side. The fact is, when you are really good at handling your professional responsibilities, when you really know that job, a course in something new can be the refreshing breeze you need. You'll meet other professionals, learn about interesting practice areas, increase your professional standing at work, and add to your marketability.

Nothing makes life more interesting than taking responsibility for your own fate. Continuing education is one way you can maintain some autonomy in your career development and increase your sense of yourself as a legal professional.

Since that article was published a whole new possibility for continuing education has come on the scene. Where can you find it? On your computer screen, of course.

The latest in continuing education is on-line learning. If you log onto NALA's, NFPA'S, or AAfPE's Web sites you will probably find a link to on-line courses as well as their listing of conferences, seminars, and classes around the country.

There's also the Consortium for Advanced Legal Education (CALE) at http://www.cale.org. This is a nonprofit educational organization that works with various paralegal education programs to offer graduate level work in areas like intellectual property law, elder law, Internet research, ADR, PACE review, and more. These courses are generally limited to twenty or fewer students and require substantial on-line time.

At the time of this writing, on-line education for paralegals is pretty new. There's not much feedback available on the courses, but they are certainly intriguing. This technology should enable you to take courses at distant schools, participate in conferences on-line, and communicate with specialists all over the country. In addition to CALE, many universities provide CLE on-line to both paralegals and attorneys. Get on-line and start your search—you may find your future specialty!

The opportunities for education are everywhere and they will continue to grow. The trick is to maintain the educable attitude. As the ABA, AAfPE, NALA, NFPA, and state and federal governments continue their dialogue regarding licensing and control of the paralegal profession, you can be sure your qualifications will be under continuing review. Continuing education is one way to ensure you'll meet the highest standards. It's your job to take the time, to make the time, and to stay on top of your game.

14 LAW OFFICE POLITICS

When it comes to managing law office politics, the beginning of wisdom is understanding just how much you don't know. If you're new to the field, you don't know much; if you're new to a particular office, you don't know much. It takes time to learn what's going on. In fact, it takes time, friends, interactions, and history. To start down the road to firm knowledge, one thing you must do is figure out who's really in charge.

You see, in law firms there are formal power structures and informal power structures. Usually they both exist in the same place and they both count. It's just not always easy to see who's who and how it all works.

Mid-size firms sometimes function through full-partnership meetings at which partners hammer out the firm's policies and major decisions by group consensus or a voting procedure. In these settings you often find an office manager or business manager who makes day-to-day decisions about business aspects of running the firm, subject to whatever limitations the partnership has put in place. Usually staffing and compensation issues are at least discussed at the partnership level. Larger firms often use executive committees, managing partners, or some other formal structure. Remember, the larger the firm the more subpowers exist. Those subpower groups or individuals often make a very real difference in the final outcome of many matters.

What's knowledge about all this got to do with you and your success? Over the course of your career it can be a critical factor. In a perfect world your law firm would be peopled by folks who are knowledgeable about paralegals and what they can do, and who are supportive of expanding paralegals' roles in the office. Because we're talking about a "perfect world," let's say they are also interested in making sure your firm's paralegals are treated fairly, even well.

In a perfect world these forward-thinking folks would have the authority to make and implement decisions and would be happy to allocate resources to paralegal education, to providing good work conditions, and to the education of attorneys on how to use paralegals. They would be interested in the implementation of a bonus plan to encourage top performance and would be happy to hear suggestions from the paralegal corps about how the firm could make it easier for them to excel as legal assistants.

Guess what? It's not like that in most places. If you want to have any effect on the way you work, where you work, your compensation, and your options, it's important that you carefully investigate how (and by whom) decisions about those things are made. You need to know who's in charge and you need to figure out how to best develop a workable relationship with that person or those people so that your ideas will be listened to and, in a best-case scenario, sought.

How do you do this? Actively investigate the firm's goals, policies, and multiple power structures. Be an avid reader of all the literature the firm puts out, including the letterhead. Keep an eye on who gets invited to what kinds of meetings and who sits on boards, brings in clients, and represents the firm at community events. Notice who talks most and who talks to greatest effect at meetings. Also notice who listens best. Of course you're bound to hear some gossip along the way.

There are so many different power structures in different firms that one single way of discovering and affecting them won't work in all cases. You will need to observe, think, build alliances, and be the kind of professional that power brokers find worthwhile and interesting if you want to get on the inside of what's happening at the firm. If you want to build a long-term, mutually profitable relationship with the partnership at your firm, getting on the inside is a wise goal. If you want to get involved in the political process of the firm, even as a junior player, here are some universals to bear in mind:

1.   Both your work product and your profitability must be beyond question. This means you not only make but exceed your billable requirements all the time, every year. Law firms are in business to provide income to the attorneys who constitute them. The firm's reputation for good work contributes to that. If you want to have real influence, you had better be giving your employers a work product they feel sure they can rely on and you had better be profitable while you do it. No exceptions.

2.   You need to be on professionally cordial terms with everybody. If you have not worked at one firm for a long time that may seem like an easy thing to achieve, but many people—both paralegals and attorneys—will tell you it can be a trick to maintain good working relationships over the long haul with a wide variety of personality types. The probability that there will be someone at your firm with whom you are not naturally simpatico is very high. The chance that someone who exercises some power over you will strike you as a less-than-attractive personality is very real. You must learn to control yourself and behave professionally—a very important skill that is addressed in more detail in the next section.

3.   What you do outside the office is just as important as what you do inside the office. Classes you take, classes you teach, committees you sit on, services you provide in your community, articles you author—all these things have a lot to do with your status at the firm and your ability to influence firm policy.

Many excellent paralegals devote all their professional efforts to their desks. They think if they always work late, go the extra mile, or become fabulous experts at what they do, someone in the firm will come into their office someday and say "Hey, we've noticed you're performing splendidly, working much harder than the other paralegals, and handling associate-level work, so we want to give you a windowed office, a big raise, and an assistant."

In this less-than-perfect world, that's not a common occurrence. Working quietly and diligently at your desk forever may not get you noticed, but you'll find that nothing impresses a partner in the firm like someone outside the firm noticing what a great professional you are. Pursue outside professional opportunities.

4. Most things take longer, often quite a bit longer, in a law firm than may seem reasonable to you. Committee decisions usually take longer than anyone, including the committee members, thinks reasonable. Even so, you will usually need to abide by their time schedules.

If you're going to ask a committee for something, plan ahead. Be persistent, but be patient. If you are involved in developing new programs, expanding technological possibilities, making library purchases, or training new personnel, expect any authorizations you need to take awhile.

5. Respecting the chain of command is almost always a good idea. No one likes to be bypassed. This means you need to find out who's in charge and what the procedures are before you go charging off with a new idea or a request.

This does not mean that you cannot make good use of other relationships in order to have all your ducks lined up when a committee or a superior reviews your request. For example, when I decided to write this book I knew I'd need a few months off to work on it. Because I work particularly closely with two attorneys at my firm, I talked to them about the leave idea before I made any formal request. I knew that if they were not happy with the idea, I would have trouble with the project. When they agreed to support my request I was in a much better position to approach the official powers. Even with their support I had to do some paralegal sleuth work to find out the formal procedure for requesting a leave.

If you aren't sure of the chain of command in your firm, keep an eye on scheduled meetings and check the firm's policy book. The personnel manager may be able to answer specific questions, but really understanding how it all works takes a lot of observation and intelligent analysis.

6. It's terrifically useful to be on very good terms with someone who has enough experience with the firm to give you some perspective on what goes on. This is a serendipitous occurrence; you can't plan to become friends with someone because that someone has firm influence or is some kind of insider. You shouldn't and probably can't fake this kind of relationship.

If you're lucky enough to come up with a real mentor or friend—someone who can give you good professional advice and clue you in to how to manage your career within the firm power structure—that relationship will really enhance your chances for success. If someone who's been around awhile and is smart and goodhearted befriends you, be grateful.

PROFESSIONAL BEHAVIOR

There's so much that goes into this topic that it's daunting to even think about writing it, but let's start with the issue of cordial relationships described in item 2 above. What do you do when you have to work with or for someone you just don't like?

Maybe your dislike is due to a personal trait, one that's annoying but not actually lethal. Maybe he doesn't listen well, she's too noisy, he always complains about his wife, she never thinks any job is actually doable. Maybe it's a personal trait but much worse than annoying—he lies, she blames her subordinates for her mistakes, he overbills constantly, she isn't careful about the work she does. Maybe the person you cannot stand is part of a faction that you think is actually bad for clients or the firm. What to do?

There are different strokes for different unbearable folks, but think about these possible responses:

For the unlikable but basically harmless person, find a coping mechanism. One coping mechanism that may work is to think of interacting with these folks like you would think of practicing your scales. If you have ever played a musical instrument you know that if you really want to play a good solo when your big opportunity comes, you need to practice a lot. You need to know every nuance of your instrument. Practicing scales will give you the capacity to hit the note you want every time you try. Likewise, if you want the internal flexibility to respond in a positive fashion to the ups and downs of professional life, you need to practice. If you let every annoying habit in the office upset your internal balance, you'll never really learn your job, let alone maintain your equanimity when you get a bad decision from a judge or when you have to deal with a screaming client or an unhappy attorney.

One thing that helps me cope when I'm feeling displeased with someone is the knowledge that I have my own annoying little ways that can get on the nerves of my coworkers. I'm pretty noisy. I try to keep it under control, but basically I'm a noisy woman. I get up and down a lot, I tend to take steps two at a time, and generally I close a door with too much enthusiasm. I talk a lot and often too quickly.

Of course this bugs some people and I appreciate those with level heads and forgiving hearts. I work hard to repay their understanding by giving them and their work assignments my complete attention and my best thinking. I forgive their little flaws, too. So when someone is making you crazy at the office, think about your own nonstandard characteristics. It might help.

What about the more troublesome traits—the folks who tell lies, blame subordinates, overbill, and the like? These traits fall under the category of failing to behave honorably and it can be quite hard to stomach this behavior. However, if you plan to work in the business you will have to deal with some people like this.

In the short term you may have to swallow your distaste, minimize any negative effects of the bad behavior, and get the job done. In the long term, you can use the tactics outlined in Chapter 7 to get on a team that is not led by or populated with people with such discouraging habits. It may take you a while, but it's an achievable goal and it will necessarily limit your contact with the folks you don't approve of. If you establish yourself as a member of a good working team, you can reasonably expect to avoid the person you have so much trouble with for weeks at a time.

It is not reasonable to expect that the partnership will rise up as a whole and expel the person you find so distasteful. This happens only on rare occasions and for grievous faults. Unless the behavior you find inappropriate endangers the firm or its clients, you shouldn't expect the firm to act. In fact, noticing the tolerance levels of partners within the firm for certain behaviors may well help you understand the politics of the place. If someone behaves in a way that bothers a lot of folks but is still around, then that person is contributing something to the firm. These people have something going for them—unusual expertise, the ability to attract clients, or something else. Open your eyes and learn.

Finally, there are some behaviors that are not okay under any circumstances and they have to be treated accordingly, on a case-by-case basis. If you discover unethical or criminal activity, you may well have to report it to appropriate authorities and I cannot promise you a happy ending. I wish you one, but I can't promise you one. Circumstances that feel professionally scary often are professionally dangerous. That doesn't mean you don't have to act. Each of us has to decide what kind of person we intend to be. Working in a law office does not absolve us of responsibility for our own actions and consciences. It does mean that taking control of your own career at an early stage and finding the right kind of people to work with is smart for a lot of reasons.

The appendices of this book contain both the NALA Code of Ethics and the NFPA Model Code of Ethics and Professional Responsibility. Even if you don't join these organizations, you should read these documents. They describe good professional guidelines for us all. Research your own state bar rules and relevant state and federal statutes. Remember, paralegals are not exempt from prosecution for tortious or criminal behavior. If you aid or abet such activity you can expect to be prosecuted along with the attorneys involved. I have learned a great deal from ethics texts in the field and I encourage you to read relevant literature and to take continuing education courses in legal ethics.

Even if you read all the codes and all the books, your desire to behave professionally and ethically will at times leave you in a bit of a sticky situation. When that happens you will have to sort it out, again on a case-by-case basis. Consider the following example:

Attorney Zed wants to take on a new matter for XYZ Corp in which XYZ is adverse to a fellow named Smith. You happen to know that Smith is CEO of ABC

Corp., a longtime client of the firm. Because of a data inputting error, Smith doesn't come up on the conflicts check, but you know that if the firm's going to take on the new work the conflict issue must be resolved. In this case it might be possible to resolve the conflict with waivers by all interested parties. In any case the situation must be reviewed and addressed.

In the real world, attorneys never really enjoy sending out conflict waiver letters to clients. Who can blame them? The letter brings to the clients' attention the fact that they are not the only clients on the attorney's mind and that the attorney has some kind of relationship with a potential adversary. But you are aware of the potential difficulty, so you go to see Attorney Zed, who does not appear enthused when you bring the potential conflict issues to light.

It takes just a minute to outline the situation. In a matter of minutes the chat's over, but you leave Attorney Zed's office unsure that the conflict waiver letter will be sent out. Have you done your duty?

I would feel obligated to follow up in some way. The exact way would be dictated by the attorney who wants to take on XYZ, the attorney who represents ABC, the amount of knowledge I actually have, etc. One way to handle this would be to mention to the ABC attorney that Smith is the potential adverse in the new XYZ matter and that a chat between the attorneys about how to handle this potential conflict may be in order. If I knew the attorneys involved well enough, I might even ask if they want me to take a shot at drafting the necessary conflict waiver letters.

It's important to remember that it could still turn out that after the matter is reviewed and analyzed, there really is some bona fide reason why a conflict waiver is not required. Remember, I didn't have all the facts when I began my response. I have, however, initiated action to responsibly protect both the clients and the firm and to do the right thing.

Notice that I have also tried to do that in a way that will not hurt my career. I have not been confrontational or accusatory. I've tried to be reasonably subtle (and any of my coworkers will tell you subtlety is not my strong suit) and right-spirited; respectful of the attorneys, the clients, and the process of conflict analysis, and effective.

No one can tell you everything you need to do or not do to handle every situation in an ethical and honorable way that does not hurt your career by alienating powerful people in your work environment. You will have to think things through. You may need to get advice. Often you will need to find the person or persons who have the responsibility and the ability to handle troublesome situations—an attorney mentor, business manager, personnel manager, or committee chair. They may be more than willing to take the heat generated by a tough situation and to ensure that the right thing happens.

If you become a superstar paralegal, you will not get through a year without facing one or more of these sticky situations. It's part of being substantively involved in a particular practice, of being actively involved in the affairs of the firm's clients, and of being the kind of professional who cares about the future of the firm, the future of the legal profession, and doing what's right.

At one point in my career I bemoaned my state as that of a paralegal with limited power to act for the firm, but with a strong sense of responsibility that stemmed directly from my active role in the firm's life. The attorney to whom I complained looked up slowly and said this: "Well, I guess if this is too tough, you could go back to your desk and put some labels on some files." I shut up and settled down to the discipline of learning the ropes in this area of firm life.

PROFESSIONAL BEHAVIOR EXTENDS TO EVERY ASPECT OF YOUR WORK LIFE

If you have a secretary you will soon learn that along with the pleasure involved in being able to delegate some tasks to subordinates comes a serious responsibility. It's likely you will be responsible for evaluating your secretary's performance. You must approach this task as one of the more important things you do in your year. Someone's career, someone's income, and perhaps even someone's job security will be affected by your evaluation. You have to be fair and honest and occasionally forgiving while you maintain reasonable standards and insure that you are able to get your work done with the person working for you. It can be harder than it looks. Be sure you are well-informed about the firm's evaluation policies. Good personnel departments distribute guidelines along with evaluation forms so you can get an idea of how your comments will be read. Remember that none of us likes to get a big, bad surprise at evaluation time.

Establish a pattern of discussing any problems in your secretary's performance as soon as practical after they come up. This will let him or her know what your concerns are and allow a fair opportunity for improvement. Choose a time to discuss these issues that provides your secretary with privacy and don't dilly-dally. It's not a comfortable situation for either of you, so just get it over as simply and quickly as possible. Such a conversation might go like this:

"Lee, I gave you the Thompson correspondence to get out last night, but I saw it on your desk when I came in today. It really needed to go last night."

"Oh gosh, I'm sorry. Mr. French had a rush and I didn't have time to get them both out before the mail left."

"Well, it's not going to work for me to give you direction if I can't count on you to follow through."

"This was really unusual. I'm really sorry. It won't happen again."

"Listen, Lee, here's what you need to do when you cannot get to something I give you. You need to find me and tell me, even before you take on someone else's rush. That way I can make the call about whether I need to get someone else on it or whether it can wait."

"Okay, sure, I'll do that. But I don't think this is going to happen again."

If your secretary's any good, it won't happen again. If it does happen again, you might have a real problem and you will need to take it up with personnel or with an attorney.

GOOD MANNERS WITH SUPPORT STAFF

Remember that, because law firms are basically hierarchical, you owe disciplined responses to everyone below you on the power ladder. The lawyer who can't control his temper and the partner who routinely yells at her paralegals are well-known objects of disdain among real professionals. They should be. You are obligated to treat your secretary, the copying staff, messengers, housekeepers, and everyone else with courtesy—even when you have to tell them that a particular performance was inadequate. There's no excuse for raising your voice, especially if the person you raise it to does not feel free to yell back. There are no jobs in the legal field that don't involve occasion for screw-ups by the people who get the mail out, copy documents, confirm meeting times, etc. Even a screw-up does not entitle you to throw a fit. Remember, someday you will make a mistake yourself. Do unto others as you would have... .

PERSONAL PROBLEMS

Another part of professional life is learning to leave your personal problems at home. Nothing is more disconcerting to someone who is deeply involved in the analysis of an important legal issue than to be confronted with a paralegal who is a) furious; b) sulking; or c) in tears. It can be upsetting personally and it certainly is a distraction from the matter at hand.

The rule, no matter how cold-hearted it may seem to you, is that if you are so upset that you cannot maintain your composure, you don't belong in the office.

Everyone who works—everyone—has times when personal concerns simply outweigh professional ones, and often they should. When this kind of thing happens it may be necessary to take some time off. Should you find yourself in a long-term situation that is bound to affect your mental state—a divorce or the death or illness of a parent—remember that work can also be therapeutic. I'm not advocating avoiding personal problems, but when there's nothing you can do to make a bad personal situation better, it may be useful to focus on work.

This kind of disciplined focus is not only possible, it may be the most restful thing you experience during a period of crisis or grief. Those of us who have worked through a divorce can testify to the usefulness of solid intellectual activity when your emotional life is turbulent. I have worked with people who were dealing with things far more tragic than divorce and have been amazed at the ability of real professionals to rise to the occasion and set their own difficulties aside while they tended to a client's problem.

SUPPORT YOUR FELLOW PARALEGALS

It is not common for paralegals to work closely together. Usually we are paired with attorneys. Days and weeks can go by with no more contact between paralegals than riding an elevator or passing in the halls. But there are times when we do find ourselves together and those times are opportunities to get to know and appreciate what paralegals in your field and often in very different fields are doing.

Encourage and support your fellow paralegals as they move out into the legal community to teach. The development of sophisticated specialties by paralegals, specialties that are rigorous and on the cutting edge, has resulted in these paralegals being tapped to give educational seminars to other paralegals and attorneys alike. If this does not impress you as an important development, you are not yet aware of the territorial instincts of many lawyers when it comes to expertise. If paralegals in your area are teaching classes, take them. You'll learn something and you'll promote solidarity among the paralegals in your firm or area.

I was remiss in supporting my local paralegal association for a long time. I joined but I did not attend meetings. If you're raising children or going to school you may also find that your schedule is so tight you just can't fit in another evening meeting. But if you do find the time, I think you will be surprised at how refreshing and inspirational it can be. I found among active association members not only top-performing paralegals, but people who care deeply about the profession and its future. I recommend checking out your local group.

Supporting other paralegals is not always a matter of professional behavior. Over the course of your career you will meet some plain terrific people who also happen to be paralegals. They will become your heroes and your friends. You'll find supporting them is one of the happiest things you get to do as a paralegal.

CLIENTS—THEY KEEP US IN BUSINESS!

It's not just that we should be consistently professionally perfect with clients because otherwise they'll fire us. That's true, but clients deserve to be treated professionally because they are our clients. They have engaged us because we have professional expertise. They are paying for that expertise. They are paying your salary.

We expect professionalism when we pay salaries. If I walk into Pamela's Pancakes in search of the perfect belgian waffle, the fact that the cook is having a bad day will not excuse a soggy mess on my plate. I'm paying for a good waffle. Clients who are paying for our services are entitled to a good waffle too—every time.

You can figure out what a good legal waffle is. Telephone calls are returned. Courtesies are extended. Work is completed on time. Lame excuses are not proffered. Clients are kept informed of the progress of their matters. They are not back-burnered. I know the attorney you work for is ultimately responsible for the treatment of clients, but you too are a professional. You too need to put the client first.

Many clients actively seek the work of paralegals on their matters. They want to control costs. They also know what good paralegals can do. If you consistently treat clients well, you may surprised at their loyalty to you. Often they will mention your expert attention to the attorneys involved in handling their matters. This is not the reason you should behave professionally toward them, but it is something to be aware of. Client compliments speak loudly to attorneys. Many clients have dealt with such good paralegals that they routinely expect that paralegals will handle their legal matters well. Do not disappoint them.

LOYALTY

Does loyalty sound like an old-fashioned idea? Old, maybe, but not out of fashion. Remember, there really are people who behave well, work hard, tell the truth, give credit where credit's due, and treat you like a human being. These fine professionals deserve your loyalty. If you have the good fortune to develop working relationships with lawyers or paralegals or secretaries or janitors who are among the class acts of the legal world, cherish those relationships and be good to the people involved. This means that you take care of all your responsibilities to these people all the time. You don't gossip about them or tell jokes at their expense or cancel lunch with them because a more prestigious invitation came your way or miss their birthdays. Watch their backs. Remember that they are one of the reasons you can get up and make it to the office day after day.

Don't forget about the loyalty you owe to the firm. You may not love everyone there or everything about the way it's run, but if you work for a good firm, acknowledge that to yourself and to the firm. Be loyal. It's awfully easy to spend the day thinking about the things you'd like to change. Many paralegals fall into the habit of sniping about these things and losing sight of what drew them to the firm in the first place.

Do not make a practice of stopping by someone's office regularly to go over (and over and over) every beef you have about working at your firm. It's an easy habit to get into and it's deadly. Your attitude will sour, your concentration will dissipate, and your billing hours will go right down the drain.

What should you do when the gripe crowd comes around? If you have work to do, mention that you do and get on with it. Move. If you don't have work, you need to spend quality time on that problem and solve it. Reread Chapter 7. You don't have to make a self-righteous speech when you leave the pity party. Be cheerful and professional. If you keep it up you won't get invited to these gripe fests often, and that's a good thing.

MEETINGS—WHAT TO BRING UP WHEN

Meetings happen. They can be fun, but often they are not. They can be useful, but sometimes they're not very useful either. However, they are a significant part of firm life and if you are invited to meetings, you should attend. Different meetings require different behaviors.

Departmental Meetings

Larger firms have departments and departments have meetings. Meetings may be held to discuss the workload of the department, to provide education to all of the department's members in their area of law, or to announce new departmental policies.

Nothing communicates a lack of interest like missing your department's educational meetings. Go to these meetings even if you think you will never use the information. You will certainly never be in a position to use it if you don't know it. Ignorance of your area of law is inexcusable. Go to the meetings even if they are held at 7 a.m. Come prepared. Participate fully, just as if you were in a class, asking questions and making comments that are relevant to the material and discussion. If you are sharp and stay with the program, eventually you will be able to use this information (and your enhanced professional reputation) to enlarge your areas of responsibilities. That means your work will be more interesting and valuable—both good things.

Meetings held to discuss department issues are not much fun and you will be tempted to miss them. "It doesn't matter what paralegals think about things," you may think. You may even be right, but it is crucial to know what's going on. If paralegal input is ever to become a relevant part of your department's political life, you are going to have to show some initiative and interest. You may have to sit quietly through many of these meetings. I hate sitting quietly through anything, but I do it. These are my superiors and my employers and I need to know what they care about and what they think about what they care about. So do you.

Informational Meetings

These meetings are usually called to announce new firm policy or tell people about a decision that has already been made by the powers that be. If your child is sick you can miss a meeting and find out later what was said, but by and large you should attend whenever you can. Every time you are there paying attention, you identify yourself as an active part of the firm.

Firmwide Meetings

Some firms have firmwide meetings to discuss the handling of conflict issues, how to avoid malpractice claims, marketing, or other firm concerns. Attend these meetings, even when they're held on Saturdays. If the meeting is important enough to the partnership to command their attention when they could be off doing weekend things, then it's important to you. The issues count and the camaraderie these meetings engender is another way to build strong working relationships.

Hot Tip: Whatever meeting you are attending, respect the subject matter and the time frame. Nothing's worse than someone who brings up work assignments at a meeting about how to file a writ.

LAW OFFICE POLITICS: THE BIG PICTURE

Last week I got a call from a young worker who was telling me about her new job. "It's so great here," she said. "There are no politics." Of course that's what she thought—she'd only been there three days. Office politics exist everywhere. You can't avoid them, but you can manage them.

You can choose where you get involved and where you steer clear. You can behave like a full-fledged adult and think in the long term. You can be disciplined and demonstrate in your own professional life the characteristics you admire in others. If you do, you'll be rewarded. If you don't, all the expertise in the world won't get you that great career.

15

A SUCCESSFUL PARALEGAL'S ALMANAC

In a successful paralegal's career, as in a garden, things have their seasons. If the right things are done at the right time, one season leads into another, producing bumper crop after bumper crop. But as in a garden, if the right things are not done, if the demands of the season are not met, no amount of effort or enthusiasm late in the year can make it all come out right. You have to think ahead. In December it will be too late—much too late—to think about December.

You might be surprised to find how easy it is to go through a whole year without taking a continuing education course, or without volunteering for a pro bono project, or without taking your children on a trip. It's easy and very unwise. This almanac is designed to help you plan your year. You'll need to customize the plan to suit your career, your firm, and your style, but the things mentioned are all things you should think about.

A year without this kind of planning is a year lost, and they can add up quickly too. When you look back five years from now or ten years from now, I don't want you to ask, "What happened? How did I end up here?"

The paralegal's almanac assumes you will be busy, moving full steam ahead with your assignments—legal projects. That's a constant in the life of all good paralegals. What sets the superstars apart is that they think about their careers too, and they act on their thinking.

JANUARY

Recovery from the holiday season is dramatic and usually visible among most of the lawyers and paralegals in the firm. Suddenly they're ready to get to work. Suddenly calendars overflow with meetings, depositions, interviews, and research assignments that were not critical last month and were set aside to accommodate December's celebrations. Suddenly everyone's in the New Year's resolution frame of mind, tempered only by the fatigue of making last year's quota of hours.

If you worked hard to make your hours for last year you may be tempted to lay back in January. Not a good idea. January's the time to think about how this year should go. What are your work goals, both for professional development and for billing hours? You need to think now about where you want to be in September.

Generally speaking, the psychological boost that a strong January will give you is hard to overrate. You can go into the year without the "catching up" mentality that is prevalent among those who never seem to make the grade. If you do not have a full plate of work, seek it immediately. January's a great time to get in on the ground floor of major projects that will be active for the next six months. Attorneys are especially receptive to the initiative factor in January. Now's the time to demonstrate yours. Remember, February is a short month. Think ahead.

Set your alarm and get to the office early at least one day a week, all month. This will give you some time to think about what you intend to accomplish this year before the phone starts ringing and lawyers start stopping by. Remind yourself that while you work for the firm, you own your career. You are responsible for moving it forward. Prioritize your professional goals and write down ideas about how to meet them. Consider what continuing education you will be involved in, both as a student and as a teacher. What new area of law will you take a look at? Is there a team of workers in the firm that you would like to get to know? How will you do that?

Get to the bookstore and pick out at least two books—one that offers good career advice and one that's substantive in your area of legal expertise. Choose one periodical and subscribe to it. Do not decide you cannot afford this right after the holiday spending spree. You cannot afford to skip this crucial step in building your career. One of the keys to getting others to see you as a professional is to see yourself as one. Professionals care about their fields, their continuing education, and their professional libraries.

If you're more experienced and can find the time it's great to take a look at new laws passed in your city, county, and state, as well as federal statutes that came into effect January first. Of course it's better to check on these before January, but if no one in your firm has prepared a summary of new legislation that may affect the kinds of people and businesses who are clients of your firm, do it. Then distribute it to attorneys and paralegals alike. This is the kind of initiative and intellectual curiosity that impresses lawyers—and it should. Perhaps your memo can be transformed into a memo to clients. Think about the possibilities.

Be sensitive to the fact that for many law firms January is a time of assessment of how the last year went. You may find the lawyers you work with somewhat preoccupied with firm matters in January. Cut them some slack; the situation will get better next month.

FEBRUARY

Enjoy the first monthly printout of the year that shows you are well on your way to exceeding the firm's expectations in the billable hour department. These same printouts will be reviewed by every partner in the firm; they tell lawyers how big their paychecks are likely to be. Do not underestimate the effect your numbers have on how you are viewed by the firm's financially important players.

Check your caseload or workload not only for how it looks this month, but for how the year looks. Give your assignments your best efforts. Think of each one as a project designed to persuade the reviewing attorney to use you again for better and even more interesting work. As long as the firm is basically healthy, if you are good, and you perform, you will get more work.

If you do not have enough work, find out why. Read Chapter 7 for help on how to do that and how to correct problems that may have developed. Be sure you're aware of when your review will come up, and if possible find out who will be evaluating your performance. Remember, you want to develop the kind of working relationship with your evaluators that will not only allow but encourage them to tell you in advance of review time about any problems that may need to be addressed.

Coming in early one morning a week is still a good idea. Use the time to do the paperwork to get funds to pay for the courses you have signed up for, to take a look at your resume to be sure it includes everything you did last year, and to review your five-year plan.

February's a short month and usually includes at least one firm holiday. Use the time you have at the office effectively. Are there changes you can make in your office setup, your relationship with your secretary, or your computer that can increase your efficiency?

February's a nice month to remember the people in your firm whose contributions are often overlooked. Do you have a dynamite receptionist who always makes clients feel good when they call? Is your support staff willing to stay late to copy documents in a crunch? These office heroes deserve recognition. Buy a box of silly valentines and some candy hearts and make up little thank-you's. Don't forget the accounts payable people who keep your vendors happy.

MARCH

Where does the time go? The first quarter is nearly over and those who didn't jump into this year with two feet and with their eyes open are waking up. You, however, are well into the year's work plan and working on something that is a happy professional preoccupation. Maybe you're setting up a new corporation for a longtime client, or preparing a challenging construction defect lawsuit, or drafting estate planning documents for people who are finally getting around to deciding what to do with a collection of rare books. Make sure that you are pushing the envelope on the assignment, learning a little more than necessary, and checking every detail twice.

If you haven't already done so, March is the time to plan your vacation. This will give you and your family something to look forward to while you complete the first half of the year. It will also allow you time to give your team workers plenty of warning. Vacations are often canceled in law offices but they shouldn't be. Don't make the mistake of routinely giving away your recreation time; in the long run everyone suffers when that happens. Planning now will also help you to be realistic about what you need to accomplish before you go.

Though it may not seem important now, check your calendar for other obligations and for health needs. It's terrible to need a root canal the night before a trial begins or to find you are without working eyeglasses because a trip to the ophthalmologist just didn't seem critical. Taking care of routine maintenance— your car's, your file system's, your body's—is a key element in long-term success. If something can break down at an inconvenient time, it will. There will be enough real emergencies to take care of while keeping up your worklife this year. Don't add to the list by failing to do the routine.

March is a good month to investigate the local paralegal associations if you are not already active. The boost to your spirits and your career may surprise you. See if there's a committee you can serve on, a talk you can give, or a newsletter you can write for. Get involved. If you meet interesting people (and you will), arrange to have lunch with them. This is how you find out about the local legal community, going pay rates for paralegals in your skill bracket, and volunteer opportunities. All of these will make a difference in your future—you just can't tell when.

March is also a good month to add a new computer skill to your professional skills list, to add forms to your form notebooks, and to take a client to lunch.

APRIL

Spring fever can hit anyone, even grown-up, success-oriented paralegals. If it hits you, relax. You're in a position to take a day off. Choose a day and enjoy yourself. You're thinking of the long term. You're treating yourself the way outstanding professionals treat themselves. Don't become one of the "I'm so busy I can't take a minute off" types. That leads directly to "I can't go to lunch" followed by "I have to work every weekend" followed by daily doses of headache medicine and personal life traumas of a sort you don't even want to contemplate.

When you get back to work go over your to-do list. Doesn't look so bad, does it? Now's the time to get together with some other paralegals in your office. Find out what's going on. Can you trade information about recent case law or new computer technology or continuing education courses? Be sure that you're aware of what's offered in-house too. If there is no in-house program, think about setting one up. Every law office is filled with expertise that is largely unarticulated to the other players on the firm's team. Talk to someone with authority about establishing a class taught by one of your firm's own lawyers or paralegals. It's number one on the list of positive things you can do to foster firm camaraderie while increasing everyone's expertise.

Spend some time evaluating the quality of your work product. Are you up to your highest standards? Stop by after work one day to ask if the attorneys you're working for agree with your analysis. Look ahead to the next quarter. Have you set up a situation that will insure your workload is adequate while allowing you to take a vacation?

As always, be sure you're meeting your quota of hours. If you need to schedule a late evening or a Saturday to catch up, do it now. You'll be more than glad you did in November. Get to the bookstore to continue your library building and read what you buy. Look for opportunities to talk about the information with paralegals and lawyers who may be interested in it. Check the Internet for the latest developments in your area of law.

In addition to your worklife, think about volunteer work this month. Maybe it will be related to your legal experience, such as working at the local legal aid clinic. However, you may find other opportunities that will make a difference in your community while refreshing your spirits and keeping you connected to the world outside the law offices. Maybe you like to tutor children or coach soccer or serve meals on wheels to senior citizens. Whatever speaks to you, follow the impulse and sign up. It's a wonderful way to help out and you will be surprised how much it does for you too. Outstanding professionals in law offices are usually outstanding people all around.

MAY

Moving into the fifth month of the fiscal year should be an event. If you plan to take a vacation sometime during the summer and spend the winter holidays with your friends and family, you are for all practical purposes halfway through your billing year. Consequently you will need to check your hours with an eye toward two or three weeks off over the course of the summer and a week or so over Thanksgiving and Christmas.

This is a great time to dive right into a big project. If you don't have one on your desk, go looking for it. Use the tactics outlined in Chapter 7 to help you approach attorneys you would like to work with. When you get the big assignment be sure to let the attorney know about any vacation plans you have so you can work together to get the job done and still enjoy your trip.

Now's the time to check out seminars and course work that will occur in the fall. Submit your request for seminar attendance now. Your superiors will be more likely to approve and finance these educational ventures now than in the fall, when a great deal of the money allocated for ongoing education has already been spent. A key to financing projects within a law firm is figuring out when the money is available. If your firm, like many, ends its fiscal year in December, you want to submit all your requests by September. After that the focus is more on meeting budget projections and December will be primarily geared toward collection efforts and closing out the books.

May is also a good month to find out which committees do what at your firm. Is there an attorney you've gotten to know whom you can talk to? How about a more senior paralegal, or for that matter a longtime, savvy secretary? Very few law firms publicize to their paralegal staffs how these committees work, but you need to find out in order to manage your career in the most advantageous way. It may save you the embarrassment of going to the wrong folks at the wrong time. Try to become informed about the powers that control many facets of your professional life.

JUNE

For at least half the firm June is one month or at most two before vacation time. Check in with coworkers to be sure you won't all be gone at the same. If an attorney you have been building a close working relationship with is set for vacation and you will be in the office, be sure to volunteer to cover any cases or follow up on any matters while he or she's gone. This will allow you to educate yourself about the case while you demonstrate your willingness to help.

It's also time to check your own half-year goals. Are your hours on track? Has your skill level actually improved from January? Have you completed some continuing education classes? Do you need to revamp your working space, your calendaring system, or your working relationship with your secretary?

Check your mental attitude. Are you proactive, thinking about how to manage your involvement in the firm's activities, or do you find yourself spending time thinking about what you have decided is wrong with the firm, your attorneys, the support staff, and the world in general? If you are slipping into the negativity pool, don't be too hard on yourself. This can happen when you've been working too hard, not doing fun things outside the office, working through lunch on a regular basis (don't do that!) and taking on more work than makes sense. You may need a three-day weekend or you may need help with a particularly burdensome project. Maybe you need the firm to treat you to a skill-building seminar. If you find that you are unable to come to work with a positive attitude, take a little time to figure out what's up and try to invent a potential solution. Usually these slumps are easier to get out of than you think.

If you haven't spent some time surfing the Net for paralegal news, the latest in on-line educational courses, and announcements of regional meetings of paralegal organizations, do it now. There's an enormous number of offerings. One of the potential dangers of a busy worklife is a sense of isolation and estrangement from what's going on in the greater professional community. A chance to schmooze with active paralegals is a great spirit booster, and it's also critical to keeping your own career moving forward.

JULY

Hang out the "Gone fishin'" sign. No kidding. Make sure you take a vacation sometime during the year. If you don't, your attitude will suffer, your work will suffer, and your loved ones will suffer. That's just common sense, but among both lawyers and paralegals failing to leave the office all year is common.

The number one reason people say they don't take a vacation is that they have too much work. They have too much to do, they say, and often they are busy. But busy or not, everyone needs a break. Take your vacation.

One of the real reasons many paralegals don't take time off is that they're afraid that when they come back they will have lost their places. They're afraid they won't have enough work, or even a desk. This fear is an outcome of a work distribution system that is fairly personalized, meaning in most cases that if no one gives you assignments you won't have work.

If this fear crops up in the back of your mind, try to face it; it's not unusual. Be nice to yourself. Be kind. Experiencing this kind of fear is quite normal in the early years of a career. If you're new you may be afraid that you haven't had time to establish yourself and to develop long-term working relationships. That may even be true, but it doesn't mean that if you take a vacation you'll end in the gutter. When you get back you will still have your job.

Don't underestimate people's abilities to see you as you are, and fairly quickly. If you're good and have the potential to get better, the attorneys you work with are likely to spot it quickly. If you have the self-confidence and good sense to take a well-earned summer vacation, they will only be confirmed in their judgment of your potential.

When you get back from vacation, July is a good time to plan the rest of the year. Now's the time to decide whether you will finish your hours in time to take time off at Christmas too, or whether this is a year when you will work the week between Christmas and New Year's and cover for the many people who will be gone. No one's terrifically excited about working over the holidays, but unless the office closes for the whole week someone will have to. Covering for colleagues over the holidays is not a bad way to establish yourself as essential to a legal team. If you're new to the field, I recommend it.

Choose one of your projects this month and give it special attention. If there's law involved that you are unfamiliar with, take some time to hit the library and get some background. This may not be time you can bill for. It's time you are investing in yourself. You are developing expertise and exhibiting expertise is how you make your living.

AUGUST

This is a truly slow month in most law offices. Many people are off on vacations and even clients are often unavailable. Many of the staff at the courthouse are on vacation, so everything takes a little longer. You may find your assignments are down. If that's so, take advantage of the opportunity to roam the halls a bit talking to people. Strengthen some professional and friendly connections. If you know that someone's usual legal assistant is on vacation, let that person know you would be happy to lend a hand with anything needing paralegal attention. This will give you experience in new areas of law, and may well lead to new working relationships.

If you did not sign up for continuing education classes in May, take a look at the fall semester's classes at local colleges. If there's something offered that will increase your value to the firm, take it. You may find the firm will pay the tuition. See Chapter 11 for tips on how to ask for the money.

You may have noticed that almost every month I suggest you check your hours to see if you are on track. That's because that's how people meet their quotas and make their hours. You can't "hope for the best" or "wait and see." That way lies mediocrity. If you want a career that really takes off, failing to make the billable requirement is more than a serious problem. It's deadly. Every paralegal who makes the required hours does not become a superstar, but all superstars make or exceed their billable hours requirements. Be sure to factor in the holidays; most firms take two days for Thanksgiving and three or more over the Christmas and New Year's holidays. That's five times eight, or forty hours you won't be billing if you take all that time off too. Plan to use September and especially October to get ahead. Think now about what projects you want on your desk for those two months!

Check your bookshelf to be sure those additions are being read. If you find you are not getting to the reading, spend one lunch hour a week this month catching up. Take one book home to read before bed. Stay with it. Keep checking the Internet for late-breaking news in your area of law. Print out what you find and give copies to attorneys and other paralegals who work in this area. If it's really new, draft a synopsis and publish it in the local bar newsletter. Yes, I said bar newsletter. Look through your old *Legal Assistant Today* magazines for "how-to's" that relate to your job. If you find a way to streamline a process or organize information, communicate that information to your team, don't just think about it. Write it up in a short memo and share it with the folks who would benefit, then volunteer to implement it. Don't forget to follow through.

Finally, August is also a good month for taking care of personal things that will be hard to get to in busier times. If you haven't done so, go to the dentist, have your physical exam, or get your car serviced. Come September, you'll be glad you did.

SEPTEMBER

We've all been out of school for awhile but there's still something about September that makes us sit up straight and sharpen our pencils. Vacations are usually over. Regular schedules kick in. It's a wonderful chance to work hard, complete assignments, and get good hours on the books. You'll find the lawyers you work with in a similar frame of mind. If you have a case that needs interrogatories drafted, or if you have clients who have been meaning to draft wills, or if you represent a public entity that's interested in getting a new law on the books, this will be the month the assignments roll in. Don't panic. It'll be fun.

Try to say yes to most of the requests you get. I don't mean you should make promises you can't keep, but you may want to schedule a few long days to get to the extra work. Attorneys always notice when you say no. Sometimes you have to do it, but it's still not a favored response, because for most of us success is tied to attorneys seeking us out to do their work. They find no's discouraging.

September's a good time to cultivate professional alliances and friendships outside the office too. Take time to have lunch with your favorite client or a paralegal or lawyer from another office. Get involved in a community project. Perhaps you can volunteer to speak at "career day" at the local high school or assist with an informational meeting put on by your paralegal education program. Think of a freebie you can provide for your firm. Perhaps your department has a stack of research memos that could be organized and indexed. If you distribute the index and save even one attorney an hour's work "reinventing the wheel," your efforts will not be overlooked.

As always, stay on top of your year's goals and your own legal development. Don't neglect your resume, which you should review and update. Take a look at your five-year-plan. You're almost one-fifth of the way there. Are you satisfied with your progress? Look over your quarterly numbers when they are published. You can be sure all the lawyers will.

OCTOBER

In some offices October feels like the last leg of a race. You can find billing printouts at the copy machines of associates who are hoping they can bill 2000 hours and get a bonus. Litigators are thinking of how they can wind up cases before the holidays, and if you ever have to prepare a case that's set for trial on December 27th you will sympathize with their efforts.

Clients whose fiscal year ends on December 31 are beginning to think of budgeting for next year's legal expenses. Although there are still three months left, it starts to feel as if the year's over, or will be over, before you can get done all the things you meant to do this year.

Hopefully you are well into your continuing education class—and liking it. Don't forget to keep your attorneys informed about your course work. Of course you'd be pleased just to get the education, but it doesn't hurt to let your boss know you are willing to devote some nonbillable hours to your joint futures.

Check with NALA, NFPE, and AAfPE for their conference schedules for the next year. In addition to the national conferences, they all have regional meetings and there may be one quite near you. You don't want to ask for financing now, but it's the right month to think about what money you want to ask for next year. You will want to have conference topics and workshop titles available when you ask for support, so get the information. These meetings are not only wonderful educational experiences, they are truly inspirational and fun. They are attended by the best people in the business and you will find that contact with these folks will boost your energy level and raise your personal expectations. Don't pass them up.

Check with your doctor to see if a flu shot or vitamins or anything else is recommended to get through the winter. Stock up on sore throat lozenges. October usually has more working days than any other month of the year, so use it well. The holidays are just around the corner and this may well be your last chance to have a banner month.

NOVEMBER

November's the evaporating month. It looks like a month but it's really only three weeks. The Thanksgiving holiday entails Thursday and Friday. Many people take Wednesday off to cook or travel. Many take Monday and Tuesday as vacation days, and those who don't often have their minds more on the holiday than on the business at hand. Even if you're at your desk you may not have secretarial or copying support and contractors like messenger services may be less reliable. That means you need to make the first two weeks of November really count. What have you left undone?

Many firms review all their paralegals annually in December. What you do now will be freshest in your boss' mind when the evaluation form hits the desk. Go through your For My Review file and pick out the best stuff. You may want to make extra copies for those who will be evaluating you. The cover memo shouldn't be pompous or overbearing, but something like, "I know evaluations are coming up. Here are some things from the past year that may be of help." You know what you are doing and the attorney knows what you are doing, but it's all being done within socially and professionally accepted parameters.

This time of year also means awards ceremonies. Many local paralegal associations sponsor Paralegal of the Year awards. Volunteer to help with the event. I can say from experience that these dinners are among the nicest professional events you will ever attend and they are worth your time and attention. Paralegals often complain that the legal profession does not give them their due, does not honor their contributions adequately. Maybe so, but until we honor our own we are in no position to seek lawyers' praise. Take time to acknowledge the work of your fellows.

By November I am usually adding up my hours every few days to be sure nothing has slipped. I have seen paralegals miss making a quota by ten hours. That's a shame. Don't let it happen to you. If you are well ahead of your quota (I hope you are!) check yourself against your own goal. But remember that logging the most hours is not always the best choice. Think about your personal obligations and the opportunities you have to enjoy people and events now that will not come again. Hard as it may be to believe, someday you will look back wistfully at your child's first orchestra concert or holiday play. Keep your life balanced.

Congratulate yourself on this year's successes. December comes next and it's a doozy; in fact it gets amplified treatment. Read on.

DECEMBER

You may be wondering why there's an expanded section for *December*. Fair question, and here's the answer: December's the end of the fiscal and hence the billing year for many law firms. It's also the end of the fiscal year for many clients, and of course it's the end of your billing year. Add to that the fact that it's a major holiday month for many people and a time of general festivity for many more, the middle of the flu season, and the month when kids are on vacation from school, and you can see why December's special. December may be festive but it can also be hectic. Some advance planning and advance action can save your professional and personal life.

Billing

Most firms have minimum billing standards for paralegals. You want to exceed the minimum. If your firm's smart it will have a bonus program to encourage you, but in any case you need to plan ahead to meet your goal. You do not want to be shopping for the holidays, fighting the sniffles, arranging extra day care for your children, and trying to make up hours in December.

Chapter 8 covers how to figure out how many hours you need to bill on a monthly and quarterly basis in order to make your annual hours. It's not as simple as dividing the total number of hours you need to bill by twelve, so if you haven't read that chapter, check it out. You have to consider vacations, illnesses, slow work periods, your family's activities, and your boss' temperament. Think ahead.

If you think ahead you will arrange things so that you are in very good shape by December. Not pretty good—*very* good. Any way you slice it, December is more than a full month. There are office parties, clients' office parties, bar association and paralegal holiday festivities, awards dinners, school concerts, your significant other's holiday office events, family gatherings, and all that shopping. A good goal is to try to go into December only 120 hours short of your annual goal.

This assumes that you actually have a goal—you haven't just waltzed along all year waiting to see how it all comes out. You've had a plan and kept very good track of your hours every month since January. You've also paid some dues to be in this enviable position on December first. You've worked some Saturdays and quite a few long days, and you've sought work as soon as you entered anything vaguely resembling a slow period. You've developed the kind of working relationships with the attorneys you assist that make enjoyable Decembers possible, even in a law office. So, congratulations. When everyone else is wearing a long face, missing the holiday fun, you will be putting on your coat and heading out in time to see your child in the *Nutcracker*.

Holiday Cards

If the firm sends out holiday cards personalized with attorney signatures, you should review the list to see if there are any that it would be appropriate for you to sign. If you find any, you'll need to approach the attorney who handles the account and discuss it. It's fairly common today for paralegals to serve as firm–client liaisons for larger clients. If you have such a role it's a very good idea to sign the card. This lets the clients know you think of them as an important professional responsibility and that you feel personally cordial also. It lets your boss know that you think like a professional who is taking responsibility for maintaining important client–firm relationships, and it lets your own psyche know you think of yourself as a grown-up professional.

You may want to buy some holiday cards to send to special clients on your own, and to attorneys and paralegals you've met in the legal community. It's your call here, but it can be a thoughtful thing to do if there's a real basis for the note. You should not routinely send out cards to everyone you've met over the course of the year, each one signed but with no personal message. It's incredibly clear to those of us who receive these cards that we are simply names on a list that is kept up by a computer or secretary and that the person who wrote the hastily scribbled name at the card's bottom has absolutely no idea who we are...and may not even be the signer. You will receive these cards yourself someday, and you will notice as you get the same meaningless note year after year that you will feel less and less like doing business with the senders ever again.

Never send a holiday card to a judge, a clerk of a court, or anyone else who has power and jurisdiction over matters you handle. It's not your business to be developing personal relationships with these people. It's unfortunate at times that you can't pursue friendships with people you admire and guess you'd like, but that's part of the discipline of professional behavior in the legal field.

Gifts for Staff and Coworkers

There is still a tradition of holiday gift giving in the legal world and it's a nice tradition. Most attorneys buy gifts for their secretaries and many do the same for their paralegals. Some host luncheons or afternoon holiday parties and of course many firms have an evening holiday party as well. Many secretaries give gifts to their bosses, attorneys and paralegals alike, and many clients send gifts to the firm. Offices with good cooks often have wonderful, fattening potluck meals with cookies for all. With all this generosity going on, are there still unspoken rules to follow and pitfalls to avoid? You bet.

If you are lucky enough to have a secretary, remember him or her. You don't have to buy a big expensive gift, just something to show he or she's on the list of people you like to remember. If you cook, you can make a delicious personal gift. Being able to think of something a coworker will really like is a test of your relationship skills. If you don't know them well enough to shop for them, you haven't been paying enough attention to the small talk that should go on between you on a regular basis.

There are many people in mid-size to large law firms who regularly help you out. These are generally called support staff and I hope you know each one by name. There's the person who sets up conference rooms with coffee and sodas and generally performs those housekeeping duties we tend to take for granted. There are people who make copies of documents you need **now** and people who route things from one desk to another and people who do accounting and help you keep track of your valuable hours and people who help the firm collect its fees (and consequently help you stay employed). Then there's the person who can tell you the name of the dental insurance representative, the person who can check on whether your outside vendor has been paid, and the librarian who finds, copies, and faxes statutes to you when you're out of the office. There are even outside vendors who regularly help you move a case along or deliver a contract safely or check a lien on a property. Should you be giving gifts to all these people too?

Well, you have to pick and choose some but a small holiday surprise, something that says "I remember you and all you do for me," is still appropriate and doesn't have to cost a fortune. Never give your support staff such extravagant gifts that they feel they must reciprocate in a way that's a burden for them. You can wrap a few holiday cookies in colored paper tied with curly ribbon and, voila, a holiday gift anyone would enjoy when the four o'clock slump hits. This year my husband and I collected bottles of hot chili sauce on various trips, each with lively wrapping and livelier names. When December rolled around I added a little ribbon and cellophane and had a dozen happy holiday gifts to share with the people in the office who make my office days brighter. These little gifts brightened up all of our Decembers—it's as much fun to give them as it is to find them on your desk!

Gifts for Clients

On this topic you really have to use your head. Generally speaking, paralegals are not expected to give gifts to clients. If gifts are appropriate, usually the firm is the giver. However, if you stay in the business a decade and work with certain clients for years you may find that a holiday remembrance becomes appropriate. A plate of cookies or a loaf of holiday bread is perfect. It communicates the fact that you find working with this client to be a source of satisfaction from a professional and personal perspective.

If you intend to give a client a gift, it's wise to discuss it briefly with the attorney in charge of the client's account. If the attorney is uncomfortable with what you have in mind, you must give way immediately. No arguments.

Some attorneys like to send a firm gift to clients and personalize it with a card. Often both the attorney and the client expect the paralegal to sign such a card. They both know that you are a critical part of the team serving the client's interests. This is a cordial and effective way to cement your relationship with the client and with your legal team. If you know a gift is going out, you may want to ask if you can sign the card. Many times attorneys welcome the idea, but have just been too busy to think of it themselves.

The Holiday Party

There's a wide variety in law office holiday celebrations these days. A tighter economy for law firms, fears of lawsuits alleging sexual harassment, and problems related to supplying employees with liquor have put the damper on some firms' holiday cheer, but others continue a fairly extravagant tradition. Whatever your firm does, you should keep a few things in mind:

1. When you're new to a firm you need to exercise real caution at social gatherings of any kind. You don't know the history, the politics, the customs, or the people involved well enough to "just be yourself." In fact, just being yourself is for the chronically naive. Anytime you are with the people who employ you, be aware that the interactions at the event could have some effect on your working situation.

In order to get the right mind-set for a holiday party that comes early in your career, think of how you would prepare for a social event with your new significant other's family. You probably would not plan to just kick back, have a few drinks, and shoot the breeze. You'd be more inclined to an alert watchfulness—trying to learn acceptable and verboten behavior.

2. A social event with the firm is often an audition for client contact. If you're able to meet new people, make pleasant and interesting conversation while balancing a plate of hors d'oeuvres, and help others feel listened to and at home, you will impress those who control client contact opportunities as someone who can be trusted to represent the firm well at business or social occasions. This is a good thing for you and your career.

3. There are still some predatory types out there who look upon office parties as a recess from normal social restraints and who will behave badly, almost always under the effect of alcohol. It's your job as a grown-up in the business world to control yourself and often others at these events. You may think it's "the firm's job" to monitor behavior at firm parties, and you might even be able to make an argument for that if a bad situation turned into a lawsuit, but you don't want that. You want to stay sober, direct conversations in cordial and appropriate directions, and mingle with the right people and have an intellectually and financially rewarding relationship with your employers.

4. An often overlooked danger of office parties is the soul who "parties hardy" and ends up dancing on the table, telling you deep dark secrets, or throwing up. Believe it or not, this is not just a problem for the festive one. It can be a problem for you, even if you are nothing more than the innocent bystander. Sooner or later Monday will come and the individual you thought was embarrassing no one but himself will have to face you and a bunch of other onlookers at the office. It may be a less than comfortable situation for you all. More than one sloshed employee has declared in torrid whispers undying love for a married boss at a holiday party—and you can bet everyone regrets it by and by.

Some firms have options for holiday events, and you may want to opt for the "during business hours" event. Sometimes these are lively, delicious potlucks meals that give you a chance to assess the culinary talents of your coworkers and to make a tasty contribution of your own. Sometimes they are afternoon receptions with tree trimming, music, and food. Whatever the venue, these are opportunities to smile and get to know the people you spend so many of your waking hours with. Does Evelyn have children, run foot races, speak Italian? Can Michael tell you the name of the person who fixed his roof after the last windstorm? Did anyone go to the same college you attended, or does someone need to buy a used computer? The small talk that goes on at these events is valuable. It helps us know each other as real human beings. Use these occasions wisely, enjoy the people you get to know, and look forward to January, when the work ethic will kick in again and everyone will be focusing on billables once more.

Family Commitments

In the legal world, commitments to family can be hard to keep at any time, but in December, with student performances, church events, and family celebrations, it can seem absolutely impossible. Remember, this is the month when you will have professional social events, and when end-of-the-year awards are handed out, and when you will be meeting those final billing requirements. Still, for everyone's sake I urge you to keep your promises to your children and to make it to family events.

You can do this if you make a firm internal commitment ("I am going to Kimberly's piano recital on December 18th"), the appropriate arrangements at the office ("My daughter's piano recital is at 2:30 on the 18th and I will be gone from 1:30 on that day to attend"), and a firm external commitment ("Kimberly, you can count on me. I've already arranged to take the afternoon off on the 18th, and after your recital we're going out for root beer floats!"). You need to do all this as soon as you know about the recital. Then you need to remind the attorneys you work with that you will be out that afternoon. You need to remind them tactfully and graciously, but at least four times. I always tell my boss about these things face-to-face the first time, then send E-mail reminders as the day approaches or leave a note as the day gets closer.

What a lot of fuss, you may be thinking, about something as simple as taking the afternoon off for a child's recital. Listen, if someone tabulated the number of kids' events that are missed by their paralegal and attorney parents because there was a change in a trial date, a last-minute emergency filing, or some other work item, you would think it's worth talking about. You need to schedule these events with the tenacity and level of intention that you employ when you calendar a mandatory settlement conference. Even if you do, you may still be tempted to think that the crisis on the horizon is so important that you have to put your family on hold, but think again. Is there someone else who can handle it? If you had appendicitis, someone else would step in. Advance planning, a professional and firm attitude, and a willingness to make up time as needed will allow you to perform as a professional at the office without sacrificing your family obligations. Think ahead. Keep your bosses and coworkers informed and keep your promises.

Health Issues

December comes with its own special health hazards and these too can affect your career. Even though the weather's worse and your calendar's full, now's the time to keep running or lifting weights or going to yoga class or doing whatever you do to maintain your health. Eat right when you can because you will have many occasions when the goodies will be so good you won't be able to resist. It's not a bad time to keep vitamins and cold pills close at hand, and speaking of hands, now's the time to wash them often and buy an extra box of tissues. Health can have a great deal to do with professional achievement. If you have good health, treasure it. If your health needs attention, see your doctor and get help. Chronic health problems like migraines and arthritis can make working under the pressure of a legal practice grueling. Every year new options for pain management and for out-and-out cures are put into practice. See your doctor.

This may be the end of your first full year of work in a law office. I want you to know that no matter what else your career brings, you will never be a first-timer again. You're one of the team now, ready to lend a hand and show a new first-timer the ropes. It's not easy to begin working in the competitive world of the law, but you did it. Good for you.

16 Your Five-Year Plan and Other Career-Building Files

Your Personal Keys to Success

Success does not just happen to people. Success—in terms of money, professional prestige, a happy personal life, and interesting and rewarding work—is the end result of a process that, at least to some extent, we control. We don't control it all, but we do control a lot of it. Most importantly we always control the way we respond to what's happening in our careers, our personal lives, and our larger world.

To help you respond effectively to what happens to you, you need to develop your own career-building files. In this chapter you will find a set that I find indispensable. Over the course of your own career you will probably come up with some more of your own. When you do, please write an article to tell the rest of us about it.

The basic files that will help you advance your career were mentioned in Chapter 5 when we talked about setting up your office. These are: Five-Year Plan, Atta-Boy Letters, Resumes, Continuing Education, Articles, and Possible Jobs. These files will do more than you think to help you create, analyze, and act on opportunities to advance your career.

Five-Year Plan

The most surprising thing at work to most people is how quickly the years go by. They work diligently, they often complain quite bitterly about their jobs, but they still wake up five or ten years later with no real change in their professional situation. Before they know it, fifteen years have gone by and they feel it's too late to make a strong career move. They may even be right. You don't have to wind up like that.

A five-year plan is a flexible working plan for moving your career forward. The legal field changes so quickly that planning in five-year increments actually makes sense. In order to do this kind of planning it's important to set aside time when you can be alone and undisturbed, relaxed, and comfortable.

You must make time to do this. You should allow at least an hour.

Before you start the actual planning session, gather books and career materials, legal magazines, college catalogues, some good paper, and the pen you most like to use. You might want food and drink, and you may even want background music; that's up to you.

If you do not own any career books or magazines and that local college catalogues and legal periodicals don't seem to find their way to your desk, correct that problem. Postpone your planning session until you have visited a good bookstore and perused its shelves. You need to begin now to build your own career library. See the appendices to help get you started. Visit the local library, local college bookstore, and your own firm's library to get more material. The more material the better—you want to be able to think big and think new when you work on your five-year plan.

When you are set to actually plan, turn off the phone, make care arrangements for your kids, tell your significant other you will be busy for awhile, and sit down where you can relax. Take a couple of deep breaths. Stretch. Let your mind wander. Then think back to when you first considered becoming a paralegal.

How did you hear about the profession? Why were you interested? Write this information down. Please take the trouble to write it down. Planning is not easy for most people. You have to convince your own psyche to take this process seriously. Otherwise you will be robbed of your own best ideas. By writing down your thoughts you will engage another part of your mind in the planning process. Remember, this is one way you invest in yourself.

Think about where you are in your career right now. Make a list of things you like about your job and your professional position. If you are new to this kind of procedure, take a look at the sample Five-Year Plan worksheets at the end of this chapter. Be concrete and fairly detailed in what you have to say but do not name names. Spend some real time on this list. Imagine a day's events from morning to evening.

Don't miss things like the amiability of support staff (isn't it nice to meet a smile when you ask for help?) or the fact that you get to work on one project at a time (if you like that) or that your firm underwrites your education by paying for computer or legal courses. Things as small as a receptionist who always handles your calls in a professional manner or as intellectually important as a boss who wants your input on which exhibits best communicate your client's case are all factors in everyday job satisfaction.

Next make a list of things you do not like about your job or where you are in your professional career. Again, be specific but do not name names. The purpose here is not to record for all posterity that you hate the way Attorney Sorenson always interrupts or ignores you. However, it's useful to note that you don't like being left out of major case discussions and that you would like a situation in which you can contribute more ideas to a team that will consider them. Maybe you do not see a way to continually grow at your current firm. Do they have strict policies on paralegal use that will prevent you from developing skills you know you have and want to use?

Okay, now get out the magazines, the newspapers, and the career books and let yourself go. Read whatever catches your eye, whatever seems interesting. Read with a pencil in your hand and a notebook nearby. Write down anything that strikes you and mark relevant pages with self-stick tabs. At some point you will notice thoughts like these:

1. It must be glamorous to work in entertainment law.

2. I wonder how much you have to travel if you work for a corporation that sells franchises in different cities?

3. If I tried to learn a whole new area of law I'd have to take more night courses and really study while Brian's still in school. I'd never see him.

4. Labor law sounds interesting to me. The cases are so fact-intensive— there's a lot for a paralegal to do.

5. If I learned Social Security law I might be able to work on my own someday.

6. Geez, I just don't know enough about computers.

7. I really want to train for a marathon next year; that means I won't be able to work a lot of overtime.

8. I need to make a lot more money if I'm going to put the kids through college.

Get it? You are your own best source for information about you—what you like, need to do, etc. The planning process is based on your own insights (which, given all you really know about yourself and your personal commitments, are quite rich) and the way those insights interact with information from the outside world.

The next thing you must do is to take another clean sheet of paper and start doodling about what you might actually like to plan toward. Good career planning is not about being a super paralegal. Instead it integrates sound career goals with the rest of your life. For instance, if you are a potential marathon runner, your five-year plan will incorporate a sort of professional rest year while you do that. If you have a third grader who needs a lot of homework help this year, you won't schedule extra classes that take you away from home three evenings a week. However, if all your kids are on their own, you may jump at the chance to get a master's degree in a subject that interfaces with your paralegal job (e.g., if you have a degree in a science you may want to refresh your knowledge base to become a specialist in natural resource law).

A five-year plan requires thinking that stretches out for five years. This may be harder than it sounds. Most people do not think five years ahead, but it's worth the effort and can be among the most beneficial things you do for your career. Maybe you can't learn a new specialty all at once, but you could take one course a semester for three semesters. Maybe you want to work locally for the next two years, but then would be free to take a job requiring travel. Just because you can't do it all this year doesn't mean you can't do it all.

There are two more steps in your five-year planning. The first is to look at your goal or goals and make a list of what you are doing or plan to do to move toward your goal. You would be amazed how many people set five-year goals and make no real effort during the first four years of the plan to accomplish steps toward the goal. Suddenly it's year five and they are surprised to see how little progress has been made. Writing down what you intend to do each year for five years will allow you to plan realistically for sensible progress and to check up on yourself.

Finally, you must resolve to keep your goal sufficiently in mind that you will notice and collect information related to the direction you have chosen. This is a critical habit to form. It will keep you up to date on what's going on and stimulate your thinking. This way you can maintain the flexibility an ever-changing working market requires.

Keep this file close at hand and add to it as new information about our changing world comes your way. Review it at least every three months! Check your performance against your goals. Revamp it as needed. Use it.

Only some of the people who have just read these pages will ever follow up on five-year planning. Some will think it's too artificial or that they will feel too silly. Some will be too lazy and some will just forget to ever do it. Those who take the time and invest in themselves will find their sense of control over their own careers and futures so enhanced that they will eventually move on and leave the others grumbling at their desks. I first thought of writing this book five years ago. You have a critical date with your destiny; don't miss it.

Atta-Boy Letters

Atta-boy letters are letters of thanks, congratulations, or commendation that over time you will receive from bosses, clients, community leaders, and others. If you prefer "atta-girl" letters, that's fine. Whatever you call them, these affirmations are gold when it comes to building a strong career. They can be used to support your position in salary negotiations, to punch up your resume, to obtain new opportunities (to speak or write articles for instance), to impress your boss generally, and to boost your own spirits.

There's a species of atta-boy letter that is fairly perfunctory and not of much use, but many are quite sincere and express genuine thanks and admiration. If you have volunteered your time and expertise, worked long hours to research information critical to a client's case, or just put in a heck of a year, these commendations record and validate your efforts. They serve as reminders of past successes. People really do forget their own victories.

You will want to keep the originals of all your atta-boy letters in pristine condition in a clean file. You should also make several copies of each. This will prevent you from giving into temptation and attaching an original to a resume or application when you're in a hurry.

Use atta-boy letters actively to build your career. It's absolutely true that nothing succeeds like success. If you have had a successful speaking experience at a local high school career day, look for opportunities to speak again, for example at an informational meeting on the paralegal program at your local college. If that goes well, perhaps you can speak to attorneys at a meeting of the local bar association on how to better use paralegals in their practices.

Each of these speaking engagements will produce an atta-boy letter and will increase your speaking skills, your confidence, and your exposure in the legal community. That kind of exposure could lead to many new opportunities.

When you receive atta-boy letters, route copies to appropriate people in your firm. I always send copies to Personnel, asking that they be included in my official personnel file. This way they will be available to the powers that be when my evaluation comes around, and I won't have to wave them myself. Don't forget to let the lawyers you work for know when you get these commendations. It will all help in your career growth.

Don't forget to provide atta-boy letters to those who help you out. This can be something as simple as a memo to the personnel department on the terrific job done by a particularly helpful copy person or as fancy as an official thank-you (in your role as committee chair) to a speaker who provided information on the Year 2000 problem to your local paralegal association. Beyond the clout these letters provide in negotiations or other career maneuvers, when they are sincere and well thought out they go a long way toward building significant professional relationships in the legal work world. It's a fast-paced, busy, busy world we work in. Atta-boy letters can slow it down to human speed once in a while.

Resumes

Read Chapter 3 for information to help you think through and devise a resume format that will work for you. Your personal Resume file should contain an original and six copies of each format of resume you have generated. In addition it should contain a floppy disk with each format ready for revision. When will you use these?

1. When someone you never expected to hear from calls with a terrific job offer but needs your resume by fax within the next 20 minutes;

2. When you see an ad for a position that suits you to a T and is only eight blocks from your house;

3. When the attorney you work with says she wants to include your resume in a proposal for services the firm is putting together;

4. When you apply to teach a seminar at a nearby university;

5. When your local paralegal association holds elections and wants you to run for the board;

6. When you pitch an article to a legal publication and they want to know something about you;

7. When a nice, "newer than you" person calls to see if you will help with his resume.

It's difficult to remember to update your resume, but you should try to keep it current. You can bet good money that the best opportunity of your career will come around on a day that is so busy you won't have time to sneeze, let alone update your resume. Being ready to take advantage of opportunities is a big secret of success! Stay current and stay ready.

Continuing Education

Continuing education is critical to career success. In today's continually evolving legal environment you must be continually educating yourself. This subject is discussed more fully in Chapter 13. Your Continuing Education file will contain three important sections: 1) catalogues, flyers, and other information about classes upcoming; 2) course material from in-house or similar seminars; 3) documentation of your continuing education by way of certificates of attendance such as those usually provided by CLE providers, or grades or transcripts.

You will use the knowledge gained in continuing education courses to increase your participation in the legal matters you handle, as well as your participation on your legal team. You will use the fact that you are involved in continuing education as a career-building tool. For example, every certificate you receive should be copied and forwarded to whomever maintains your personnel file, as well as to attorneys you work with. If you have been looking for an entree to a new team or a new legal field, send a copy of your course documentation with a short note to the attorneys in your firm who do that kind of work. Let them know you are available to assist them in future matters.

Remember, putting off continuing education equals putting off your career. How would you view someone in the medical field who did not keep up on the latest developments or someone in the computer field who simply said he's learned enough? Do not expect your employers—current or prospective—to have more faith in you or more respect for your professionalism than you would have for a paramedic who decided to rest on her laurels.

As you acquire real expertise, try to become involved in continuing education as a teacher. Volunteer. The old saying—that if you want to really learn something you should teach it—is true.

When you teach, be sure that you do a splendid job. Prepare, prepare, prepare. Be sure to document these experiences too, and let the appropriate people know about your foray into this new area. Being established as a teacher in a law-related area will do a great deal to enhance your stature within your firm and the legal community.

Articles

Of course, right behind teaching comes writing. The legal world is a world of words. We depend on articles in legal publications to keep us up to date and informed. As you develop a specialty and stay informed yourself, you may well come across opportunities to write for legal professionals.

Be creative when looking for these opportunities. You may work in an area of law that's being revamped as we speak. Let's face it, you're going to have to learn it all anyway; why not write it up for others too? Your paralegal association newsletter may have a column that invites guest writers. When you have had some success in your local venues, consider publications for national associations.

Publishing is a surefire way to boost your confidence and create something that will provide further career opportunities. Keep copies, send copies, and enjoy the thrill of seeing your words in print.

Possible Jobs

After all the work you put into your five-year plan, this file may seem a bit redundant—but it's not. Don't neglect it. This file is a collection point for all the information that will come your way over the course of your career about other things you can do. Some of the jobs will be special kinds of paralegal positions, but not all of them will fall so soundly into the paralegal or even the legal arena.

This is a fun and important file because it encourages you to think creatively about yourself and your future. Maybe you work with a terrific jury service vendor who has a graphic arts person who does wonderful trial exhibits. You always liked graphic arts and now you can see how you could combine your legal, computer, and artistic skills in a new profession. It may not happen now, this year, or ever, but you are free to consider the possibility and you should. A brochure from this firm goes into your file.

Perhaps your firm represents a large corporation that has a separate job description for someone who manages corporate generosity and reviews requests for contributions and grants. Maybe you'd like to give away corporate money to do good works. A word about this job goes in the file.

Maybe you read an article about in-house counsel for a major sports team or a research institute, or maybe you'll want to work in a paralegal education program someday. Articles and program brochures all go into this file.

Someday when your children leave home or you finish your undergraduate degree or you just get itchy, you will find yourself getting out this file. Ideas you saved from the great abyss of lost opportunities will be there for you to peruse and maybe to act on. Use this file.

Be sure to find a convenient place to house your personal files. A desk file drawer is perfect but even a cardboard accordion file will work. These files form the core of your future professional plans. Ten years from now you will not believe you ever lived without them.

FIVE-YEAR PLAN WORKSHEETS

My paralegal history:

I first heard about this profession:

Things I really like about it:

Things I really hate about it:

Continued Five-Year Plan Work

Things I could possibly sometime do:

Things I'd like to try but don't see how I can do:

Schools/classes/opportunities/volunteer work?

Goals I *might* set:

Goals I *have* set:

Plan to get there:

Year One

Year Two

Year Three

Year Four

Year Five

17

The Evolution of Paralegal Careers Inside the Firm

This article was originally published in *Legal Assistant Today* magazine under the title "Paralegals make 'Partner'" (May/June 1996, vol. 13, no. 5).

Here's the scenario: You've just finished a complex bit of research and analysis which, it turns out, saves the day for your client. The attorney you are working with turns to you with a surprised and relieved grin and says, "This is great—this is just what I needed. You're good. You should go to law school."

From that attorney's perspective you have just been paid the ultimate compliment. This is the old "paralegals are wannabe lawyers" mentality. There's no explaining that you didn't miss going to law school through some small lapse in attention. You *chose* to be a paralegal, you *want* to be a paralegal, and you hope that the field will continue to develop in a way that will use and reward your growing expertise.

Good news! There have been recent sightings of innovative law firms responding to the changing legal and business environment by raising the level of their paralegals' work responsibilities and paying them a fair salary for handling the increased load. Some have even adopted formal career tracks for paralegals, tracks that are not so very different from those they offer associates. Common workplace benefits include secretarial support, office space, computers, and support for continuing education. Senior positions often include health club memberships, *Martindale-Hubbell* listings, access to the firm's bonus pool, and associate-level compensation packages. These beefed-up paralegal programs reflect a new level of respect for the contributions of experienced paralegals.

Legal Assistant Today (*LAT*) spoke with five firms that are working with paralegals in new ways. The firms differ in size (from three people to several hundred), structure, history, philosophies, and specialties, but they all have this in common: They know that better use of paralegals is one of the keys to their future success.

Cooley, Godward, Castro, Huddlestom & Tatum, a San Francisco—based firm with offices as far-flung as Boulder, CO and San Diego, CA, is a front-runner in paralegal use and management. Their aggressive paralegal program is headed by Susan Chen-Wong, who came to the firm from the paralegal placement field and had been exposed to a wide range of attitudes regarding paralegals. Her interview with Cooley Godward convinced her she'd found a firm that not only appreciated the benefits of retaining good people, but was willing to fund a program that would do it.

At Cooley Godward, paralegals actually have a career track that officially begins at paralegal, graduates to senior paralegal, and finally peaks at a specialist position. In addition the firm hires document clerks to assist paralegals and attorneys. Chen-Wong says the document clerk position is open to those who do not meet the bachelor's and certificate requirement for entry into the paralegal track. Those hired as document clerks cannot expect any kind of automatic promotion to paralegal, says Chen-Wong, but those who meet paralegal standards can progress to senior paralegal and finally to the specialist position.

Perks for those on track are many. Beyond having an office and secretarial support, which Chen-Wong proudly notes is the norm for paralegals at her firm, senior and specialist paralegals have window offices and a chance to share in their own special bonus pool, and are included in the firm's *Martindale-Hubbell* listing. Even more impressive is that fact that specialist salaries at Cooley Godward are in line with those of third-year associates, putting them in the mid-$80,000 range. This is a firm that rewards expertise.

Chen-Wong stresses that the specialist title is earned only by the very best. The firm employs ninety paralegals, but only five are specialists. Each specialist has a minimum of twelve years' experience and in-depth knowledge of a specialty area. Specialist's duties include serving as a resource for other Cooley Godward professionals, teaching in-house seminars, mentoring other paralegals, and answering client questions. The firm values these non-billable contributions enough to include them as hours that go toward meeting a 1950-hour billable requirement.

Cooley Godward's program has the potential to provide a several-decade career of professional growth for paralegals who climb the ladder. It's designed to meet the needs of the firm for continuity and expertise while meeting the needs of the paralegals for continuing development and compensation that realistically reflects their contributions.

Another firm that has taken the role of its paralegals seriously—and backed it up with substantial pay and low attorney to paralegal ratios—is Ziffren, Brittenham, Branca and Fischer in Los Angeles. The entertainment specialist decided some time ago to staff its firm with mostly partners and paralegals; they hire few associates. Tara Flynn, an administrator at Ziffren, says the sixteen-partner firm currently employs seven paralegals and two associates. The most senior paralegals earn six-figure salaries and bonuses as large as $20,000 for handling highly sophisticated work.

Although Ziffren's use of paralegals is still unusual, the associate to paralegal ratio is something that many firms are adjusting. Venture Law Group (VLG), another leader in advanced career tracking for paralegals, reports that 1996 is the "year of the paralegal" at its firm. They anticipate hiring a substantial number of paralegals this year to lower the current ratio of one paralegal for every three attorneys, a ratio they find too high.

Formed in 1993, VLG is located in California's Silicon Valley, home to the computer chip industry. From its inception, this firm intended to try nonconventional staffing and employee utilization to meet the needs of its clients—sophisticated consumers who want to watch their legal costs and who know that a well-trained, experienced paralegal is likely to turn out a quality piece of work more quickly than an associate fresh out of law school.

Debbie Wilkins, VLG's first senior paralegal, takes a leading role in paralegal recruitment. The attorneys at VLG, prior to coming to the firm, had the usual range of experience with paralegals at their former firms—from excellent to definitely not-so-good, she says. To encourage the attorneys to rely appropriately on the paralegals they hired, VLG wanted to get the *best* paralegals available on their team, and they wanted to keep them. To do that they developed a paralegal program that offers the opportunity for high-level work responsibilities, a home computer to help shoulder those responsibilities, secretarial and paralegal-clerk support to maximize productivity, and open-ended compensation. The potential to approach six figures as a senior paralegal at VLG is real for those who meet the highest standards. The title senior paralegal is not bestowed casually. Currently only four of VLG's 15 paralegals are seniors.

Paralegal retention is a high priority at VLG, and a major component of the retention program is flexibility in job structuring. Every paralegal must be both good and profitable, but not every one is a "superstar." The firm recognizes that highly competent paralegals who want to work standard hours are still valuable to the practice and at Venture they are respected as contributing team players. Wilkins credits this innovative approach with stopping the revolving-door syndrome faced by so many firms when paralegals job-shop every year or two to see what else is out there.

Additionally, the firm works hard to come up with incentives for paralegals. Wilkins reports that cash continues to be the most effective inducement: Paralegals at her firm haven't shown interest in perks like car phones or the other professional trappings of attorneys. What they want, she says, is to perform at a high level during the workday, be respected, and be paid accordingly.

The firm that takes the cake in paying paralegals according to performance is the Benefits Department, a Pittsburgh firm headed by attorney Hollis Hurd. Not only is this firm on the cutting edge in its practice, but it was founded on the concept that paralegals and lawyers could work together in an association that benefits both and exploits neither. Paralegals here are truly partners.

Practicing exclusively in the employment benefits area, the firm was formed, in part, as a response to competition lawyers faced from actuarial and consultant firms that entered the ERISA arena in the early 1980s. These consulting firms offered a full range of employee benefit services to clients, writing plans, advising on tax consequences, and obtaining favorable determination letters from the IRS. Their clients would often ask, "Shouldn't we have a lawyer?" so consulting firms hired lawyers to work in-house.

Hurd decided that the nonlawyer-lawyer combination being developed within consulting firms could work just as well, or better, in the law firm. After all, the legal field already had a job title for nonlawyers with special expertise—*paralegal*. Hurd knew a paralegal at Coopers Lybrand, Lori Recktenwald, who seemed a likely candidate for such a venture.

He ran the idea by Recktenwald at lunch one day and she was enthused. The two formed the Benefits Department in February 1991. Since then they've added another paralegal to their team and the three share responsibilities for marketing, running the business, serving clients, and dividing the profits.

Hurd's philosophy, which he admits is radical in the legal field, is that no one should be making money off other people's work—each should benefit according to the work he or she generates. There are no set salaries at the Benefits Department. Compensation is determined by a mathematical formula (based on billing rate and hours worked) that is applied each month to the dollars billed to clients. This format matches Hurd's compensation philosophy and provides flexibility for each of the participants. If someone needs to take time off to teach or spend time with family, he or she can do so. The result will be lower compensation during that time, but the choice remains with the individual.

Hurd says the key to this kind of teamwork is finding the right people for the job. Paralegals in this setting not only need to be skilled in their fields, they need to be personable, feel comfortable extending themselves to clients, and must relish being responsible for their own fate. In return, not only is the compensation philosophy years before its time, but Hurd ensures that everyone in the office is equipped to be totally independent and productive—from personal desktop computers and laptops to fax machines and printers.

The legal staff are so self-sufficient at the Benefits Department that they hire no secretaries. At the same time Hurd provides supervision. The firm has regularly scheduled meetings and Hurd also meets with each of the paralegals individually to review work and answer questions. Recktenwald credits Hurd with pulling her through her former fear of speaking in public. In addition to being a spirited marketer for the firm, she now gives seminars and consults with the IRS.

Robins, Kaplan, Miller & Ceresi, a Minneapolis-centered law firm that has offices in seven other cities, has had a formally adopted paralegal program with a component called Career Pathing and Retention for a number of years. In 1991, *LAT* reported on the success of Deborah Wahl, Robins' first and current paralegal manager, in dramatically reducing paralegal turnover. Wahl attributed that decrease to an enhanced work environment.

Making the workplace a more desirable place means not only updating salaries and benefits, but also developing job descriptions that allow individuals to grow at the firm. To jumpstart its program, Robins Kaplan provided each paralegal with a personal computer and offered in-house training on Westlaw, LEXIS, WordPerfect, and Lotus. But the most surprising innovation is the establishment of paralegal retreats that, says Wahl, the partnership saw as an investment, rather than as a costly luxury. At the 1991 retreat, paralegals from all of Robins' eight offices met in Minneapolis to hear about the firm's progress, participate in educational sessions, and share experiences. The increased communication and general lift in morale, says Wahl, helped make the paralegal corps a successful profit center for Robins Kaplan.

Today, the Career Pathing and Retention Program is thriving—and so are the paralegals. Robins Kaplan has increased the number of paralegals from 33 (1991) to 81 (early 1996) and maintains excellent profitability. Wahl's own areas of responsibility have been narrowed to allow her to focus on the needs and potential of the paralegal corps. She has created comprehensive paralegal job descriptions that accurately reflect both the complexity and the value of the tasks paralegals perform. These same job descriptions are used by Wahl as educational tools when working with attorneys and clients. Wahl frequently makes presentations to clients on how their legal matters will be efficiently and effectively staffed, and client response is great.

Another addition to the firm's program is the establishment of paralegal committees that encourage the development of leadership skills in the senior paralegals. One of the most exciting of these ventures is the paralegal-managed Internship Committee. Committee members contact local paralegal schools, interview and hire interns, staff projects appropriately, and manage the firm's intern work flow. An additional benefit of the program is that it allows the firm to assess potential job applicants for the future.

Robins Kaplan is serious about providing recognition for professional development and dedication to the firm. Senior titles are earned through a process established by the Professional Development Committee, focusing on continued career development through increasingly substantive responsibilities and recognition. There are sixteen seniors in the Minneapolis office and Wahl says the title means a lot. Attorneys and clients recognize the expertise of these paralegals, and the paralegals are expected to make a greater contribution to projects and undertake new responsibilities, like speaking to attorney groups and making client presentations.

For the future, Wahl sees the need to provide nonmonetary incentives to paralegals to avoid raising paralegal costs to associate levels. Even so, in 1996 Robins Kaplan is considering adding a bonus program to the benefits senior paralegals receive.

Retaining good paralegals is a plus for law firms on several fronts. Losing good employees adds significantly to the costs of running any business (incurring recruitment, interviewing, training, and orientation costs, as well as a substantial work flow interruption). But while reducing turnover is a benefit sought by most businesses, the retention of smart, experienced paralegals does more than simply reduce the cost of doing business—it helps firms to maintain income.

First, it's good basic economics. Today's business-savvy clients have had enough exposure to paralegals to know that much of their legal work can be accomplished by these effective assistants at reduced rates from those charged by attorneys at the same firm. Interested in keeping their legal costs down, these clients are no longer willing to pay for the training of associates and are no longer shy about questioning bills that include hours of research in an area in which a firm claims expertise. In many case it's better business for law firms to assign the work to an experienced paralegal.

Second, there's a greater chance for continuity. Associates tend to move on and develop their own clientele, but when a business client develops a successful working relationship with a highly trained, accessible paralegal, its principals can look forward to years of working with the same individual, whose background knowledge of their firm's needs is constantly growing.

Third, a major advantage for law firms that is rarely voiced aloud is that paralegals do not "grow up to be partners" (that is unless Hurd's way of doing business catches on!). Generally paralegals know from day one that full financial partnership is not likely to be part of their futures. Even so, many are willing to stay with a firm for the long haul, contributing substantially to its success, if the work is sufficiently interesting and the money is right.

Overall, the appropriate use of paralegals indicates to clients that their attorney is interested in helping them control costs and is even willing to change the way the way the work gets done in order to keep the client's business. When firms keep great paralegals on board, the paralegals help the firm keep clients.

This new way of looking at paralegals—as professionals who have undertaken long-term careers—is just what the doctor ordered for older, experienced paralegals who are frustrated by the level of work they are assigned and are at a dead end in the salary department.

It's not uncommon for paralegals to find themselves leaving one job for a not-too-different new job because, bored with their work, they need the refreshment of a new environment. If they feel unfairly compensated, they find they are no longer willing to bring to their assignments the commitment and intensity that produces exceptional work and brings professional satisfaction.

Valuable contributors need ongoing challenges and emphatic economic acknowledgment of their contributions to the firm's success. Today's competitive economy is encouraging law firms to meet those needs. Retaining competent, trained professionals will increase profits.

Here's a short quiz to see if you've been paying attention.

Career tracks for paralegals benefit:

a. law firms

b. paralegals

c. clients

d. all of the above

If you chose d, go to the head of the class. The paralegal profession is emerging from adolescence with a much clearer idea of what place it should occupy in the adult legal world. Lawyers too are seeing the benefits of new working arrangements and the firms highlighted here all recognize the need for change in the ways paralegals are utilized and compensated. They've undertaken varied, creative, and exciting experiments and are reaping big rewards. This is intelligent management. We wish them continued success and look forward to future developments.

Clearly, paralegal career tracking is beneficial to longtime experienced paralegals, to the lawyers who employ them, and to the clients they serve. Would you be surprised to learn these programs meet the needs of entry level paralegals at the same time?

Originally most paralegal students were age thirty and up. Many were changing careers and had years of life experience to draw on when they took on their first assignments. As paralegal education in the United States has flourished it has attracted younger students, some of whom enter junior college programs right out of high school.

These graduating paralegals are not only short on experience on the legal world, they often have little work experience, period. But with time they can become the "seniors" of tomorrow. Thus firms like Venture Law Group, Cooley Godward, and Robins Kaplan have not only added senior positions to their career ladders, they've also created paralegal clerk positions at the bottom. This provides a manageable entry point for new program graduates who may not otherwise have enough experience to land a job.

As paralegal clerks, newcomers have a chance to work for and with senior paralegals whose help and advice can give them a boost. The positions give them a chance to get their feet wet in the back room before they find themselves in the courtroom or the boardroom. They also are less likely to encounter the dreaded paralegal burnout (what we older paralegals experience when we pull out our hair and shriek, "No, no, please don't give me another deposition to summarize").

Think about it. Those who enter the profession at twenty five will have fifteen years of experience by the time they are forty. As more firms see what advanced paralegals can do, these younger paralegals can look forward to a career of increasingly interesting responsibilities, new challenges, and rewarding compensation.

Since that article was published, the opportunities for career paralegals have continued to increase but not in an easily recognizable pattern. Instead it's as if law offices are like mini-climates, organic and each growing its own species of paralegal–attorney relationship. This is an important concept for you to grasp as a career paralegal.

When the articles and career columns announce that the demand for corporate paralegals is high, or that firms are offering big hiring bonuses, or that you should fear a big downsizing event, take in what they report but make sure you look around yourself. Firms in the same area, even firms in the same building, offer different salaries, different kinds of work, different perks, and very different working relationships and opportunities for advancement to their paralegals.

If you have developed an excellent working relationship with good people, you have nothing to fear when downsizing hits the magazines and newspapers. Just as importantly, if you have not developed strong skills and a solid reputation for professional performance, all the hiring bonuses in the world will not do you a lot of good.

The legal field continues to change rapidly, but that does not mean that some things don't stay the same. It still takes common sense and good judgment to know if you have found a good spot in the world to sell your skills and services. It still takes experience and persistence to learn to work with others in a way that maximizes everyone's productivity and future good. You should never underestimate your own abilities or your value to a thriving legal practice. You can create opportunities for yourself even when the newspaper says nothing's cooking. Likewise, you should not abandon a good firm with potential for growth to go running after every hot new bit of career news as if the "expert" knows more about what you are living with every day than you do.

Most importantly, you need to decide what you need to have a career that satisfies you over the long haul. If you want the biggest paycheck and are willing to relocate and work long hours to get it, then direct your career accordingly. If you want more time and energy for an active personal life, you need to choose a career path that allows you weekends to go scuba diving or to play the flute or to watch your children's soccer games. There's a place out there where your style will fit. Read the expert's reports and assess what they have to say, but don't forget to think realistically and for yourself.

18 CROSSOVER HITS

This article first appeared in *Legal Assistant Today* magazine (Nov/Dec, 1995 vol. 13, no. 2).

It's 7:30 a.m. You're driving to work, one hand gripping the steering wheel, the other wrapped around a coffee to go, when you pass a corner crowded with fourteen-year-olds who probably will not make it to school that day. "I wish I could do something for kids like that," you think, but a busy day awaits. The impulse to put your considerable skills at organization and persuasion to work for the social good is drowned in the demands of deposition preparation, witness interviews, and case strategy meetings. Before you know it, it's 5:30 p.m. and you're driving past the same corner, no longer surprised to see some of the same kids glued to the sidewalk. They need help, but you're bushed and your own kids wait at home. You don't have the time or the energy—unless you're Gail Harper, Executive Director of Kids in Need of Dreams. Harper transformed her career as a litigation paralegal at the Atlanta law firm of Alston & Bird into a public service career heading up a truancy intervention program staffed by attorney and nonattorney volunteers. Harper's former employer, Alston & Bird, celebrated its centennial by making a $175,000 financial commitment to fund a comprehensive assistance package for truant kids and their families in and around Atlanta. A longtime volunteer, Harper had already helped develop a pro bono project for the Atlanta Legal Aid Society and the Atlanta Volunteers Lawyers Foundation. When Kids in Need of Dreams got off the ground, she was on hand and clearly qualified to direct its good work. She's headed up the program since 1993 and is working this year with a staff of two to further implement K.I.N.D.'s goals, which include cloning the project in other parts of the country. Harper is more than enthusiastic about her career change and the program's success.

All over the country, paralegals are leaving law offices to pursue new and exciting careers. The exodus is prompted less by dissatisfaction with their paralegal positions than by the excitement of the career opportunities that beckon. They are finding that the writing, researching, organizational, and client management skills they developed as legal assistants are highly valued by a wide variety of outside employers. Consider the case of Lisa Hjulberg.

Hjulberg works in an office right across the street from the law firm where she was a paralegal for thirteen years. Although the distance between the two offices is short, the atmosphere and career advancement possibilities are miles apart. Hjulberg, formerly a litigation paralegal in Riverside, California, developed a law firm niche as an eminent domain specialist. Trained by an expert eminent domain lawyer, she mastered the complicated property acquisition procedures required of public agencies by state law, and developed professional relationships with appraisers, title officers, and independent property acquisition agents. Hjulberg earned her paralegal certificate at the University of California at Riverside and returned to college last year to complete a bachelor's degree with plans to eventually hang out her own shingle as a consultant. However, before she finished her degree work, she received a phone call from a client. Did she know, he asked, that the City of Riverside was looking for a property acquisition agent? The caller had worked with Hjulberg for years and thought she was clearly qualified for the position. The City of Riverside agreed, choosing Hjulberg over the two hundred other applicants for the job. She knew her stuff and the professional skills she had developed at the law firm were just what the City needed.

Although the professional responsibilities of her new position were not new to Hjulberg, she was pleasantly surprised by the City's attractive compensation program and work atmosphere. Like many paralegals who have left traditional law firm employment behind, Hjulberg enjoys having her contributions evaluated without reference to whether or not she went to law school.

The switch to a non–law office career for paralegals has never been more possible or made more sense. Although the word *paralegal* puzzled many people ten years ago, today's paralegals are definitely visible and if folks don't know just what they do, they know paralegals are on the front line of the legal community's efforts to make legal services cost-effective. This critical piece of information makes paralegals instantly interesting to hiring divisions of corporate and governmental entities. Add to this the fact that many of these employers have worked with expert paralegals in their own attorney's offices and it is not hard to see why the business world is interested in former paralegals. Business folks know that professional expertise and efficiency, resulting in a cost-effective product or service, are critical to competing in today's economy.

Do You Have the Itch to Switch?

Are you interested in a career change, but find yourself humming, "The water is wide, I cannot get o'er"? In a survey of twenty former paralegals who have successfully forded the river separating the law office from the greater world of employers, three success strategies emerged.

- *Direct Skills Transfer:* If your law firm expertise is in corporate matters, employment law, benefits administration, or public entity representation, you already have skills that transfer directly to the kinds of entities your law firm currently serves. Beth Kramer works in corporate securities and finance for American General Corporation in Houston, Texas, performing many of the same functions in-house for AGC that corporate paralegals in law firms do for corporate clients. Kramer prepares SEC filings and debt and equity registration statements and assists with mergers, divestitures, and acquisitions. She cites a good salary and benefit package and the chance to have a life outside the office as advantages of working for a corporation.

  Other areas of expertise transfer directly to both corporate and governmental settings. The knowledge required to administrate employee benefits programs for business clients is an entry into thousands of human resource departments. Contract review and regulatory compliance assurance skills are needed in almost every agency in America. If you can draft an ordinance, review CEQA guidelines, research Fair Political Practice questions, summarize legislation, or draft agenda items to advise legislators, you are eligible for positions with cities, counties, and state and federal agencies.

- *Indirect Skills Transfer:* Litigation paralegals often feel their skills can't be marketed outside a law firm. Not so! The person who gathers background information, prepares analytical summaries, does research, and organizes the presentation of evidence to juries is very well-equipped to work for corporations, nonprofits, and government entities. Sherry Strimling, currently an account executive with Sutter Health, entered the risk management field from a law firm position in medical malpractice. Strimling works directly with health care recipients to resolve their concerns and assess potential exposure for Sutter. She uses the same case valuation skills she developed while directly involved in litigation to execute her risk management responsibilities at Sutter Health.

  To land corporate or government jobs, litigation paralegals need resumes that describe the abilities they have developed in preparing cases for trial in language the business community calls its own. Some translations are suggested here, but don't let them limit you. If you can prepare a trial budget, manage a computer document control system, prepare witnesses for trial, communicate with experts, design exhibits, insure that court deadlines are met, and generally keep your head in the uncertain world of the courtroom, your skills and professional presence are needed in hundreds of business or government offices. A case manager in a litigation setting is a project manager for a development company, a senior analyst in a government office, and an administrative assistant for a CEO who reports to a board of directors. Don't let language pigeonhole you.

Hot Tip: Say it so they can hear it! If you can assist an attorney with the presentation of a complicated lawsuit at trial, you have skills that are highly valued in corporate America. It's all how you say it.

Paralegalese	Corporatalk
Interview witnesses and factual investigation	Fact-gathering and background research; prepare report
Summarize depositions and expert reports	Analyze background materials for executive summary purposes
Prepare discovery and trial budgets, compare to exposure	Cost–benefit analysis
Discovery plans, generation and response	Project planning, management and follow-up
Prepare exhibits and trial notebooks	Report generation for board presentations, backup
Supervise support and consultants in trial preparation	Personnel management and project coordination

- *Giving Yourself an Edge:* Many paralegals have made successful switches to new careers by arming themselves with a little more special knowledge. Debbie Brazill, a public law paralegal interested in government employment, obtained a master's in urban planning while still employed at a law firm. When she applied for her first city planning position, her paralegal experience coupled with the master's degree put her ahead of many candidates who had significant planning experience.

Don't discount the impact of a bachelor's degree on your resume. The research and writing skills required to earn a journalism degree will impress any firm that needs market research. Science degrees provide an entry to the thousands of companies emerging in the science and technology field; art degrees will influence museums and art foundations who need help complying with state and federal requirements to maintain their financing. Educational degrees help candidates land jobs that include training responsibilities. Add a degree in library science to paralegal experience and you are a natural for running the local law library.

Where Are All the Jobs?

If you're considering the switch to a non–law firm setting, start by perusing the non–law office sections of the want ads. Don't even pass up the restaurant section; all those jobs aren't for waiters. Terms like administrative assistant, senior analyst, project manager, research analyst, and communications specialist should all catch your eye. Think creatively. California Pizza recently advertised for someone to help them locate sites for new franchises and review real estate contracts. A paralegal with a real estate background who likes travel would be perfect for the spot. A local foundation in Boulder, Colorado wants a communications specialist to help them inform high school students about the dangers of drug and alcohol use. If you care about this issue, can communicate persuasively, and like to spend time on campus, this might be for you.

Let your own interests direct your search. The Sierra Club has positions for conservation assistants who track legislation, train volunteers, lobby congressional aides, and write articles. The March of Dimes recently advertised for a Chapter Director to direct activities in Riverside and San Bernardino counties in Southern California. They needed someone to develop and maintain relationships with volunteers, the local business community, professional organizations, and government agencies. If you have experience marketing your firm and maintaining established client relationships, you're qualified. Lucas Films, the Association for Prevention of Cruelty to Animals, the Catholic Church, Greenpeace, and National Public Radio are only a few of the many entities that need project management, contract review, research and writing, and public relations help. If you are interested in them, they will be more inclined to be interested in you.

Listen to the people around you. What do they do? How did they get into the field and how could someone like you fit into their organization? Your work may bring you into contact with legal vendors that need people who understand lawyers to sell their products. Ask questions and make contacts. Westlaw and Information America, Lexis/Nexus, and countless other databases need salespeople and trainers to convince law firms to use their products. Insurance companies need adjustors who are trained to assess the value of a claim or to negotiate settlements. Title companies need escrow officers who can read and understand detailed material on property matters and shepherd anxious individuals through complex real estate transactions. Good journalism is based on research and writing skills you should have developed in the law office. How many legal publications can you name? Human resource departments need individuals to document compliance with required procedures, interview job candidates, and run training programs. Every day you are exposed to job leads. Your job is to notice them—and follow up.

Judy Quan maintains her position as Administrative Coordinator for the Alternate Dispute Resolution practice group with Gibson, Dunn and Crutcher's Houston office while she sits as an arbitrator on the National Panel for Consumer Arbitrators. Her life as an arbitrator began when her boss could not attend a seminar on arbitration. Since the fees had been paid, Quan was sent in his stead. She found the whole business fascinating and used contacts made at that seminar to get in touch with the organization's training program, eventually qualifying as an arbitrator herself. She extended this career move even further when she authored *Legal Assistant's Guide to Alternative Dispute Resolution*. Her achievements are impressive. They are also replicable.

Don't forget the consultants with whom you work. Do you like computer graphics and know a firm that prepares trial exhibits? Legal software companies, court reporting services, public relations firms, environmental agencies and consultants, personnel agencies, the banking industry, real estate firms, developers, property management firms, third-party claim administrators, and risk management consultant firms all need people with skills that are foundational in the paralegal world. If you have developed an expertise in dealing with these industries, exploit it.

Remember that positions in public agencies are not limited to city and state governments. Investigate state university and community college systems, public health departments, the Federal Drug Administration, the FBI, the Government Accounting Office, the National Endowment for the Arts, and of course, the court system. Open your phone book to the listings of community services in your area. You will be amazed at the number of potential employers that need well-organized communicators who can deal with details, regulations, and the public. You may want a career helping potential parents wend their way through the labyrinth of adoption rules and regulations, or helping frustrated consumers obtain relief. If you are interested in these agencies, take the initiative and call their personnel departments. They maintain phone lines and mailing lists that advertise openings, but don't stop there. See if someone in personnel will give you twenty minutes to come in and discuss your interest in the agency and your impressive list of skills. If they invite you in, take the time to prepare by researching their services and functions and customizing your resume.

Consider a visit to an employment specialist (your friendly neighborhood headhunter). These professionals are trained to evaluate your skills and abilities and match them up to as many employment opportunities as possible. They invented the phrase "transferable skills" and may be able to point you in directions that are new and exciting and that combine your professional skills with your other areas of interest. They will also help you incorporate into your job search some elements that you cannot always consider when applying for law office jobs. Do you need a job that lets you walk out the door at five o'clock, one that provides variety and freedom in planning your week, one that's within walking distance of your house, or one that gets you the highest possible salary while your children are in college? One of the attractions of working outside the law office is that you can factor these kinds of variables into the overall job equation.

Don't forget the old standby, networking. It's still a great job search tool, but you have to know what it really means. It is not enough to hand your business card to an interesting speaker or business contact. Be politely aggressive and set a lunch date to find out more about interesting fields and the people who work in them. Ask serious, well-thought-out questions about job requirements and opportunities. Let people know you are interested in making a switch to a new career and that you'd appreciate any pointers they can give you.

Finally, be ready for the serendipity of the job search. Debra Hammond left her law firm position as a litigation specialist to work for Simplex Time Recorder Co. because it was five minutes from her home and she was tired of a long commute. She found the position also offered a better salary and benefits and enabled her to branch out and learn about different areas of law. Her Simplex position includes litigation, contract review, employment law, construction law, bankruptcy, collection, and real estate work. Although she was originally looking for a way to eliminate time on the turnpike, she finds the variety in these assignments adds to the interest of her workweek.

Ethical Obligations

Given all this good news about what you can do to expand your career horizons, don't forget the ethical obligation you owe your current employer. Many paralegals develop relationships with their firm's clients that include an element of personal respect and camaraderie. These relationships can lead to jobs, but if they do, they must not harm the firm's relationship with the client. When Lisa Hjulberg and Sherry Strimling got calls from clients about possible jobs, they knew their law firms would lose valuable professionals when they left (that would be them!), but they also knew the move would not contribute to a loss of business for the firms. Occasionally clients make offers that are not so clean and well-intentioned. These proposals are built around getting the law firm's expertise without going through the firm. If a job offer you receive based on a law firm contact is of this sort and would be detrimental to your employer, you must not go forward with the deal. There are plenty of opportunities to move out into the business community without biting the hand that is feeding you. If you think a job offer isn't clean, let it go.

Change Built on Tradition

The migration from law office to the outside work world as a trend is here to stay. Competent and efficient legal assistants are no longer hidden away in back offices putting documents in chronological order. They are visible, working directly with clients and marketing their firms' services to the community. Smart businesspeople, corporate administrators and executives, financial officers, title company executives, and government supervisors were bound to notice. If you're seriously considering a move, bring to your job search the enthusiasm, initiative, and creative thinking that has infused the best paralegal professional attitudes for the last two decades. This profession rests on the shoulders of pioneers who created a legal specialty through the sheer force of their intelligence, diligence, and undeniable professional contributions to the legal practice. Their followers who are taking those same attributes to the greater professional marketplace are experiencing genuine success. If you want a new career, you can make it happen.

19

Compulsory Computers and Other High-Tech Help

Nothing's more daunting than writing about computers a year and a half before a book will hit the stands. Much of what was relevant six months ago is now old hat! What's a writer to do?

The first thing is to identify what's lasting in the legal computer world. Number one, they are here to stay and, as you've read elsewhere in this book,

> No computer skills equals no career.

Notice that I wrote "no career," not "no job." There are people who will keep jobs and perhaps even get new ones—with very limited computer skills. But jobs are not careers. Those who are not computer skilled will not have great careers.

Legal employers want paralegals who can produce much of their own work and who are comfortable using a variety of software to make that happen. It's not actually enough to know specific programs. Most people know how to use a few software programs, and that's basic. What you need is the "computer comfortable attitude" that will make you optimistic and enthusiastic when you are introduced to new programs and may even help you think of a few new application possibilities on your own.

None of us who work as legal assistants can learn all about computers, know all the different programs used in every office, or even predict what new technology will come our way next. We can, however—and we must—achieve an attitude of openness and a willingness to learn that will make us computer-hip in our professional environment. What does this mean?

1. If you are unsure of your own computer prowess you must take immediate steps to cure your insecurities. Take this seriously. It's understandable that those of us who didn't study computer science might feel surprised and a little

dismayed that this new technology is such a critical part of our jobs. You may think the time it takes to learn about computers could be better spent billing hours or reading treatises or even taking clients to lunch. But computer skills, like the other skills you use every day, deserve their share of your time and attention. It takes time to develop skills, good old nonbillable time.

Remember, this is time invested in yourself, in your professional future. It's a critical investment. Your own firm may have a computer department that can help with training, but you can also investigate classes at local colleges, CLE courses, and—you guessed it—classes on the Net. Take classes, learn things, and get comfortable. Your future depends on it.

2.   When you begin a new project, stop to think if there is a way you can use tables, graphs, slide shows, spreadsheets, or other computer capabilities to help you. It's almost always difficult to add in these helpers once you have started recording information, so consult with the savvy people in your firm (or in your family) and get help setting it up. You will be amazed at the response you'll get from the attorneys and clients with whom you work when they see the information they need organized in slick, high-tech fashion.

3.   When you get your next research assignment, consider using the Internet first. See the next section for some tips on how to get information out of cyberspace and onto your desk. The Internet is useful for researching both legal and factual material so don't forget it when you have a statute or case to look up. You will find the complete text of many bills, along with legislative history and related material, right on the Net.

4.   Get ready for change and more change. That means that we all have to get used to the fact that as soon as we learn one generation of computer technology, another will be heading our way. Train yourself to greet these new advances with an open mind and a burst of energy. Think of how terrible it would be if we all had to go back to selectric typewriters. (For my younger readers, a typewriter is—er, was—a machine with a keyboard that looks sort of like a computer keyboard and that made letter marks on paper by means of a key striking an inked ribbon!) Still, I can remember that when computers were first introduced into offices there were secretaries who wanted to ship them right back to Silicon Valley.

5.   Consider becoming the firm expert at one or another software application. Perhaps you want to keep up the database used by your litigation department to input factual case material and track depositions and witnesses. Or maybe you want to learn to access the court dockets for your local courts. What if you became the one everyone turns to when they need the complete history of a piece of legislation?

Each of these spots is a terrific area of responsibility for a paralegal and one you can master quickly. The information you input or organize or access will be useful to many of the lawyers in your firm, which means you'll be valuable too. Perhaps you have an eye for graphics and want to learn how to use the new software that allows us to create exhibits for presentations and trials right in our offices. This is usually much cheaper than having outside consultants create your exhibits and the money you save the firm will be appreciated.

6. Whatever skill development you choose in the computer field, be sure you document it. Write a memo to your Annual Review file. If the skill may be helpful to attorneys who don't know you have it, draft a short memo outlining what you can do and circulate it.

7. Have some fun with your computer. Take a little time to play with the equipment. There are some things you don't have to do in life, like learning to eat with chopsticks. It's not mandatory but it is fun. Likewise there are some things you really don't have to learn to do on the computer, but you might want to just for fun. Give yourself a gift of two hours of "goofing off" with the software. Create a valentine or a slide show for your kids or a card for your secretary! This playful attitude is one thing that will help you learn quickly; ask any six-year-old you see at a keyboard!

THE INTERNET

The Internet—how did we ever live without it? If you don't have access, you're already behind. If your firm does not provide an Internet account for you, you need to get one yourself (this presupposes you have a home computer—another must). User accounts are very affordable and the information is incredibly broad and helpful. Like most ambitious paralegals I've been collecting useful Web sites for some time. You will find some of my favorites listed in the appendices. But Web sites come and go, overlap, and lead you around the Net like a treasure map. Once you start looking for information you'll see what I mean.

On April 16, 1998 I typed "Law" into my Internet "search the Net" option. I received 19,321 "hits." Then I typed "Legal Sites" into the same slot. I got 13,798,872 hits. That's right. Each of these sites will have links to lots of related sites. In fact there are sites that provide directories of legal sites.

Most court decisions, legislation, and serious newspapers and journals are available on the Net. Many full-text versions exist. These days most states, counties, and cities have public records on-line; the federal material is all on-line. You can find out what Congress did yesterday and what they intend to consider tomorrow. You can check for the availability of corporate names or find assets or get drivers license information. You can research Social Security benefits, employment law, law firms, attorneys, or judges. General and very specific information about science, medicine, real estate trends, universities, and areas of law are all available.

The search methods are easy and search engines are wonderful tools. You simply ask for all the data on "computer crime" or "Catholic high schools" or "corporate takeovers" and that little box on your desk will spit back tons of information. "Oh, no!" you may cry, "What do I do with all that data?" The answer is that you learn to refine your searches, read the summaries of the various entries, and pick and choose what you will use. It's great fun.

You can also get directions and a map to your next meeting, order plane tickets, apply for a credit card, buy books, check out restaurants, talk to your kids, get on lists to receive current information, and enter into discussions with folks who do what you do and care about what you care about.

I was first introduced to the Internet at a firm lunch meeting chaired by the head of our MIS department. He showed us exactly how to log on and did a quick run through on how to call up the text of the *New York Times*, and then said, "There!" I asked him how I would become trained to access and use this vast sea of information. He gave me one of those cryptic MIS smiles and said, "Oh, you just play with it; you'll figure it out."

Strangely, he was right. Like everyone else I have my favorite sites, my points of entry into the maze of information that has allowed me to get the facts first on more than one occasion. I have had attorneys ask me a question, then call up an hour later to say, "What have you got for me Detective Bogen?" I usually have quite a bit, and the reputation of being someone who can get the facts—and fast—is a help in any paralegal career. I have fun with it.

You will too. You'll learn tricks like omitting the "http" when you use Netscape or Internet Explorer (they add it automatically), or turning the graphics option off for faster page loading. You'll learn to be careful when you download and to check everything for viruses. Eventually you'll get a folder and start keeping site addresses and tricks of the trade and you'll find that all of them are not job-related. Some will be priceless information that will enrich your own life and that you can share with like-minded coworkers and clients to enrich and strengthen these important working relationships.

Don't forget to use the Net to keep track of what your national organizations are doing. NFPA, NALA, and AAfPE all have sites. Of course the ABA has many, including one on the Standing Committee on Legal Assistants. You can also track job opportunities on the Internet and get on lists (listserves) to receive E-mail postings from groups that interest you. If you get on a list for a group that regulates a business that many of your clients are involved in, or provides updates in your area of law, you may find yourself providing new information to lawyers, paralegals, and clients that will advance your career while you forward their interests.

TROUBLE IN VIRTUAL PARADISE

Not everything in the fast-paced world of computers is sunny and bright. We have to keep our heads on straight and use caution. There can be trouble in virtual paradise. Today's computer brains can bring problems of their own—some cute and funny, some embarrassing and inconvenient, and some dangerous and likely to lead to malpractice claims. Here are some things to think about the next time you get your hands on a mouse.

E-Mail

The funny and legally less-serious downside of E-mail is all over your office. Those who are not too motivated to be productive anyway, those who are bored with their work, those who are naturally chatty and just plain friendly can often be found doing the office version of "writing notes in class." This frittering-away-time phenomenon may mean that your secretary is not getting all your work done, or that you are getting more fun and friendly E-mails than you can answer if you intend to get your own assignments completed and meet your billing requirements. It's hard to police this kind of chatting since it looks a lot like word processing, but it can, over the course of a year, have a definite and negative effect on the amount of work accomplished in your office.

Your part, if you want to have a positive impact on this effect, is to master the artful dodge when you get more gossipy missives than you can handle. The dodge must convey your desire to chat but your regretful realization that you have to get your work done or your children will not be able to register for next quarter's college classes. An invitation to continue the talk over lunch is often a good way to go. A gentle talk with your secretary will let him or her know that while you understand the interest in the Halloween costumes of coworkers' kids, you are under the gun to meet important deadlines and need help to maintain your productivity. This is an E-mail problem you can solve.

A mid-level, politically serious E-mail problem is the inadvertent sending of mail to addressees you did not intend to include. While some incidents are merely funny, others can lead to real credibility problems. Use care in issuing junkmail, telling jokes over the E-mail lines, and advertising your old furniture. People who will be making decisions about your future see these things and amend their opinions of you accordingly. No matter how lenient the official policy, very few law firm partners like to think of their staff time and office resources being used for personal reasons. Be aware that E-mail can be forwarded to people you did not want to see it. This actually happens more with E-mail messages than with written notes. Use discretion. I have seen some humdinger "confidential" E-mails printed out and forgotten at the printer, where those waiting for a document pass the time perusing what's lying about. This kind of thing can be more than embarrassing.

Some people get carried away on E-mail and say things they would never say face-to-face, making later personal contact less than comfortable. Relaying personal information, facts about your family troubles, weight gain, desire to become pregnant, or confessions about questionable behavior are inappropriate. Careless statements about the character of someone you work with are just plain stupid. The successful practice of law assumes discretion as a basic building block. A successful career requires the same thing. Do not think of E-mail as a quick, erasable note. It's not.

E-mail can make a lasting impression. Typos and spelling errors are bad news. Although most of us would never allow a regular memo, much less a finished document, off our desks with spelling errors or typos, it's not uncommon for E-mail messages to bounce around the office in a dreadful state. If it's important enough for someone to read, it's important enough for you to proofread.

The Games People Play

Computer games are everywhere and that includes the office. Solitaire and bridge are often brought in by trainers to get people comfortable using a mouse. Usually when the trainer leaves, these games stay on the company computers.

I don't recommend ever playing computer games at the office. If you decide to do it anyway, be aware of when you play. Frankly, it looks bad to walk by someone's desk on office time and see them running "simulation pilot." The fact that you often work on firm matters during the weekends and evenings doesn't really help. Your bosses and coworkers don't see that. Lawyers are usually quite keen on maintaining a professional environment; they do not want to walk clients past a desk whose occupant is deeply involved in Tetrus. It may seem like a small thing, but this will affect the way you are seen at work.

Spelling

The spell check feature is another technological time bomb. How many times have you finished a document, run the spell check, and, buoyed by a false sense of security, sent your boss the document without a final "real live human being with a brain" proofreading? Spell check systems do not know what you are trying to say; it's all the same to them if you say "sine" or "since." They are both words, both spelled correctly. Your reader will not find deciphering these miswordings any fun at all. (Your reader wilt net fund deciphering these misreadings ant fun at ill!) I work in the area of public law and live in fear that some day my spell check feature will allow me to write a memo on "pubic law." Spell check features don't think.

Spelling errors create chaos in another area too. Document organization and management applications depend on correct data input for correct functioning—that is, for data retrieval. Data input always requires care, but sometimes, even with care and the best intentions, it's just plain impossible. Let's say you have received 12 banker's boxes of documents on a multimillion dollar case with 45 major witnesses. An attorney calls you in to explain that this is going to be a very exciting case to work on, that it is important to the firm, high-profile in the legal community, that you are going to love being part of the team, *and* that the first thing she needs you to do is input those documents "into the system" (a phrase loosely translated as, "I have no idea what I am talking about but I want you to go away and make this happen without any more help from me"). You are not naive. When you begin your review of the paper and the "inputting into the system" you are careful to note names and check the typing (spelling) of names and other important words you will later use as search terms to capture relevant data. Even so, as you hit box three you will find Mr. Frankel's name spelled as "Frankil," or is it Mr. Frankil's name spelled as "Frankel?" If you are sufficiently alert after hours of data input to pick up on the fact that these two spellings probably refer to the same person, and if you can find the attorney who gave you the case to ask her about it, you will find out that she does not know which spelling is correct. When you call the paralegal at the firm who had the case before you, you will find out he is too busy to return your call. If Mr. Frankel or Frankil is on your side you will finally call him, because you must be sure, but it's not a happy situation.

Finally, because this is how life is, you will find out that the correct spelling is not the one you have used in detailing the first three boxes of documents. There is only one thing to do, and yes, it is as bad as you think. You go back and correct field entries while you cry into your Diet Mountain Dew. Of course the flip side of this problem is running a search with a misspelled search term. The machine won't think, it will just carry out the search. It won't find anything authored by "Frankel." Scary, isn't it?

CONFIDENTIALLY SPEAKING

The more vendors we include in our practice management, the more careful we need to be about confidentiality. Be sure firms that provide videoconferencing or imaging have reliable policies and reputations. Remember that sometimes even the fact that a meeting took place is confidential, so if you videoconference from a professional location outside the office, check it out for exposure to the public. Be aware that some legal vendors get substantial portions of their business from one or a few firms, which could potentially lead to personal relationships between principals at the two businesses that are potentially compromising. I once was arranging for videotaping of case material that would be shown to mock juries. The case was a large and important one for the client and the firm and the mock jury demonstration included all of our major arguments and strategies. By chance we discovered the video firm I had contacted did a lot of work for opposing counsel in the case. Although there was no concrete reason to expect that our strategies would be communicated to the other side—in fact I think they would not have been—the prudent choice in this case was to go with another service that had no particular relationship to any parties or firms involved.

Similar care must be exercised if your law firm has established E-mail links with clients. Do not assume that what you send via that E-mail line can be protected from disclosure. If it is printed at the client's end, then allowed to remain at the printer for hours, you may end up quite unsure about who has read your comments, or who a court will allow to read them in the future.

FAX OF LIFE

How did we practice without fax machines? I have no idea, but fax filing with courts and fax exchanges with opposing counsel are not without risk. One potential problem is that the knowledge that an item can be faxed may make us complacent about deadlines. If we finish it late and the fax is inoperable, what is our recourse?

Fax exchanges with opposing counsel can also be problematic. Consider this: You and opposing counsel agree to fax final offers of compromise at 12 noon. You dutifully fax yours off, then spend the next 40 minutes calling the other side to complain that their document has not arrived. They say they sent it. Only later do you learn that the attorney who tried to fax it did not understand that the machine simply put it into memory to be sent later.

MALPRACTICE

Technology's place in standards of practice is not yet defined, which makes it all the more dicey in techno-land. You cannot assume anything. If a firm failed to do any discovery in representing a client in a lawsuit, most likely it would be considered delinquent in its duty. Do litigation firms now have a duty to do computer discovery, and if so, how will that occur? Are you aware of what kind of searches your clients must undertake to respond to discovery requests? Is it enough to run your fingers through the file cabinets or do you need to access their computer systems? Are there dependable parameters for when this expensive discovery makes sense? Keeping up with new techniques, vendors, and consultants can be a full-time job as well as a new area of specialty for paralegals. But keeping generally informed in this new area is yet another nonbillable task we have to accomplish. Entire magazines are currently devoted to legal technology, and that's actual paper copy; think of what's on-line.

If a firm is sued by a client for malpractice, will the firm's computer tapes become discoverable? These tapes retain information you may think was erased. A horror story we all want to avoid is the following: Firm XYZ was sued for malpractice by its former client; computer discovery commenced. Among the E-mail messages recovered from the firm's computer tapes were the following: "Please review the depos and summarize so it will look like we are doing something on this case" and "I don't know, maybe our guy really did it." You may think comments like these are never committed to paper or E-mail, but somewhere out there in the world today, someone is typing something just that damaging. Use your head.

THE BIG CRASH

Most of us have experienced the Crash Phenomenon. This occurs about 11:00 a.m. when you have been working all morning on a long document that, bless your heart, you have forgotten to save along the way. You are looking forward to getting this baby done and heading off to lunch when—wham—your screen freezes. You can't do a thing. You get no response from your keyboard or your mouse. Nothing, nothing, nothing.

Most frightening is the realization that you can't save your document. You grab the phone and call your computer wizards but the line is busy. Somehow, somewhere in the vast reaches of your firm's bit of cyperspace, someone has done something that has crashed the system and there is nothing for you to do but turn off the machine and go to lunch, where you can drown your sorrow in Diet Coke and nachos. While you do so those mysterious folks who keep your firm's computer system going will do the secret, magical things they do to "bring it back up." This, however, rarely means recovering a document you never saved. You will have to begin again.

Another instance of crash disaster is this: Working on a megabucks, multi-issue case that involved 45 depositions, you will quite naturally put them all on a data management software system. This can be a great help in cases when the issues are complex, because using search keys allows you to get any witness' testimony on a certain issue or about a certain person or document or date or whatever, in no time.

However, you must be aware that sometimes those deposition transcripts may "disappear" from the system. It can happen, even when the computer experts cannot explain it. If you are close to trial you may have sent disks of the testimony on to cocounsel. Retrieving the disks is possible of course, but time-consuming and embarrassing. Moral of this story? Back up everything. In this case you might also load the transcripts on your laptop; then you can reconstruct the system from those records. Remember, never count exclusively, or even too heavily, on electric techno-based data systems. When the power goes out or the big crash hits, papers may get shuffled, but they are still there.

THE COPY CAT BLUES

Even before computers became our best friends, creating legal documents entirely from scratch was rare. Legal writing is often an elegant and careful sort of copying and clients expect—and often request—that we use forms where it's appropriate to shorten the time and expense related to document creation. Now more than ever, it's possible to miss making a necessary change in a document you are revising. Why? In the "olden days" we would often read a document as we dictated, revising as we noticed each needed change. Now we can copy a complete document to a new document number and then word process the changes ourselves. How easy it is, how incredibly and dangerously easy, to miss changing one paragraph that includes, for example, the effective date of a document.

Another potential problem comes from the ease with which we download from the C: drive to floppy. You can stick the floppy disk in your wallet, take it home for the weekend, make substantial changes on Saturday before you head out for a hike, then forget to take it back to the office with you Monday morning. This presents two possibilities for disaster. In scenario number one you realize you have a couple of days to finish the document, move on to other projects, and eventually become unclear about which version of the document is the latest and best. Solution: extra work and extra time to sort it out. In the other scenario, you need the document finished by noon. Solution: You can get moving and hope you can recreate the Saturday work quickly at the office, or you can get into your car and go home to get it. Neither of these solutions is fun or billable. We have to develop good habits, but the chances to slip are certainly there.

IMAGE THIS

It's all the rage, and perfect for some practices, but the imaging of documents is also a new world for most of us. Usually it involves a large matter, a client with substantial money, and interfacing with a whole new world of legal vendors. Imaging can be helpful when storing, duplicating, organizing, and searching in large document matters; but limitations in the equipment's ability to read handwriting or dirty documents is a real limitation. When you have to search in imaged documents, be careful. Even if you are spelling things correctly when you input the search query, if the document misspells important names or key words you can have trouble.

Another potential problem with this new technique is that it usually requires that your documents—your important evidence—leave your office. Often this occurs at a critical time in terms of discovery, so if you find yourself involved with imaging, think hard and think ahead. Develop close working relationships with the vendors and arrange in advance for how emergencies will be addressed.

CAR 54, WHERE ARE YOU?

Car phones and cell phones are everywhere...in your purse, for example. They can be great for quick contact with your boss or secretary when you're on the road, but convenient as they may be, they too have a downside. Who wants to be constantly available? There was a time when you could graciously gain valuable time because your boss could not be reached. (Which sounds better: "I won't be able to speak to Ms. Mills until tomorrow" or "Gee, we really haven't had time to figure out just how the law applies in your case"?) These days people expect that you and the attorneys and paralegals you work with can be reached in, at most, a few hours. This is a reality we all have to live with. Be sure to let clients know there are some meetings that cannot be interrupted and that, important as they are, very few judges appreciate pagers or cell phones going off in court or even in a settlement conference. These phones are like fire: a good thing when used well, but don't let them get the upper hand in your day.

DON'T LET BIG BROTHER DO YOUR THINKING

No, this is not a bit of sixties rhetoric with no relevance to the twenty-first century. As we learn to live with, work with, and depend upon our wonderful new technological aids, we are going to have to work hard to remember who's in charge. No matter how sophisticated your document organization and retrieval system, there is no substitute for good, old-fashioned human brain work. Analysis still requires sitting down and reading the documents, making extra copies to mark up, comparing what you have in your hands with something you vaguely remember seeing two weeks ago. In short, you still need to know your case, the facts, the law, and the outcome of mixing them up. You still need to assess the credibility and attractiveness of witnesses and you still need to figure out how best to present your client's position. If you are not involved in a lawsuit these factors still matter. If you are negotiating a contract you still need to try to "read" the other side.

If you produce contracts, wills, or other documents for clients that contain what is foolishly called boilerplate language, you will have to be more careful than ever before that the current computer-produced version you are using is truly customized for that client's needs. This means more than just editing a document. You must be sure the model you work from is complete enough to provide all the necessary choices. This requires that you think as hard and as carefully as if you were creating the document from scratch.

Be especially careful if you are using mass-produced forms from software companies. Are there local or state laws or filing requirements that are not reflected in the generic document? The client is relying on you to think of all the potential options or potential problems that may apply to the situation. You are not entitled to rely on a software company to do that thinking for you.

BRAVE NEW WORLD

It really is a new legal and technological world, and the practice of law will never be the same. But while the techniques change, our jobs remain surprisingly constant: to represent clients' interests in the manner best suited to help them achieve their goals. No matter how fancy the trappings, the core of a successful practice is still a team of bright, dedicated individuals who are committed to excellence. Bring to the computer age your enthusiasm, your curiosity, and your willingness to adapt, but most of all, bring your intelligence. Now more than ever, the practice of law depends on careful use of resources directed by a lively intellect and a focused mind.

Do enter into it all. Explore the new technologies, build and rebuild your skill base. Develop areas of expertise. The opportunities are exciting and the cost of opting out is being left behind until you simply are no longer considered a valuable player.

Keeping Up with What's New

How do you keep on top of this amazing flow of information? Staying on-line will keep you fairly current with the Internet, but don't stop there. Many firms have MIS or computer-related bulletins that provide up-to-date information on new Web sites of value. If you are active on-line, you may be able to add to these lists yourself.

Don't limit your interest areas. My firm's January newsletter alerted me to a good source for legal information on Mexico and Canada, but it also gave me a great site for writers of children's books as well as a fitness site that contains hot news on the health front. The newsletter also let me know I can enroll in in-house classes in QuattroPro to learn how to create, format, edit, and print spreadsheets, and classes in Presentations to learn how to plan and implement slide shows on my computer. In February it let me know about a good site for tax queries as well as links to state and federal tax sites and a *Doonesbury* site to ease the pain. It also started explaining Wide Area Networks (WANs), which the firm intends to implement soon. You get the picture.

If your firm doesn't have such a newsletter, considering putting one out yourself. Link up with the most talented computer nuts at your firm (every firm has some!) and schedule a lunch meeting to discuss it. Decide which partners might support your project and put together a proposal. This is a great example of how investing in yourself and the firm can dovetail. Don't forget, you can include exercises to keep your coworkers' backs, shoulders, and wrists healthy, updates about the firm's computer policies, and computer humor—because we all need a cyber-giggle once in a while.

Consider your computers—both the firm's and your own—basic career-building tools. A laptop can contain much more than a briefcase, and a computer database can organize more data than any filing cabinet you can ever keep organized. Your computer can make you independent and able to access incredible resources on your own at the same time it allows you to join forces with friends and colleagues all over the globe. While writing this chapter I've searched dozens of sites on the Internet and "talked" via Internet E-mail to professionals, friends, and family in six states and one foreign country—and that was just this morning!

20 FAMILY, HEALTH, AND HAPPINESS

"Good health and good sense are two of life's greatest blessings."
Publius Syrus, 42 BC

This chapter probably belongs at the front of the book. Officially it's not a part of anyone's paralegal career, but thinking about our personal lives in conjunction with our career plans is one of the really critical things we can learn to do.

Take note: A fulfilling, worthwhile personal life is not necessary for a terrifically successful paralegal career. That's right. You can be a successful, noteworthy paralegal and have a miserable, discouraging home life. In fact, some folks are doing that right now.

What I want to emphasize is that it's not necessary to neglect your personal life to succeed as a legal professional. It's not necessary and it's not smart. You don't have to work till midnight three nights a week, worry constantly, ruin your health, and fall into bed a wreck, ignoring your kids and your spouse, to be a terrific paralegal. You can manage your career as a top-notch legal assistant, rather than have your career manage you.

Easier said than done? Maybe, but there's a lot you can do to perform splendidly, promote your own career, and take good care of yourself and your family. Here are some things to think about.

SET REALISTIC GOALS

Set your annual and quarterly goals early and figure out exactly how you will meet them. Of course the plan will have to be amended along the way. It's better to have a plan and amend it than to go merrily down the road with no forethought. This means you cannot wait until December to "find out" how many hours you have billed this year. In December you should be happily patting yourself on the back for a great year and planning your goals for the next year.

Decide how many hours you must bill. Be realistic. Analyze both your financial needs and the special needs of your family during the year. Is this the year your child enters school or has to undergo surgery or learn to deal with braces, glasses, and acne? Is this the year your significant other is returning to school or changing jobs? Is this the last chance you'll all have to take a family trip before the offspring graduate and move out? Is this a year when family dinners are more important than ever because your oldest is starting junior high? Is this the year you need to put away as much money as possible in preparation for college payments?

Think about your own non-work goals. Do you want to finish your bachelor's degree or get a master's degree? Are you in dire need of time at the gym or on the track? Is this the year you are going to take piano lessons, learn to play racquetball, volunteer at the legal clinic, edit a newsletter, or solve your migraine headache problems?

If you're married or otherwise significantly involved, do not forget the significance of that other. Is this the year you two learn to dance? Or does your spouse need time when you cover the home bases so he or she can expand a career or get an education? Have you decided to take that trip to Paris? If you're not significantly involved but wish you were, are you prepared to spend enough time away from your desk to meet folks?

Think these things through before you plan your work year. Do not think they will all just fall into place because you love your family or want to stay in shape. If this is the last year you have to watch your high schooler run track, plan a way to be out of the office and at the track at 4 p.m. on ten afternoons during track season. That kind of thing never works out without planning.

THINK "PROFESSIONAL GROWTH"

Getting the job that's on your desk right now done is important—even critical— but it is not enough. Successful, happy paralegals have an ongoing interest in where their careers are headed.

Think about what professional growth you plan to accomplish this year. Consider your professional associations. Do you want to serve on the board? Have you had an idea for a class you could teach rattling around your brain? Do you want to expand your expertise in a new area of law? Is there a class you need to take?

Talk to your boss or whoever reviews your performance and ask if that person thinks you are making good choices and will support your plans. This is an opportunity to coordinate the firm's needs and your own goals—a sure avenue to success.

GUARD YOUR HEALTH

A busy legal career is hard on your body. Sitting at a desk, handling the stress of deadlines, adversarial situations, and public performances—these all take a toll. So does skipping lunch or eating too many french fries. Your health is your responsibility and as important to your happiness and career as anything else. It's also critical if you intend to raise great kids or be any fun on a weekend in the Poconos. Do not leave your health to chance and do not wait until your body breaks down to get it serviced!

See the eye doctor. We use our eyes constantly in this business and eye professionals report seeing stress-related problems at earlier and earlier ages as the computer generation enters the workplace. Ask about lighting, different lenses for computer distance reading, and exercises that may relieve eyestrain. Ask about nutrition and vitamins.

Get a complete physical exam. Ask your doctor about your weight and if you need to lose a few pounds, get with a program. Discuss posture problems that may result from sitting at your desk. Get some advice about lifting (those heavy boxes full of documents) and any wrist pain you may have. Ask about shoes. Ask about nutrition. Ask about flu shots and tetanus shots and TB tests. Again, ask about vitamins. Discuss exercise.

Assuming your doctor okays exercise, join a gym. If you work for an enlightened firm that provides help with gym membership fees, take advantage of that and write the partners a thank-you letter. Otherwise, cough up the cash and get involved. If you aren't a gym-rat, then figure out what your exercise program will be. Walk to work, run, take yoga, or play soccer. You must do something.

If you cannot think of any physical activity you might enjoy, pick the one that sounds the least noxious and give it a try. Assign yourself a certain number of months before you can quit. It takes time to experience the pleasures of sweating, but once you do you will be amazed. My husband and I often substitute a gym date for a movie date. We meet, work out (and chat), shower, and leave feeling great—and totally justified in stopping for a frozen yogurt on the way home.

See the dentist before the pain hits. It's amazing how difficult it is to fit a routine dental appointment into the life of a working adult. This must be true because the number of adults who don't see their dentists till the pain is unbearable is astonishing. They have to have root canals the night before a big argument or get a filling redone just before a client reception. Everybody has a slow season in this legal business; just make the appointment and go.

All these health ideas are good for anyone any time, but they do have special professional significance for you if you have serious goals in the legal field. Health is an automatic advantage in the competitive world of law. Even looking lean and mean can be a psychological advantage.

EXPECT SOME STRESS

In a well-organized, well-run career there will still be days and sometimes weeks of long hours and stress. Trials, closings, probates, significant issues within the corporate structure of client companies, significant issues within your own firm, all come with built-in intensity and time requirements that can't be avoided.

When you're in the midst of one of these events you'll be glad you expected it and planned ahead. You'll be very glad you chose to maintain, rather than just repair, your health. You'll be glad you saw your ten-year-old's clarinet concert in the fall if you have to miss a soccer game in May. The way you handle your year is important to you. It can also be a teaching tool to those whose futures you will help shape. Teach well.

HAPPINESS

What can we say about happiness? For one thing, think about it. Really do. Figure out how your career fits into your idea of overall happiness. What do you want to accomplish in your life? You have to think about billable hours and getting ahead, but that's not what you have to think about all the time. What else do you want to do and learn? The answers will be different for each of us, but consider that many high achievers in the legal field have entire other worlds of interest.

Legal professionals write plays, volunteer in adult literacy programs, hike mountain ranges, play in orchestras, invent gadgets, head up Scout troops, swim competitively, raise money for the Leukemia Foundation, collect old china, rollerblade, review restaurants, study medieval science, organize ten-K races, sing in choirs, raise horses, swing dance, restore Victorian homes, run writing groups, and take classes at their local universities. They find that the effort expended and pleasure gained from these activities goes a long way toward keeping them alive, alert, and refreshed when they go back to the office.

DO NOT THINK "IT COULDN'T HAPPEN TO ME"

Legal careers, like many others, are potentially damaging to personal lives. They don't have to be, but they can be. It's your job to be sure your life stays on track, is fun and rewarding and right. If you like your work and have a lot of it, working late too often is easy to do. If you are having troubles at home, working late can be even easier. It can even be easy to work too much if you have a happy home life filled with understanding people who don't give you much grief about your schedule. Those hours when you should be home but are at your desk will take a toll. You are not immune. Guard your life.

The message of this book is not that you will attain career success as a paralegal by devoting all your time and all your energy to your job. A lot of time must be devoted, but the goal is to devote that time intelligently and selectively so that you accomplish your goals with time and energy to spare. This is a realistic, grounded goal for you. I wish you happy, healthy pursuit!

21 A SAMPLER OF SUPERSTARS

"It takes a long time to bring excellence to maturity."
Publius Syrus, 42 BC

Here's what one top litigator says about being a superstar paralegal:

"The trick is to get the basic work done flawlessly (document production, witness binders, etc.) but also come up with creative ideas that win cases. Some legal assistants try too hard on the second part; they think they are smarter and better than the lawyers and really prefer that kind of work—so the basic work gets shorted. On the other hand, some, if not most, legal assistants just focus on the first part, grinding out the basic work but without any spark.

"But the superstar does both. The hard part is to provide the creative ideas without shorting the first part, and to do so in a nonthreatening way. Litigators spend a lot of time coming up with sound bites, themes that encapsulate the case for the jury. You don't have to be a lawyer to be good at it—and sometimes being a lawyer is a handicap. Superstar legal assistants both know the case from the bottom up and can provide a nice sound bite."

Sound like a tall order? Here's what a great municipal lawyer looks for in her paralegals:

"In our office a legal assistant works for several attorneys and the ability to juggle is a major factor in success, or lack thereof. Humor—another not-strictly-legal characteristic—is another thing that greases the wheels and helps communication.

"It is so important that the legal assistant get the assignment right so that he does what is really needed. This is not always easy—particularly if the attorney is not clear, which sometimes happens in the early stages of a project. So it's important for the legal assistant to feed the assignment back to the attorney to make sure that what the attorney asked for is understood and to make sure the attorney asked for what she really wanted.

"Also, it is really helpful if the legal assistant has skill at evaluating urgency, and the willingness and ability to buy into the justified feeling of urgency held by the assigning attorney."

Piece of cake, right? All you have to do is take care of all the routine stuff, do some case-winning creative thinking, listen perfectly and feed back what you hear, and, oh yes, buy into the attorney's sense of urgency. While you do this you should remember your twenty-five other assignments and tell a joke. Of course, it helps if you can tap-dance too.

Can you do all that? Sure you can, that and a whole lot more. Here are some superstars who have made careers out of fulfilling and exceeding these kinds of requirements—all while keeping an eye on their own futures and dreams!

Diane Petropulos, Trailblazer
Current Position: Program Coordinator

Diane Petropulos is a well-known name to those who've been around the paralegal world a while. She heads up the paralegal education program at Sonoma State University (SSU) in California, but that's just her day-gig. Petropulos' contributions to the paralegal profession have involved a lot of professional overtime. She is and has been active in the national paralegal arena for many years, serving on task forces and committees with national organizations, heading up an effort to establish baseline criteria for entry-level paralegals, and pursuing other ventures that have an impact on the present and future of the paralegal field. She also writes a regular column, the "Student's Workshop," in *Legal Assistant Today* magazine. Pretty heavy stuff, but once upon a time she was a beginner too.

In fact, when she graduated from Pomona College she was a pre-beginner. After graduation, she spent some time at UCLA doing graduate work in French, but somehow she wasn't loving it. Some part of her mind was open to other possibilities and then she saw an ad from the Philadelphia Institute, one of the first paralegal education programs in the United States. The ad described an educational program training people to become paralegals and included a brief description of the job. Diane had never heard of paralegals till then, but the job sounded "interesting."

Not too long after that Petropulos moved to Minnesota where, as luck (fate?) would have it, another of the nation's early paralegal education programs was busy training paralegals. This time she thought, "Interesting" and, "Good idea" and entered the program to earn a paralegal certificate at the University of Minnesota.

Her first legal job landed her squarely in the world of criminal defense and Federal Indian Law. Petropulos was even involved in preparation for the famous Wounded Knee case. Exciting as all that was, her personal life required that she be pretty much in motion for the next few years. Soon she found herself headed back to the San Joaquin Valley in California armed with a certificate and some experience.

When Petropulos found out she was moving back to California, she fired off a letter to the law firm where she'd previously taken an assignment as a temporary legal secretary. She proposed to the partners that they needed a full-fledged paralegal. Those of us who know Diane are not surprised that the partners were convinced. They created their first official paralegal position in the litigation department and hired her.

Writing to her former employer and marketing herself and the new legal animal called a paralegal is a wonderful example of taking the initiative in a situation where a lesser soul might feel initiative was impossible. Taking the initiative, coupled with the creative act of recognizing an opportunity for herself and others, is a pattern in

Petropulos' career that has been a real part of her impressive success. Her work at the Fresno firm gave her income and experience. By the time she next moved, this time to Humboldt County in northern California, she was ready to freelance.

Diane's Humboldt County freelance practice involved criminal defense, plaintiff personal injury, and once again Federal Indian law. She also worked as a court-appointed investigator and paralegal with the criminal defense bureau. One of the cases she worked on was a murder case, a landmark event in itself, but this case was unusual even for a matter involving murder: there was no body to produce as evidence. The case proceeded to trial and resulted in a guilty verdict. The body was actually recovered some time later.

Another significant part of Petropulos' freelance period was work she did for a firm in which each of the three partners was Native American. This firm served as general counsel for a number of Indian tribes and entities. Petropulos was involved in several significant actions, including assisting one tribe in getting congressional legislation passed to recover reservation land.

Eventually Diane signed on as a full-time employee with this firm, but once again a family relocation created job change. Her next paralegal spot was as a full-time assistant in City Hall in Calistoga, California. Here her time was split between assisting the City Administrator and the City Attorney. The exposure to work factors, politics, and policy outside a traditional law office setting served her well because, although she didn't know it, she was just a year away from the career move that would bring her to Sonoma State as Coordinator of the Attorney Assistant Program.

By this time Diane was not only a paralegal, she was a mother. She liked her Calistoga job but she wanted interesting part-time work. She had a child care helper who was also actively involved in career evolution and a job search of her own. This meant the "nanny" was watching the want ads and ended up passing on the SSU job lead to Diane.

Late on a Thursday Diane got the word from her son's nanny that Sonoma State was looking for a paralegal program coordinator. It was an interesting and exciting job lead and a part-time spot. The next day after she left her office she drove straight to the college campus to apply. The human resources worker handed her an application form that Diane proceeded to fill out, but she could tell at a glance that the form provided by personnel could never communicate what she had in mind for a paralegal program. She already had ideas about a program that would "teach it like it is" in the real paralegal world, but it was not a simple idea. She needed some time and space to express it.

Petropulos explained her problem to the human resources staff, that is, that she was very interested in the program and in the job and was eager to communicate her ideas and to make a good impression. She told the personnel person that she was pretty sure a handwritten application form wouldn't allow her to do that. Both Diane's initiative and her training in making an argument came in handy that late afternoon. The personnel worker agreed that Diane could supplement her application with a statement about what she saw for the program and how she wanted to implement her vision, as long as the complete package was returned to personnel before 8 a.m. the following Monday.

Petropulos went home and spent the weekend thinking through and writing up her ideas. The rest, as they say, is history. She not only got the interview; she got the job. The initiative she took to go the extra step, to find and maximize the opportunity, was not only critical but probably decisive. Her efforts said clearly what a resume can only hope to convey: I am qualified and I can get the job done.

That same initiative and a lot of hard work carried Diane to national leadership in the paralegal profession in this country. She is an active member and past president of AAfPE (American Association for Paralegal Education). She's also made her vision for a paralegal program that "teaches it like it is" a reality. In SSU's attorney assistant certificate program, practicing attorneys and paralegals share the teaching load and provide students with real exposure to roles they can expect to play in a legal practice. Internships in real legal settings are an important and required part of the program. As the times have changed, Petropulos has made sure SSU's program has changed too, incorporating computer training that allows paralegals to go out into the work world with a handle on the kinds of applications they'll be required to perform on the job.

Maximizing opportunity and creating her own future are key elements in Petropulos' successful and noteworthy career. The long, steady climb to excellence and professional prominence has been regularly injected with strong shots of that potent career cocktail—vision plus action.

Donald Swanson
Current Position: President, Five Star Legal and Compliance Systems, Inc.

Many of today's most successful professionals in the paralegal field didn't plan to have a legal career at all. The careers found them. Don Swanson, now president of a California company that provides temporary and full-time paralegal placement services, highly technical computerized litigation support (including training, consulting, and software sales), and government contracting, began his adult working life with a fish company. This Northern California family-owned business generated millions of dollars in revenue each year. Swanson was the assistant to the president. The recession of the 1980s had a major impact on this company and Swanson, like so many others in the late 80s, was laid off.

Swanson's father had heard of a new legal profession, one that was predicted to be one of the fastest-growing occupations in the 90s. He suggested to his son that a paralegal degree might be helpful for future employment.

Swanson thought his father might be right. He enrolled in the paralegal program at the University of San Diego. In 1987 the market for paralegals was hot; every graduate was getting a job offer. An on-campus interview with San Diego Gas & Electric led to a great first job. Swanson was assigned research and writing projects and work on a computerized database. This was his first substantial exposure to personal computers and the impact they would have on the legal world was not lost on Swanson. A year later he moved to New England where he became the senior and only paralegal at Boston Edison. That job provided Swanson with the chance to implement computerized litigation support for the company. He hired and supervised 50 temporary paralegals to work on a nuclear power outage case. This team handled over 4000 interrogatories, 4 million pages of discovery, and 200 transcripts of testimony. Swanson supervised the effort and saved the firm $1 million. The five-year Boston experience also provided know-how he would use later in founding his own company.

Like all superstars, Swanson's interest in his own education didn't end when he got his paralegal certificate. While at Edison he earned a master of finance degree from Boston College which, coupled with his paralegal experience, equipped him to go out on his own. In April of 1992, just five years after Swanson earned a paralegal certificate, Five Star opened for business. This company now serves Fortune 500 companies and law firm clients from New England to Hawaii. What accounts for Don's incredible success?

When you meet Don you realize immediately that he loves what he does. He likes to find people jobs and he likes to teach professionals about new technology that can revolutionize their businesses. He's excited about what can happen next and after you talk to him for ten minutes, you notice you're excited too.

Swanson's an example of what can happen when a paralegal knows his strengths, is willing to work hard to learn about the world, and has the courage to take well-thought-out risks designed to take advantage of the changing legal landscape. He has advice for today's paralegals worth listening to: "Serve attorneys with an extraordinary degree of responsibility, resourcefulness, and organization, and offer the excellent oral and written communication skills and superior legal research abilities." He knows that what attorneys need in an assistant is someone who can work well under pressure, someone who will solve the problem at hand.

Clearly Swanson also believes in the power of investing in yourself through continuing education and promoting the paralegal profession in the community. His company sponsors a prestigious competition designed to honor outstanding paralegals in Southern California, the Five Star Paralegal of the Year award. Just as importantly, Swanson gives his own time to work with other community leaders on programs designed to help the children of Los Angeles.

Swanson sees great things in your future. Traditional paralegals, he says, will be offered greater responsibilities that will bring new job opportunities. He sees clients as paralegal advocates because they demand cost-effective legal services; he knows attorneys need good paralegals in order to make the most of their own talents. Swanson is an exciting example of what vision and hard work can accomplish.

Susan Nauss Exon
Current Position: Director of Law and Public Policy, University of California, Riverside Extension

In 1976, two weeks after her high school graduation ceremony, Susan Nauss Exon entered the paralegal education program at Central Pennsylvania Business School. Sound unusual, ambitious, well-organized, and disciplined? That's Susan—that and quite a bit more. Since that graduation day she's been a student, a paralegal, a lawyer, and an educator. Who knows what's next?

Like Petropulos, Nauss Exon attended one of the country's first ABA-approved paralegal education programs. It was an intense full-time program; the class schedule was all day, Tuesdays through Fridays. Eighteen-year-old Nauss Exon was also working at McDonald's to help cover expenses. That left evenings for homework, which in Susan's case was done on a manual typewriter at her parents' kitchen table. But she's a hard worker; she persevered and in December of 1977 she began an internship.

The Advantage of Internships

In 1978 few attorneys were familiar with paralegals and fewer still understood what paralegals could really do. Susan's internship was with a three-person law office in downtown Harrisburg, Pennsylvania's capital, and the firm was starting a legal search and assistance corporation. Susan's job, as the only paralegal, was to set up and manage this business, providing services to corporations around the country: UCC lien research and research and confirmation of other information contained in the states' corporation and UCC bureaus.

Nauss Exon's clients were all located somewhere else. They did business with her over the phone lines and Susan learned that an ability to establish a favorable client relationship quickly went a long way toward keeping the business going. She also learned the importance of developing a strong rapport with the staffs at the various state agencies she researched. This is not to discount the importance of good skills, but as this book has stressed, professional relationships count for a lot too.

Relationships affect our careers in other ways. Nauss Exon's Harrisburg internship turned into a job but romance took her to Rochester, New York where she took a job at the Rochester Institute for Technology. This position was not a paralegal job. It was secretarial and administrative, but Susan stayed with it because she was lucky enough to work for a boss who was a terrific professional mentor. Clint Wallington taught her supervisory and managerial skills that have served Nauss Exon well for over twenty years. She credits Wallington with reinforcing the strong work ethic that has been a mainstay of her career. He supported her efforts to grow professionally by allowing her time to take criminal justice courses during the workday. Susan made up the time she missed by staying late and working during lunch hours. She says Wallington taught her that if you are good to employees, they will usually repay you well.

Get Your Foot in the Door—Then Move Up

Nauss Exon stayed for two years in Rochester, then moved to Wyoming where she worked for a public defender's office. This position illustrates another Nauss Exon success tool: Get your foot in the door and then improve your situation. Susan took the job as a legal secretary with bump-up potential. It wasn't long before she was bumped to a criminal investigation and general litigation paralegal spot. Also of note was the salary change; her salary there doubled in one year.

In 1980 Nauss Exon moved to Laramie, Wyoming. Her reputation preceded her. Susan arrived in Laramie on a Saturday. By Tuesday the local public defender was at her door with a job offer. That job was in Cheyenne, which was farther than she wanted to commute, so she turned it down and took a job with the English department at the local college. As it turned out the college job bored her silly, and like so many highly motivated paralegals, Susan finally opted for more interesting work even though it involved a long commute. A large Denver, Colorado firm was opening an office in Cheyenne and hired Susan.

Susan's career took off at this job. She found herself doing research and drafting while also running the library, establishing form files, updating the firm's lawyers on bulletins from agencies that made policy affecting the firm's clients, and reviewing the *Federal Register* daily and summarizing important cases. She coordinated a system of opinion letters (which she often drafted) that the firm sent out to clients whose interests might be affected by the new case law or by developing policy. The work was exciting and fun but the hours were grueling. Nauss Exon remembers a nine-month billing period in which she billed 180 hours a month while doing 40 hours of administrative work too. She was getting great experience but she was usually tired.

After three years, Susan moved to Rock Springs. She started over, knocking on doors, her impressive portfolio of work in hand. In just a few days she had established a network of part-time contract jobs with seven law firms. Some of that work was for the county prosecutor's office. Three months later they offered her a full-time job, and she took it.

Nauss Exon had always wanted to go to law school. Now 27, she thought the time was ripe and she applied to, and was accepted at, the University of Wyoming School of Law. She rented a room in Laramie and commuted home to Rock Springs on the weekends. Given her track record, you won't be surprised to hear that at the end of her first year Susan was fifth in her class. She made *Law Review* and received a scholarship for her second year. During her third year she stayed on *Law Review* as staff and was a teaching assistant. After graduation she was recruited by a Southern California law firm, Best, Best & Krieger, LLP.

Susan had never intended to practice law for her entire working career. She had always intended to teach and had in fact started law school with the idea of returning to Rock Springs to start and develop a paralegal education program. But at Best, Best & Krieger she got to combine her litigation skills with her interest in public agencies and environmental law. She liked it so much that she stayed for six years.

Sometime in 1993 Susan realized that the time was ripe to make her teaching dream come true. She had been teaching courses in the Legal Assistantship program at the University of California, Riverside Extension for some time. Nauss Exon began perusing the *Chronicle of Higher Education* for other teaching spots. She came across a new junior college being developed in Texas. A review of the position openings revealed that they didn't have a paralegal program at all. Nauss Exon wrote them a letter.

Create Your Own Opportunity

The letter, perhaps not unlike the one Petropulos wrote to Sonoma State, detailed the projections for paralegal career growth and recommended such a program as ideal for this new institution. The academic powers agreed and decided to develop a program and hire someone to run it. Eventually they offered Nauss Exon the teaching spot.

At this point Nauss Exon made a call to her contacts at UCR. She wanted to get advice about whether to take the job. When UCR's administrators realized she was serious about closing her law practice to devote her time to paralegal education, they made an offer of their own and in 1995 Susan took over as the Coordinator of the Legal Assistantship Certificate Program.

Not surprisingly, Susan's leadership in the program has been energetic and inspiring, to great and positive effect. She established an Advisory Committee for the program that includes judges, private and public lawyers, paralegals, community members, and students. Nauss Exon initiated the process of obtaining ABA approval for the program (a process now in its final stages) and spent a great deal of time in education, both formally and informally. She teaches in the program and also spends time meeting with local attorneys. Nauss Exon has been the featured speaker at several bar association meetings, explaining the program and promoting the use of paralegals in local law practices. In addition, Nauss Exon's influence in the program is evidenced by the talented instructors she's hired and by the active continuing education program for paralegals and attorneys she has developed. She also established Internet and computer education programs for all legal professionals and was so successful that UCR changed the name of her department to Law and Public Policy, upgrading her position to Director.

Nobody knows what's next for Susan. She may not know even herself. Her success is built on a practice of noticing openings and turning them into splendid opportunities. She's been actively keeping an eye out, working hard, and getting results since she was 18. I think we can expect more surprises and more exciting accomplishments from this leader in the paralegal field.

Beth Agre, Career Paralegal, Creates a Life of Her Own
Current Position: Paralegal at Litvin, Blumberg, Matusow & Young

Beth Agre grew up in Philadelphia, Pennsylvania. When she entered Penn State in the fall of 1969 she knew what she wanted to study—English and education—because Beth also knew what she wanted to do after college: She wanted to teach. She graduated with her English and Education major, but even the best laid plans can run smack into history. In this case it was the end of the Vietnam War. No one anticipated the effect that event would have on teaching jobs. Suddenly lots of veterans were coming home, earning credentials themselves, and flooding the teaching market. Full-time teaching jobs were hard to come by. Beth found herself substituting, but that was not what she had in mind. She moved to California hoping to find more teaching opportunities, but the situation there was the same as in the East.

Beth headed straight to the library for a research session. What Agre wanted to know was what other jobs were available to English majors; guess what was on the list? Lawyer. Beth knew that lawyers worked in offices, a setting she'd never experienced and one she was not sure she'd like. She decided she should take a field trip and do some real-life research into how she might like law office life before she went to law school.

Real-World Research

One thing you notice right away when talking to Beth Agre is that she's as straightforward as they come. Her post-library visit to an employment agency was no exception. She told them she had no office experience and no real office skills, but that she wanted to see what office life, and specifically law office life, was like. The agency sent her off to interview for a word processing editor position at Security Pacific Bank in San Francisco. That position seemed all wrong, so she was sent to the legal department to see if she could fill a need there.

The vice president who interviewed her told Beth he could tell she didn't really want to be a legal secretary but that they'd "find something" for her to do. That was an auspicious beginning. The legal world has continued to find things for Agre to do for twenty years. She's a career paralegal who has created a dynamic and diverse working life. Because she's a self-directed, independent thinker, she even found a way to incorporate her love of teaching into her paralegal practice.

Agre was fortunate at Security Pacific. Her boss was a teacher at heart and a paralegal position opened up a after a short time. Her boss became the kind of mentor that paralegals thrive on, encouraging her to become a paralegal, encouraging her independence, and pushing her out from behind a desk into the law library. He also taught her that lawyers are "just people" and that she would do well to approach them as coworkers, not as miniature gods. Agre took this advice and says it has helped her establish rapport with attorneys and others in law offices through the years.

Security Pacific was a good working environment for Beth, even supporting her further education by paying for courses in San Francisco State's paralegal education program. However, Agre found that the education she'd gotten on the job had already prepared her to tackle the paralegal job market; she left the SF program without a certificate. Although Beth liked her coworkers at Security Pacific, she decided the banking industry simply did not pay well enough. After four years she knew she was qualified to look for new challenges. She moved on.

Agre's first stab at a new spot was with a multinational corporation. She reports that the work there was fascinating but the atmosphere was oppressive. She wanted a job at which the people and the work were congenial. Unwilling to settle for half of what she wanted, she decided to give a traditional law firm a try. Like other topnotch paralegals, Beth had kept the names and numbers of useful contacts from her former jobs. She got in touch with Broad, Schulz, Larson & Wineberg, a firm she knew from her Security Pacific days, and soon was a member of their team. Beth loved the people and the environment at Broad Schulz enough to stay for three years, but eventually she found the work itself too limiting. She was still searching for the perfect fit.

Those Who Can Do, Teach Too

Remember Agre's teaching dream? She remembered it too. In 1983 she decided that paralegal education might offer a venue for her teaching skills. Like the other paralegals interviewed here, a key element in Agre's success is initiative. When she was ready to try teaching, Beth wrote a letter and enclosed not only her resume but also a detailed course proposal to Sonoma State's Attorney Assistant Program. It must have been an impressive package because she was soon teaching legal research and writing in the program. She has continued to teach—and love it—for fourteen years.

Persistence Carries the Day

Teaching was not a full-time job, so Agre's "regular" paralegal life continued. Although she didn't know it, she was about to find the job she'd been looking for—good folks and great work. Agre read that Memel, Jacobs, Pierno & Gersh, a national firm, was opening a San Francisco office. They planned to open their SF operation with one attorney, one paralegal, and one secretary. This is where Agre's persistence in finding what she really wanted paid off. She jumped into the paralegal spot and took off like a rocket. The San Francisco office of Memel Jacobs focused on bank defense. Agre was responsible for about 150 such cases at a time, handling the base camp client contact, research, and writing while the attorney flew around the state for court appearances and depositions.

Agre was happy and satisfied with both the work and the people at this job. Unfortunately, the Memel Jacobs partners were not all happy with each other. In 1987, just a few years after finding this dream spot, Agre faced the situation paralegals dread. The firm blew up, and Agre's dream job was destroyed in the crossfire. Beth landed on her feet, this time as an independent contractor with Fireman's Fund Insurance. At Fireman's she was involved in a class action matter that was in the process of settling (Fireman's was settling and pursuing damages against other parties in subrogation actions). The experience was great. Beth worked for an hourly fee plus expenses, but she had office space and some office support. She had responsibility and autonomy, and this project foreshadowed Agre's later leap into independence.

In 1988 Agre relocated to Sonoma County. She took a job with the litigation firm of Senneff, Bernheim, Emery and Kelly. She worked there, productively and happily, until 1992 when once again a partner separation created the need for change. Agre decided she was tired of having her job dictated by the vicissitudes of lawyer partnerships. She decided to strike out on her own.

Like successful entrepreneurs before her, Agre wrote to everyone she'd ever met in the business, letting them know she was available for contract work. It was not long before her contracting paralegal plate was full, a little overfull perhaps, and she was earning more and enjoying more autonomy than she ever had as a law firm or corporate employee. Agre visited her client lawyers to pick up the work, then returned to either her home or office to work uninterrupted! You can see the appeal.

Good Paralegals Are Always in Demand

A good paralegal is always in demand in some law office or other. It wasn't long before Agre got a call from a Santa Rosa lawyer with an offer she had to consider. They met to talk and the straight-shooting Agre started out by letting the partners know just how independent she'd become. She said she just wanted to work, "with no one bugging me." They said, "We won't bug you" and they kept their word. That was a happy arrangement, but change seems always in the offing for Agre. This time it was a change of heart—an old friendship evolved into a strong romance.

The Freedom to Follow Your Heart

That romance took Agre back to Philadelphia, where you won't be surprised to hear she found employment right away. Agre is working as a paralegal and continues to teach. She has this advice for paralegals just entering the field: Maintain a flexible attitude, a willingness to learn, and most of all, a sense of humor. None of us can say exactly why a sense of humor is so critical in this business, but many outstanding paralegals will tell you that it's crucial to success. Maybe it provides a perspective from which to view life in the legal world as part of life in our larger world. Beth's work life, her personal and professional success, also communicate something. They demonstrate the wisdom not only of being flexible, but of looking for new opportunities and holding out for what you really want. Beth could have stuck it out at several jobs that met some of her "great job" criteria, but she kept looking for the situation that provided both good working conditions and great coworkers, as well as interesting, stimulating work and the autonomy to get it done. There seems to be one constant in Agre's career strategy: She's always willing to try something new if it looks as if it might make things better.

22

SPECIAL PERFORMANCES AND DEVELOPING YOUR OWN AREA OF EXPERTISE

Before you can take off and build your superstar career, you need rock-solid job security. Of course, nothing's totally secure in this world, but to the extent that any of us can feel secure in our work or in our jobs, you want that. It will give you a solid base from which to grow, to launch new ideas, and to develop ever more interesting versions of your professional self.

One of the surest ways to obtain this kind of job security is to develop an expertise that provides you an area of responsibility within your firm's practice. This is a set of tasks that are crucial to the firm, that must be done, and that you can do flawlessly. This area will be your professional turf. You and your employer will expect that you are the firm's professional in charge of getting this critical work done.

This chapter contains examples of areas of expertise that are useful to law firms and accessible to you. If none of them fits into your firm's practice, look to the underlying principles that produced them. You will find a way to apply those principles to your firm's practice and carve out an area of professional responsibility that will serve as the base from which your career can grow.

CLIENT LIAISON

A client liaison is the person responsible for managing the firm's work for a particular client. Clients requiring liaisons are usually large clients requiring a lot of legal advice. They generate substantial amounts of work and therefore are financially significant to the firm. If you become the person who knows that client (meaning the client's staff) well, who understands the client's goals, budget constraints, political constraints, philosophies, etc., you will find that you have become quite valuable to your employer. How do you get this kind of spot? What do you do once you have it?

A client liaison position is usually assigned by the attorney responsible for the client. Even if many attorneys in a firm work on one client's matters (and that's usually the case), there is one attorney who has special responsibility for that client and the firm's work for it. It may be the attorney who brought in the client or it may be the attorney who has the greatest expertise in the kind of work the client requires. In any case, if your firm has a large client for which it does a fair amount of work, it should not be that hard to find out which attorney is in charge of the client's work. That's the person you must see about becoming the liaison.

Getting the client liaison assignment requires an in-house interview. You need to convince the right person or persons that you should be trusted as the firm's connection for this important client. The key to success is preparation. Before you talk to the person in charge of the client, do some background research. Take notes on salient facts about the client—the size of the company, the work the client does, the kinds of legal work it needs done, and the fees generated for the firm in a year. Talk to the people who work on this client's matters. See what they think about the client and about how your firm's service to the client can be improved. What you are doing is imagining the role you could play that will increase the firm's ability to serve this client.

When you talk to the attorney in charge of the client, go armed with this information. If your firm does not already assign paralegals liaison duties, you may have to begin by selling the concept. Provide examples of what you could do, for instance tracking work assignments, contacting associates when their assignments are late, arranging for the prompt delivery of finished work, responding to routine staff inquiries about the status of assignments, answering client questions on bills, etc. These administrative duties are anathema to most attorneys. They are often anathema to paralegals too, but if you can show that you will handle them cheerfully and well, you will get the job. Later on you can expand your functions.

It takes a lot of tracking and related administrative follow-up to organize the work firms do for large clients. If the client is a public agency or sizable corporation, the work flow will be further complicated by the fact that several individuals at the client's office may generate work requests and that the work schedule will have to be coordinated with client-scheduled board meetings. These clients and the lawyers who work for them need a point person who tracks work, communicates policies, watches for hot issues, and generally makes sure that all the client's work is done promptly and well and that any special requirements of the client are met.

Client liaisons usually work closely with the attorney who is in charge of the client account, reporting on work assignments, communicating reminders to associates who may have back-burnered an assignment because they got too busy, coordinating the efforts of lawyers so that duplication doesn't occur, generally assessing the client's needs and determining how the firm will meet those needs. This provides a further opportunity for you—the chance to develop a close working relationship with the attorney in charge and to understand better the way the firm works.

The client liaison usually works closely with the client's staff also, checking in to be sure the client is being kept informed of the status of assignments, learning something about the client's long-term goals and budgets, perhaps assisting with reports to the client's board or governing body, meeting with departmental staff to plan ahead to meet future legal needs, and the like.

This is a particularly fun part of the job. It will take you out of the office to where your client lives—where the work goes. You will get to meet the people behind the voices on the telephone and will get an understanding of the client's point of view. It's also an opportunity to learn the art of combining social and business occasions. Taking a client to lunch is an art. In this job you will get the chance to perfect it.

There is a great deal of artful badgering involved in being the client liaison. You will need to know what's going on with the various assignments and when the attorneys and paralegals doing the work think they can get it done. You will need to communicate all that to the attorney who is responsible for the client, and you will have to communicate to the worker bees the time schedules that must be met.

You will also have to communicate the "why" behind many assignments. It is usually very helpful to an attorney drafting an ordinance or contract to have a clear idea of what exactly the document being drafted is supposed to accomplish, but unless someone has a special responsibility to be sure everyone's clear, misunderstandings can and often do occur. The liaison's job includes minimizing those misunderstandings, which will eliminate wasted effort and wasted money.

All that reminding, organizing, and keeping track of things requires a sense of humor, a strong sense of when things are critical and when they are not, and a willingness to keep notes, lists, and charts to keep you and everybody else straight on what's going on. It also means you will spend time on the phone with staffers at the client's office and time roaming the halls of your own office gently reminding lawyers and paralegals that in our business the clock is always running. It takes tact, tenacity, and the ability to find new avenues to get the work done when the normal path develops a snag.

In addition to all this, the critical thing you will need as a client liaison is good judgment. You will need to know when to handle something yourself and when to contact the lead attorney immediately. You may need to know how to deal with the press. You will certainly need to know how to handle very confidential and sensitive matters.

What does this kind of work have to offer the list-keeper, the ego-soother, the emergency technician, and den mother? It offers the chance to see how legal services are provided in a real-world setting, outside the courtroom so to speak. Coming up with a code enforcement program and accompanying local legislation that will satisfy five city council members, a city manager, staff, and the city's residents is no easy task. The perspectives of many groups and many individuals will have to be reviewed. Compromises will have to be negotiated. Tangential issues have to be addressed and serious social issues that are in some way related, like drug enforcement policies, also have to be integrated into the final work product. Orchestrating the mechanics of such a process is no easy task. Doing so in a way that includes all the players and facilitates real communication is a major undertaking.

If you take on this kind of work and keep your eyes and ears open, you will learn a lot quickly. You will develop professional poise and maturity. Finally, this service is worth a great deal to your firm. If you can successfully manage the work flow for a major client, with all the finesse and expertise required, your contribution will be appreciated. Consider this position as a possible area of responsibility for you.

PUBLIC LAW SPECIALIST

Some public law specialists are client liaisons too. They work for law firms that work as contract (outside) counsel to public entities. Other public law paralegals work in-house for public entities, for example in the city attorney's department of a city government or for county counsel. In either case the paralegal must become adept at working with public employees, handling contact with the public, and assisting governmental boards and their employees in legislative and other matters.

Public law paralegals often handle the processing of claims made against a public agency. There are statutes in various jurisdictions governing the processing of such claims, but generally a public law paralegal can expect to log claims, review claims for completeness, initiate a factual investigation, draft related correspondence and reports to the manager or governing body, draft rejections as needed, calendar claims to watch for resulting litigation, and work with staff to make sure the entity adopts all possible protections from claims.

This work often leads into assisting the entity's risk management office with an assessment of particular and aggregate potential liability. The paralegal often drafts confidential reports to management and the governing body, as well as working with those responsible for budgeting these matters.

Preparing closed-session memoranda regarding pending or potential litigation is another aspect of this job slot. Confidentiality is extremely important and the paralegal is often responsible for retrieving copies of these memoranda to ensure that leaks do not occur. This requires tact and tenacity. The paralegal usually works with the clerk's office to make sure such confidential material does not become public, while ensuring that required records are kept.

Public law paralegals become expert at reviewing requests by the public for information. The inadvertent release of material that is exempt from disclosure may be deemed a waiver of the exempt status of a document. This is serious business.

Many public law paralegals work with law enforcement agencies on such matters as hearings regarding gun confiscations or complaints by citizens of disturbances. They also work with code enforcement personnel to see that the entity's governing codes (building, health and safety, etc.) are enforced. Public law paralegals also become familiar with environmental requirements affecting their clients and are often involved in drafting environmental guidelines and policies.

This job also involves knowledge of personnel law. Public law paralegals often work with agency staff to review requests for personnel files and to draft and distribute policies to agency employees. Staff education is a rewarding part of the job, as is the development of procedures that prevent lawsuits and other problems for the client. Each year the federal government passes legislation affecting local governments, for example, drug and alcohol testing procedures. These laws must be integrated into the life of a local government, and the paralegal can play a major part in making sure the agency is in compliance.

A public law paralegal who has litigation training may be involved in defending the agency when it is sued or assisting it when it exercises its power of eminent domain. A paralegal who has contract expertise will be useful in helping an agency draft, negotiate, and manage its many contracts.

The chief joy in becoming a specialist in this area is the exposure you get to how human beings have organized their community lives to promote shared interests and benefit and protect individuals. As you are aware, incredibly difficult issues arise whenever groups of people must work together. This job gives you a chance to learn firsthand how those difficulties can be addressed. It's exciting to see how your work as a legal professional actually has an impact on the lives of people in towns and counties and states across America. If you like variety in your work and a chance to participate in the life of the community, consider this specialty.

AUDIT LETTER SPECIALIST

Another area of expertise and responsibility that you may wish to develop is that of audit letter preparation. Audit letters are letters prepared by law firms in response to requests from clients and their auditors that provide information about the client's legal affairs that are relevant to an audit of its financial status.

This article first appeared in *Legal Assistant Today* (March/April 1996, vol. 13, no. 4).

Learning to write audit letters is like getting a flu shot. The inoculation process isn't exactly a barrel of laughs, but when everyone else is dying in the trenches (or in this case, committing malpractice), you're glad you took one. So be brave and read on.

Many of your firm's clients undergo audits of their financial records each year. These are important events that actually affect whether the clients stay in business. Let's say a business is in generally good financial shape, but is facing a potential judgment that would wipe out all cash reserves. When a company is undergoing an audit, a good faith audit must take that potential judgment into account.

Therefore, someone at your law firm is writing audit letters—letters that respond to requests for the release of information about a client's loss contingencies (potential financial losses; defined further below). If you don't draft audit letters, you are probably responding to in-house surveys that provide the information that goes into them. If you do write these valuable letters, you have discovered that they are a good bread-and-butter sideline for paralegals. Learn to do them well and you provide a valuable service to clients, strengthen your own position in the firm, and scare a lot of folks who don't have a clue what audit letters are.

Audit letters present a significant opportunity for malpractice. The release of information to a third party (the auditor) may result in a claim of waiver of attorney–client privilege. If the letter falls into the wrong hands, information disclosed may even be held to be an admission by your client. In order to respond to requests for loss contingency information, the request must come from the client—not the auditor—and be signed by someone who is authorized to direct you to release information that would otherwise be privileged.

Naturally, the line separating appropriate disclosure of information and violation of a client's privilege is very fine. It s so fine that in the mid-1970s that line became the subject of policy statements from both the American Bar Association (ABA) and the American Institute of Certified Public Accountants (AICPA). These statements, collectively referred to as the "Treaty," outline the respective duties of attorneys and accountants in the auditing process. The Treaty's guidelines are accepted by both professional groups, and language from the ABA's Statement of Policy regarding Lawyer's Responses to Auditor's Requests for Information is often incorporated into the body of audit letters (which is where most of the cumbersome language comes in).

With such high-stakes odds, why do I recommend learning to write these things?

1.   Never underestimate the wisdom of a sideline specialty. Requests for audit letters come in all year. They are there to keep your hours strong when your big case settles.

2.   They're a real service to the firm's clients. Audits and audit letters must be completed and must be done correctly, by someone with know-how.

3.   You'll learn more about your client's business concerns by writing these letters, and if you're smart you'll take time to think through issues of privilege and due diligence.

In this chapter I cannot give you all the information you need to meet disclosure obligations without violating professional confidences. What I can do is alert you to critical issues and terms of art.

Before you produce your first audit letter, educate yourself with source material provided by the ABA. See the *Auditor's Letter Handbook*, available for $10 from the ABA, 750 North Lake Shore Drive, Chicago, IL 60611 (312) 988-5000 (refer to publication 507-0014).

When writing audit letters it is impossible to write in plain English and avoid legalese. This is contrary to most current legal writing advice, but the fact remains that no one can recommend short, direct sentences for audit letters because the ABA and the AICPA have agreed on language that fixes the parameters of important aspects of audit letters. The language is difficult and cumbersome, but you must use it if you are to protect both the client and the firm. Your job, your challenge as a writer of audit letters, is to untangle these unwieldy sentences so that they make sense in your own head. (If you don't, their convoluted verbosity will lull you into a false sense of security.)

For example, audit letters ask for information about loss contingencies, a term that has been defined by the accounting profession as "...an existing condition, situation or set of circumstances involving uncertainty as to possible loss to an enterprise that will ultimately be resolved when one or more events occur or fail to occur. Resolution of the uncertainty may confirm the loss or impairment of an asset or the incurrence of a liability." Phrases like these are typical of the little devils you deal with when writing audit letters.

You also must compile information for your response. Gathering the information from all the attorneys and paralegals in your firm who may know about matters that should be disclosed in an audit letter is both an art and a science. This is the due diligence process, and methods differ according to the size of the firm and the amount of work undertaken for a particular client. Larger firms use E-mail, paper surveys, oral inquiries, and reviews of billings; smaller firms may use less formal methods. However it is done, once the facts have been gathered and the letter writing commences, you must remain alert to the implications of each phrase of the request you are responding to—and that's easier said than done.

These steps should help you through the audit letter process:

1. *Read the request carefully.* They can all look a lot alike, but depending on the sophistication of your client they will differ. As mentioned previously, the letter must come from the client, not the auditor, and be signed by someone authorized to direct you to release information that would otherwise be privileged. If you're not sure the individual who signed the letter can authorize the release of information, check with the responsible attorney.

2. *Check dates first.* Good requests give dates that govern what you disclose. For example, a client request may read, "Our auditors are engaged in a review of our financial statements at June 30, 1996 and for the fiscal year then ended. Your response should include matters that existed at that date and up to the date of your response." What this means is that if your response goes out on September 29, 1996, matters that fit the rest of the limiting parameters of the request and existed on June 30, 1996 or at any time up to and including September 29, 1996 must be reviewed for possible disclosure. Keep in mind the date the client wants the letter to go to the auditor. You will not endear yourself to the client or your boss if you delay the successful completion of an audit.

3. *Specify materiality parameters.* Good requests specify materiality parameters. For example, "For the purpose of your response assume claims in excess of $15,000 individually or in the aggregate are material." This means that information on claims totaling less than $15,000 individually or in the aggregate need not be disclosed in your response. However, when you gather information from the attorney and paralegals in your firm you must get everything out there. You cannot assess aggregate potential liability unless you know the whole story, and since outcomes in litigation are notoriously unpredictable you do not want to fail to disclose something that later turns out to create a loss in excess of the audit letter's parameters. Auditors and attorneys have agreed that litigation is so unpredictable that there are very few cases in which a negative outcome can responsibly be labeled "probable" or "remote" (both terms of art, so see the *Auditor's Letter Handbook*). Usually attorneys conclude that "it is premature to predict the likelihood of an unfavorable outcome," and usually they are right. As mentioned earlier, the release of information to a third party (the auditor) may result in a claim of waiver of attorney–client privilege.

4. *Know what to disclose.* Disclose pending litigation or claims. The standard request letter does not, in and of itself, authorize you to release confidential information. The Treaty requires that the client be fully informed of the legal consequences of the release of information held in confidence prior to the disclosure. When information that is not a matter of record must be disclosed, many attorneys prefer to send a draft of the letter to the client before releasing it to the auditor. This allows for full discussion of the consequences of making the disclosure. As a general rule, include only the case name and number and a short description of the contentions of the parties. This will duplicate information contained in the pleadings, which are public records. If the auditor feels unsatisfied with the information provided, rest assured you will hear about it. The disclosure of further information can be discussed then.

5. *Check for unasserted claims.* Many request letters ask for disclosure of "unasserted claims probable of assertion." The decision to disclose unasserted claims is the client's. If you or someone else in your firm thinks there is an unasserted matter that should be disclosed, take it up immediately with the attorney who will sign and be responsible for the letter. That attorney will decide whether this must be discussed with the client.

Most request letters seek confirmation of the fact that when the attorney "forms a professional conclusion" that there is an unasserted claim requiring disclosure, the attorney will consult with the client in that regard. The language confirming this understanding is straight out of the ABA *Auditor's Letter Handbook* and is conveyed in a 113-word sentence. This is an important confirmation for your client's purpose—obtaining an audit that is issued without reservation by the auditors.

If the attorney and the client finally disagree about the disclosure of an unasserted claim, the attorney may be forced to resign representation. Attorneys may not abet clients in frustrating the purposes of the audit.

6. *Include limitations.* Be sure to include the *Auditor's Letter Handbook* language limiting your firm's exposure. This will include:

- that your firm's representation of the client is limited to certain matters;
- that you have made no independent review of the client's affairs;
- that you have endeavored to find out from the attorneys currently with your firm whether they are aware of disclosable matters;
- that all the limitations set out in the ABA Statement of Policy regarding Lawyers' Responses to Auditors' Requests for Information (Dec. 1975) apply (if they do);
- that the information is as of the date of the letter (be sure to disclaim any undertaking to report later changes);
- that the information provided is intended for audit purposes and may not be provided to others without notice, a court order, or to defend a challenge of the audit by the client;
- that the client does not intend to waive any applicable privileges; and
- that the firm does not intend to waive attorney work product or other privileges with regard to these matters or any other matters regarding the client.

Sound scary? If not, I haven't done my job. The audit letter process is complicated and filled with opportunities for malpractice. Failure in due diligence, the release of unauthorized information, or the failure to counsel the client on the legal consequences of disclosing particular matters just begin the list of potential problems.

Some auditors are more concerned with meeting their deadlines than with helping you serve the client. They often have clients sign requests for audit responses as much as a year in advance, then house those letters in their own files and mail them to attorneys in client envelopes a year later. Occasionally the person who signed the letter has moved on, or worse, been fired.

Because the letters look similar from year to year it's easy for the client, or even your boss, to forget they require careful attention that translates into hours—and a bill for the client. You cannot let the client's idea that this is a boilerplate item dilute your diligence.

Remember, the benefits are worthwhile and the process is occasionally fun. Finding your way through the maze of professional obligations presented by these letters is a challenge. And paralegals like that, remember?

THE LITIGATION SPECIALIST

Litigation is the old standby. No matter what else changes in this world, people keep generating disputes that have to be settled, insuring that this is one area of practice that never really fades away. Paralegal litigation specialists have historically always been in demand, because a litigation practice is filled with important jobs that attorneys hate to handle and that legal assistants handle particularly well.

Everyone who has worked a case knows what I'm talking about. Discovery, the heart of a lawsuit, involves hours of sifting through documents—both your client's and the opponent's—to sort out what happened and what can be proved. This task has both a clerical and a high-tech thinking aspect to it. The documents must be physically organized; data must be collected, organized, analyzed, and stored; timelines must be made; and often certified copies must be obtained for use in court.

Before you even get to court, witnesses must be interviewed and opponents must be deposed, all of which requires a review of the case and the paper it is based on so the attorneys who will ask all the questions know what on earth to ask about.

Sound interesting? It is. It's also fun and a good area of responsibility with room for incredible professional growth. The following articles detail two different aspects of the litigation specialist job. Take a look at them to see if this might be the area you want to work in.

This article first appeared in *Legal Assistant Today* magazine (May/June 1998, vol. 15, no. 5).

Taking the Show on the Road

Stay in the business long enough and it will happen to you—opposing counsel makes a motion for change of venue and wins. With the stroke of a judge's pen, you no longer have the home court advantage.

Fair? Maybe not, but who said litigation was fair. Litigation's not about being fair; it's a small war. Given the risk, the expense, and the anxiety the client faces—given everything that argues against taking a case into a courtroom—if a matter gets to trial it's a serious fight. Only fools think they can afford to go in unprepared.

How do you prepare to try a case in a distant city? What do you have to think about? How is the paralegal's trial support role affected?

When you try a case in a new and distant venue the paralegal's role is expanded exponentially. While the trial lawyer's mind is on a myriad of specific matters—everything from expert depositions to the closing argument—the paralegal must keep an eye on the big picture and take care of the smallest detail. There's more to think about, less room for error, fewer alternatives in getting the jobs done, no established rapport with local court personnel, no network of home-team secretaries, runners, copiers, and proofreaders, and often a command center that looks a whole lot like a hotel room.

It can be an exciting time, a challenge to your resourcefulness and a change of pace that spices up the year, but everything depends on how prepared you are going in. How prepared do you have to be? Very, very prepared.

What You'll Need to Win the Distant Venue Trial

A Committed Team. The team will have to be set early on. You and the client need to know who will try the case, who will sit second chair, and who will back them up. This is usually a partner-associate-paralegal team. The case team should remain fixed for a number of reasons.

The more experience any one person has in a new court and a new town, the greater the comfort level will be. This will improve performances at trial time. The same lawyer who argues motions before the unfamiliar judge should also try the case. Few judges are pleased with changes in attorney personnel and some even have local rules requiring a particular attorney to take responsibility for trying the case early on. You're ahead of the game when you anticipate this attitude and make the hard decision that once someone is assigned to the case he or she's on the team until the case is resolved.

The team has to be ready to pack up and go when you get a start date. That means colleagues, clients, and your family all have to be ready to wave a cheerful goodbye when distant justice calls. This fact often has a great deal to do with deciding who should be on the team in the first place. If you're assigned to work on a case that will be tried out of town, take the assignment seriously. If you have family obligations that make it impossible for you to commit to carrying the case through to completion, tell the powers that be right away. Do not get on board with the idea that the case will probably settle just before trial and that consequently you won't really have to leave your five-year-old during her first week of kindergarten. Cases do go to trial. You must be prepared to take the case all the way.

The team members must work well together. Chances are they will not only be living inside each other's heads during the weeks before trial, they will also be living in close quarters while it's in session. All will be doing their parts under less than optimum circumstances. Remember, all trial preparation is demanding. People get cranky and tempers can flare. The pressures that cause this will be exaggerated when trying a case on unfamiliar terrain. Trial team members will need to know each other well. They should have tried a case together before. That way even if the judge's expectations are new and confusing, the attorneys' won't be.

Support during the actual trial will be totally different when you are far from the home office. Library access and access to secretarial support, printers, computers, copiers, exhibit boards, banking, supplies, food, coffee, parking, and phones will all be new or nonexistent.

Imagine this: You're up late one night putting together a last-minute motion that includes six exhibits. Will you be able to find extra exhibit tabs? When you need to find a particular case in half an hour, will you be familiar enough with the courthouse law library to do it, and have time to photocopy it for the judge? Do you know where you can find a copy machine in the courthouse you can use? How many copies of each document does the judge require? Is there an ELMO machine or an overhead projector in the courtroom? Do the bathrooms require change for the doors?

It's impossible to predict everything that will come up. For instance, an attorney can fly to another state to try a case and forget to bring any shoes for court. In fact, this has actually happened. Did the paralegal have to find a place to buy new shoes at 8 p.m.? You betcha!

When you're out of town the trial team needs to think everything through much sooner than in a local case. This includes the order in which you present your case. Which witnesses will you need? What order will you put them on in? How will you contact them? When will they come? Where will they stay? What kind of leeway will the judge give you in producing them?

You must investigate the travel possibilities. Can you drive and pack the cars full of trial boxes? If your most important witness flies in, will she be stuck in freeway traffic and not make it to court after all? Do any of your witnesses refuse to fly? If you need to dry clean a suit overnight, where can you do it? You may need to rent a van to carry large exhibits. You will have to figure out where you'll stay. Find out all the details—how much will it cost, what the checkout times are. Talk to your attorney to find out if you must clear the costs with the client before you make the reservations. Don't forget to find out what the motel's cancellation policies are.

Think about the time of year your trial is set for. What kind of a jury pool are you likely to get in this locale? Will holidays intervene? Do cases go out quickly in this county? Is your opponent well-known, liked, or disliked there? Is there an active criminal calendar that takes priority over civil matters? Does your judge usually go fishing for two weeks every August? Will you have to transport all your materials through rain or snow?

Although you won't be able to nail all this down, you need to think of as many of these things as possible in advance. If you wait until you get there it may be too late to make adjustments to your case or to mitigate difficulties. Making an effort to find out what your attorneys, your client, and your witnesses can expect will go a long way toward smoothing things along later when the inevitable changes occur.

Lots of Pretrial Contact. When it comes to getting things done easily—or at all—cordial relationships still count for a lot. The more people you are on good terms with in your distant venue, the better. It costs money to accomplish this, but if a case is worth trying out of town it's worth the investment of pretrial visits.

Contact a good legal secretarial service and investigate the options for using their services. Check the Yellow Pages and the local legal directories, or call the local bar association office. They may have a roster of available services. There are legal secretarial services that contract on an hourly basis and a good one can be a lifesaver when the unexpected occurs. These services are also often excellent sources for other information about your new locale. They've been around. They know the ropes. Learn from them.

You'll need some kind of office space. Find out if the hotel or motel you're using has office suites. You may need to rent an office near the courthouse. Be sure you have enough phone lines to allow for phone calls to be made while someone else is hooked up to the home office via modem. Make sure there's enough power for a portable copying machine, fax machine, or other equipment you bring from home. Check the lighting, especially if you're using a hotel suite. You don't want mood lighting to get ready for trial. Either visit the local office supply store and buy some lamps or bring them with you.

You need enough space to house boxes of stuff. Every night you will have to take home whatever you need to prepare for the next day of trial, plus whatever you don't want anyone else looking at while you're not there and whatever the judge doesn't want propped up against the walls of the courtroom. Many judges are quite particular about this. Your goal is to comply amiably with every court order. Large exhibits are always a hassle, but they are still part of most trial presentations. Make sure your vehicles and your office space will accommodate them.

You need desks, or at least tables. It is no fun to try to work with files and computers on motel beds. You can live without bookshelves, but a cheap set from a supply or import store is often worthwhile, because pawing through piles of reference books stacked all over the floor gets in the way of everybody's concentration.

Library access is critical. Sometimes you can find friendly counsel in another county who will open their library to you. I've found firms who will provide library access for a fee as well. Some courthouse law libraries are sufficient to augment what you bring from home, but you have to check the hours carefully. Think about what will happen if you need a book at 2 a.m. If there's a law school in the area, that may solve your problem. They're usually good, and they stay open on weekends and at night. In the age of the Internet we can all find a lot of law with our computers, but a library is still mandatory. Be sure to find one.

You need to master a hundred mundane details about the local geography. Find out where you can blow up an exhibit in half an hour, grab an espresso, call your kids, park your car, eat a nutritious breakfast, or discuss the case calmly and confidentially with the attorney or the client. You need to know where the pay phones are, where the local bookstores are, and where the ATM machines are located. These may seem like routine peripheral matters but they can take center stage when you're late for court in "the city of a hundred one-way streets" and there's no parking lot in sight. Don't forget to locate the local emergency room.

Don't underestimate the positive effect of small comforts. I've seen trial teams eat lunch—the same lunch—in the same restaurant every day for a week during a trial. Why would they do such a boring thing? Because while they're in trial their lives are already exciting enough. They have to be on their toes and ready for a big surprise the entire time they are in court. They have to try to read the jury, read the judge, and maintain cordiality with the court reporter, the bailiff, the clerk, and opposing counsel. Sometimes the same waitress bringing the same chicken salad for a few days running is all the routine they are going to get. They enjoy the nod of recognition they get walking through the door, the fact that the bathroom is easy to find, and that they can call their significant others without standing in line. One of your jobs supporting a trial team is making their home-away-from-home as pleasant as possible; that might well include finding a comfortable restaurant.

It's absolutely critical that you have firsthand experience at filing documents, paying fees, and talking to the bailiff, the judge's clerk and secretary, the court reporter, the law librarian, and the janitor. You don't want to find out while you are complying with the judge's explicit order to "file documents by 10 a.m." that the clerk usually heads out for a cigarette at 9:50. You don't want to turn in an exhibit book for the judge only to hear the clerk say, "Judge Foster likes all the tabs at the bottom of the book." While we all know court personnel are not in the business of pulling for one side or the other during a trial, it doesn't hurt if they like you. There's a better chance of that if you invest some time up front in finding out who they are and what their habits are. Don't stand on procedures and rules with these folks if you don't have to. If you can comply easily with their preferences, for heaven's sake do so.

You and your attorneys must all see the courtroom. Is there an overhead projector, an ELMO, a chalkboard, a flip chart? Does plaintiff or defendant sit closest to the jury? Who can see the jury members' faces most easily (and inconspicuously) during trial? Where will the exhibits be stacked or stored when not in use? Does the courtroom look formal or informal? Are there windows that will cast a glare on your witnesses or distract the jury?

You need both the local and the local local rules. Since the local locals are not all written down, you'll need to investigate. Does the judge want an exhibit notebook? Does she have a trial management order requiring joint submissions? Do you need an extra cover sheet on everything you file? How much does he hate it if you're late? Must exhibits be prenumbered? Is she prejudiced against out-of-town counsel? Is he pro-defense or pro-plaintiff? Does she like or hate governmental agencies? Where did he go to school? What kind of practice did she have? Can you get on good enough terms with any local attorneys to find out more? Does he have a lot of experience with this area of law or not?

Global Packing. This may seem like a funny topic, but don't laugh too hard. You have to think of everything.

When you pack, make a packing list for every team member, including the secretaries back home. This is not to help them; it's to help you. They can review it. They can tell you what you have forgotten—and you *will* forget something.

Most trial paralegals will tell you that they have total responsibility for the documents when they go to trial. The attorney expects that when he or she says, "I need the original motion to exclude testimony to file this morning, and three copies," you will be able to produce them before the elevator comes. As important as that is at home, it is critically important when the show's on the road. There's no way you can "run it over" in a few minutes. There's no room for error here.

Create a special box or folder that contains all your important original exhibit documents, things like the original contract or the certified notice of pendency of action or the original copy of the smoking gun. This box will never leave your thoughts and rarely leave your side. Get used to it. Feel naked without it. This box contains the heart of your client's case. You have been entrusted with its safekeeping. Guard it well.

You need boxes that will serve as file drawers for all your pleadings and for discovery materials. Pack everything you've already exchanged or filed and your yet-to-be-filed motions in limine, witness list, exhibit list, requested jury instructions, voir dire, joint filings, trial briefs, statements of the case, objections to the other side's exhibits, etc. Include boxes for your experts' files and for your files on their experts, for your witness files, for issues files, and for any other case management format you and your trial team use.

Pack multiple copies of all the depositions. You need boxes that are big enough to house three-ring binders for trial notebooks, notebooks for the judge, small-size versions of large exhibits, and documents you will provide to the other side during trial. I've found it helpful to make more copies than the attorneys I work with request. They are thinking about their openings, their exams, and their arguments. They can't think about all the logistical and practical matters too. You do that. Err on the side of having too many copies.

Don't forget, most attorneys have some books they don't go to trial without. They are personal volumes and they are tabbed and stickered. They will be useful and a major source of efficiency and comfort when you're out of town. Bring multiple copies of the judicial profile on your judge, the local rules, and any other rules or trial management orders that may apply. Bring any of your own books that you may conceivably need. There may be volumes your attorney wants to borrow from your firm's library too. Find out.

Include boxes to house office supplies: extra blue backs, yellow pads, felt-tip pens, regular pens, pencils, tape, staplers, staples, scissors, large paper clips, small paper clips, folders, binders, clips, red rope file buckets, transparencies, exhibit tabs (the court's and yours), three-hole punches, two-hole punches, staple remover, glue sticks, blue pens, black pens, pleading paper, typing paper. Whatever you might run to the supply room for at home, you need with you. Don't forget supplies you would take for granted at home—tissues, sewing supplies, Band-Aids, antacids, headache medicine, vitamins, cold and flu medicine. You need a roll of quarters and although some people consider them optional, I always take candy bars.

It's your job to be sure the communication lines are in place. Every firm has its own mechanisms. Be sure you know all your options. Does everyone have a calling card? Are there firm cell phones you should use?

Pack extra surge protectors, floppy disks, batteries, and modems for the laptops. Don't forget the manuals. You need the books (manuals) for your computers as well as for the word processing and other software you use. Critically important is a list with phone numbers for your computer support people.

Are you settled on where you will stay while you're there? We've touched on this under the office issue, but be sure you investigate all the possibilities and get clear authorization from the attorney heading the team. Get commitments from the hotel and your client concerning the final arrangements. Decide how you will get from hotel to court each day. Find out if you will come home on the weekends or work there.

Make sure everyone packs what they need for personal health, including medications (especially what they like for handling colds and their hayfever drugs) and extra eyeglasses. Do not assume the attorneys you work for will think of this. If they wear contact lenses, make sure they have their glasses as well as lens solution. Trials are hard on the eyes. Contact lenses almost always give their wearers some trouble there. Think ahead.

Get a recent phone book for your new locale long before you go. Read the first 20 pages. You'll find maps, government phone directories, emergency medical help, and other useful information. Look up copying services and couriers. Copy their names and numbers into your personal phone book and keep it with you at all times. Pack a recent phone book from your hometown. You never know when it will come in handy. Get all the relevant Thomas Brothers maps and any other maps you need. Don't forget to scout gas stations and convenience stores.

Once again, be sure you can reach your computer support people immediately. You need every number they have, including beepers. You need fax and modem numbers. Frankly, you need home phone numbers, and most of these folks will generously provide them. Don't abuse their kindness but do make sure that when your ability to cope with technology ends, you have backup.

The Martha Stewart of Scheduling. Be graciously efficient every step of the way. You must have all the phone numbers: Be sure you have your secretary's home phone number; the attorneys' secretaries' home numbers; the attorneys' home and car phones; everybody's beepers; witnesses' business, car, and home phones; opposing counsel's office phone; and any others you can get. Don't forget the home phones of several associates you can call for research support in the evening. For everyone named above you also need fax numbers.

Get everyone's addresses (home and business) as well as their schedules. Pay special attention to your witnesses' scheduled plans. You need to be aware of the times any of your staff (secretaries or attorneys) will be off for vacation or other known absences. What hours does your boss' secretary work—does she go home at 4:30? Be sure you have E-mail addresses for as many people as possible. You may need to send off an E-mail message at 2 a.m. that will be read at 8 the next morning while you are in court.

You need an address sheet for the courthouse (with directions and maps) to give to your team and to send to your witnesses. Include parking information, bathroom locations, law library locations, bank locations, and where you can most likely be found. You need a beeper number yourself and you need to give everyone that number as well as your home phone, your E-mail address, the number where you are staying during trial, and your secretary's number. You are the point of connection; decisions may be made by the attorneys but communication goes through you. You must be available. Be sure the receptionist at your office knows what's going on and has a copy of your phone lists. Receptionists are usually scrupulous about not giving out phone numbers to unknown callers, so be sure you are clear about the people you want her to give these numbers to.

Find out if the judge's courtroom is dark on any days. Does he or she hear motions or other matters some mornings? Are there other calendar peculiarities that will affect your scheduling during trial?

When in Rome... Get a feel for the local style. Imagine this case: Out-of-state defense lawyers show up in force at a small country courtroom, each in a serious suit, with a serious briefcase and serious, expensive shoes. Every time one of them opens a fancy briefcase to shuffle among the papers, the judge sighs. Only one of them speaks. The others just open and close their briefcases and then sit there looking suave.

The defense lawyers haven't done anything particularly wrong, but their attitude and appearance are not congenial to this venue. Finally, lone counsel for the plaintiff stands up and begins with, "I don't know how they do things in your state, but here we still care about a little thing called constitutional rights." The judge smiles. The jury smiles. The audience smiles. The out-of-state lawyers can get on their chartered plane and go home to tell the client it should consider settlement. It isn't that the case is all that bad. It's that they exude an opinion: "This is a hick town, a hick judge, and a hick lawyer." They tick off the judge, who can make their case a lot more difficult than it might have been.

You have to get a feel for how things are done in your new venue. Is it formal? Are paralegals allowed at counsel table? Can you store exhibits in the courtroom if you keep them covered? Does the judge decide pretrial motions in limine before jury selection? Are there special filing requirements? Avoid violating the local customs. Doing so will not necessarily torpedo your case, but it will make your job harder and increase your client's risk of a bad outcome.

When outside the courtroom, comport yourself as if you are on display—even if you think you're not. At breakfast, at lunch, and at dinner, in the evenings, and always, behave as if judge and jury are watching you. Be smart enough to stay out of bars and other night spots. Do not discuss the case with anyone—not a waitress, not the clerk at the bookstore, no one.

Observe the community. Do women run in shorts in this town? Do women wear pantsuits to court or do they all wear dresses? This is not the time for you to take a stand on women's rights issues. Your client's position and money are on the line; you are not entitled to jeopardize them by dressing in a way that violates a town custom.

In Trial, Finally... The actual trial may feel much like a local trial except that you are the conduit back to the mother ship. Sometimes you are the mother ship. Back at the motel (or at your legal secretarial support office or at a friendly local counsel's office) your E-mail connection is on. Your pockets are filled with change. Your notebook with every phone number you could possibly need is in your hands. You have all the exhibits, the deposition transcripts, the physical evidence, the motions in limine, the witness and exhibits lists, the statement of the case, the trial brief, the request for jury instructions (and motions to back them up), any special verdict forms, the local legal directory, the supplies box, the carefully covered blow-ups, medical supplies, and tissues.

Organize and orchestrate the arrival of witnesses. Take notes on testimony. Feed back to your attorneys what the jury is doing. Talk quietly to the client during breaks, dispense aspirin and Band-Aids as needed, buy sodas, pre-order lunch, etc. Anticipate the needs of your team.

Check in with your secretary and with the attorney's secretaries twice daily to make sure disasters are not cropping up in other cases. You will need to find out how your attorney wants this handled. Some attorneys want to hear every detail. Others are comfortable relying on you to make the right decision about when they need to be interrupted. If you can, direct problems not related to this case to someone else, but do not overstep your bounds. This is one more reason why out-of-town teams should be comprised of people who know each other and the practices involved well.

Keep a notebook with your time, significant expenses, unexpected expenses, the experts' time, and anything else you will have to go over with the client later. Note things that come up that increase costs but are not in your control. This is important. Many clients are gung-ho before and during the trial and horrified later at the cost. Be prepared to tell them what they bought with their money.

After the ball is over, what does the local court require?

After closing arguments, the lawyers and the client will be going through re-entry. For days or weeks they have been living in that separate and isolated world called the courtroom. Now they can let down their guards, slump a little, relax, even forget something. You, on the other hand, don't get to let down yet. There actually are courts that make you pack all your files up as soon as the closing arguments are over. Have a van ready to pick everything up. Do you have anyone to help you? Find out what you'll have to do and plan ahead.

You'll probably be in charge of packing up the motel or office space you've been using. Who's in charge of settling the bill? If it is on a firm credit card, be sure your attorney doesn't head down the road to visit family before you get a signature. If the client is covering the bill directly, you will have to address this tactfully. Do it quickly, while the enthusiasm of trial and the feeling of fighting the good fight is still fresh. It will all seem a lot worse the next day.

Find out if the judge requires the attorneys to wait around while the jury deliberates. This can be a real drag but many judges do require it. If yours does, you will have lots of time to pack up while your coworkers pace the floor, call their families, pace again, call people they went to college with who happen to live in this town, pace the floor, and complain about the fact that they can't go anywhere or do anything. Somehow they will fail to be very useful in the clean-up action. They're too busy worrying about the outcome. If you find a way to distract them and yourself, good for you. Eventually the phone will ring.

Settle up with all your contractors (legal secretarial support, any copy service bills, etc.) before you leave town. Make sure they feel comfortable that they will get paid—and be sure they do. It's tempting to forget these people as soon as you get back to home base. Your desk will be full, but do the right thing. If they took care of you, take care of them.

Taking the show on the road is a lot of work, but the experience will increase your expertise and your confidence. It can also do a great deal to make you an important member of the litigation team. It's an opportunity to build—skills, self-assurance, and valuable professional friendships. Your working relationships and your job may never be the same again.

SAMPLE MASTER DATA SHEET

Client:

XYZ Corp.
2376 Via Zurita
Braeton, CA 94639
ph: 939 685-2003
fx: 939 685-2004

President/Contact
James Richardson
home: 177 Portola Dr.
Granada, CA 94522
ph: 939 677-2005
bpr: 939 455-2039
fx: 939 677-2394
secretary: Cheryl/ 685-2014

Opposing Side:

Frank De Vita
153 Franklin Lane
Summerville, CA 94666
ph: 919 644-2034

Counsel for De Vita
James Henderson
Henderson & Maloney LLP
200 Manor Avenue, Ste. A
Braeton, CA 94639
ph: 919 644-5000
fx: 919 644-7000
secretary: Pam 644-5124

Our Team:

George -	hm: 939 677-2386
	car: 344-1054
	bpr: 666-3984
Mark -	hm: 922 588-3843
	car: 344 2857
	bpr: 666-3769
Deb -	hm: 939 687-1995
	car: 344-9976
	bpr: 666-4973
Evelyn -	hm: 922 588-2002

Courthouse

14066 Wilderton Avenue
(Corner Wilderton and Main)
Verdant, CA 94577
Clerk 919 644-6000 (no fax filing)
Dept. 3, Judge David Caspar
Second floor, room 222
Clerk: Janelle Peters
ph: 919 644-6078
Bailiff: Jacob French
Secretary: Terry Jones
ph: 919 644-6079
Dark Fridays

Our Experts:

Joseph Vendell & Mickey Roberts
Vendall, Roberts and Casey
Personnel Resource Analysts
222 Western Ave.
Braeton, CA 94639
ph: 939 677-3029; fx: 677-3129
hm phs: Joe 687-2948; Mickey 687-2354
bprs: Joe 315-6754; Mickey 315-5843

Their Expert:

Frederick Wilson
Human Resources Inc.
4392 15th Avenue
Summerville, CA 92374
ph: 919 533-2699
fx: 919 533-2600

Check-Off Lists

Find Out ASAP:

1. Courthouse location, department location, clerk's name and phone number, requirements for pleading headings, special rules or requirements; calendar issues

2. Directions on ground travel to city and courthouse

3. Information for air or train travel to city/ who flies when

4. Available places to stay near courthouse/get five different bids

5. Local legal secretarial services/office space

6. Locations:
   copy service
   courier service
   bank
   hospital/urgent care
   office supply store
   library/regular and law
   grocery/drug stores
   restaurants
   gas stations

See 6.1-6.15 below for related packaging list

Maps—Lists—Indices

1. Map of courthouse location w/ street and freeway information

2. Phone/address sheet (see sample) expansive—includes all team personnel

3. Map of interior of courthouse w/ dept/filing desks/ phones/ library/ restrooms

4. Case-specific calendar for all team members
   Includes case deadlines and other commitments of team members

5. Index of all case materials

6. Packing list

Equipment

1. Laptops - 3

2. Modems, printer, fax

3. Portable copy machine

4. Lamps, bookcases, tables, chairs

5. Cell phones

6. Trial cases

7. Luggage/briefcase carriers

8. Tripod, flip chart, TV, VCR

Packing List

6.1   clips: pleadings, correspondence, memos and note, discovery, research

6.2   client docs (originals), smoking guns, other evidence

6.3   witness files, issues files

6.4   our expert material

6.5   their expert material

6.6   motions in limine, witness list, exhibit list, statement of the case, trial brief, issues briefs, voir dire, jury instructions, objections, special verdict

6.7   judicial profile, local rules, trial management order

6.8   Judge's notebook, Attorney trial notebook, Deb's trial notebook, exhibit notebook

6.9   large exhibits, small exhibits, copies for other side and court

6.10 supplies (pens, pencils, yellow pads [two sizes], felt-tip pens, tape, stapler, staples, scissors, paper clips, all size stickies, folders, two- and three-hole punches, exhibit tabs, file buckets, pleading paper, regular paper, expense vouchers, transparency sheets, large flip chart, Acco fasteners, three-ring binders, blue backs, envelopes, fax cover sheets)

6.11 more supplies (tissues, gum, antacids, headache medicine, vitamins, sewing kit, Band-Aids, antibiotic cream, flu medicine, allergy medicine, flashlight, coins)

6.12 extra batteries, surge protectors, floppy disks, modems, computer manuals, cell phones

6.13 Five-in-One Code book, special texts on relevant issues, favorite personal books, material on trial procedure, voir dire, witness examination, etc.

6.14 phone books, Thomas Bros. maps, other maps, local chamber of commerce material, local legal directories

6.15 extra glasses, personal medications, doctor's phones

BECOME A SETTLEMENT EXPERT

There's another special area of expertise for litigation paralegals and it may surprise you. It's not about what to do to get ready for trial, it's about what to do when you settle. Handling the postsettlement chores is an excellent way to convince a top-notch litigator to make you part of the team. The natural energy flow of a litigator is toward the fight. Once the fight's over, tying up the loose ends is a lot less inspiring. If you take it on you will impress your boss.

Typically you find out your case has settled just after you have done incredible amounts of work getting ready to go to trial. Don't despair; it does not mean all your work was for naught. The only way to get a settlement that is worth your client's time and trouble is to prepare the case fully and well so that the other side knows you mean business and can make your points.

If you've done well and obtained a good settlement for the client, rejoice. Then have a cup of coffee and get out your phone list. You have a busy day ahead of you.

The first thing to think about is money. Don't spend another penny. Call your experts first. Tell them the case has settled and that you will be calling them back later with details. Be sure they understand that they are not to do any more work on the project until further notice.

If you have court reporters transcribing material, phone them to cancel the work. Check with any paralegals or attorneys who are summarizing or reviewing testimony, creating exhibits, drafting jury instructions, or preparing witnesses. Let them know the case is settled and they can turn their attention and their billing clocks in another direction. Check with the word processing department to see if any attorneys or paralegals have turned in dictation that is now obsolete.

If any court appearances are scheduled for that day or the next, make sure you call the court and let the clerk know what's happening. Even though you will be filing official papers later, this will protect your working relationships with the court's overworked personnel. If you have lodged exhibits with the bailiff, call to make arrangements to pick them up. Call your witnesses and let them know they need not appear.

It may or may not be appropriate for you to call the client. If you have had a close working relationship with the client, you might want to check in to see if anything new has occurred that the attorney should know about.

Be sure the client will be in town to sign settlement documents once they are drafted. You should be able to draft these documents yourself. If you do not have a form file of settlement documents, begin one now. Include a variety of settlement and release documents. Just be sure that you don't rely so heavily on the forms that you forget to think through carefully and critically each element of the settlement as proposed and how your client will be affected.

Usually settlement documents must be reviewed by several parties and their counsel before a final version is agreed on. Create a history of this review by using red-line versions so deletions and additions are clear, and make notes about who wanted what changes. Keep everything until the final version is executed. I have been involved in cases in which a Post-It -note with a dollar figure written on it had to be retrieved to facilitate negotiations. It's never over till it's signed, sealed, and delivered.

Keep on top of the exchange of versions of settlement documents; make sure they don't sit on an attorney's desk for three weeks. When the final version is executed, be sure you know who is to have the original, whether it needs to be filed with the court, etc. As the settlement specialist, you are responsible for dotting the i's and crossing the t's. Be careful.

If the client will be writing a check to settle the case, arrange to handle the transaction through your office. Be sure you don't release funds until all appropriate releases have been executed. If the other side is dismissing, be sure to follow up on the filing and obtain a conformed copy for your file and for your client.

Once the settlement agreement has been finalized and the parties have all signed off, supervise the closing of the file. Check with accounts receivable on the outstanding bills. If there is an amount in trust due to the client, be sure a check is issued. Keep the physical file open for a month or so to include follow-up correspondence. Be sure the files are eventually boxed up and labeled for storage.

Before you actually close the boxes, take a little time to make sure they are orderly. If you have the client's original documents, speak to the attorney in charge of the matter about them. Usually you should make copies and return the originals. Get a receipt for those originals and file it in the box too. This can avoid a nasty argument about who lost what later on.

Touch bases with all the coworkers who helped you with this matter and thank them for their hard work. Add any motions or pleadings you think you can use as forms to your form notebook. Provide your boss with a memo outlining what has been done to close the case and asking if there's anything you forgot.

COMPUTER MAVEN

If you have a talent for working with technology you will find the computer specialty a particularly important one. As we each become more computer independent, we also become more computer dependent. People who can solve computer problems are increasingly valuable in law offices.

You can establish your expertise by taking classes at institutions designed to educate folks about computers, by taking courses in a local university paralegal program, or by working with your firm's computer professionals. If you have a bent in the right direction, just getting some extra software loaded onto your computer and playing with it until you figure it out may be all it takes.

Computer experts come in several flavors: those who can solve computer malfunctions, those who have mastered various programs the firm uses, those who can locate information on the Internet quickly, and those who can design custom databases and programs that will help the firm solve a particular problem or track particular data. A final specialty in this area may be the paralegal who can calmly and clearly educate others on how to use this technology in our work. If you have ever seen a busy attorney facing a computer glitch on a day when she has to be in court in ten minutes, you know that someone who can intervene and educate calmly is a dream come true. If you like teaching you may want to contact computer companies for training on how to teach their software to others.

INVENT YOUR OWN SPECIALTY

You're in charge of your career. You're smart and you can think. You're observant. These specialties are just examples. You can use your skills and your head to respond to your clients' needs and create your own area of expertise. The same anthropological skills that tell you about the workplace, the attorneys, and the firm's standards can tell you how to create your specialty. Pay attention to what goes on with clients and to what the clients want to accomplish, and your area of expertise will invent itself.

You cannot afford to drift from one assignment to another without developing strong working relationships with particular individuals who look to you for particular and expert help. You need to be someone who can answer questions and get things done, someone who can solve problems rather than pass them to a real problem solver. Keep an active and interested eye on the office and make your move. Educate yourself. Volunteer. Do what it takes to develop an area of responsibility you can call your own.

A

GLOSSARY

ABA: American Bar Association

ABA approval: Used with regard to paralegal educational programs, this designation means the program has undergone and passed the ABA review process for paralegal programs.

ADR: Alternate Dispute Resolution. A set of methods including mediation and arbitration designed to resolve disputes without going through all phases of the formal litigation process.

Appeal: An appeal from a decision of one adjudicating entity to the entity authorized to review such decisions. For example, a superior court decision may be appealable to the appellate court; the decision of a hearing officer may be appealable to a city council or board of supervisors.

Arbitration: A form of alternate dispute resolution. Arbitration may be binding or nonbinding. It may be voluntary, contractual, or court ordered.

Associates: Attorneys who work for firms but are not partners. Usually associate attorneys are on track to be considered for partnership at a later date, but nonpartnership track associate positions (sometimes called permanent associates) are becoming more common.

Attorney of record: The attorney on record with the court as representing a party before the court.

Attorney–client privilege: The confidentiality privilege that exists regarding communications between client and attorney. This privilege belongs to the client and may only be waived by the client. The obligation to hold in confidence all such matters extends to the attorney's staff. Paralegals and other staff members must be diligent in the maintenance of this privilege which exists for the benefit of the client.

Bate-stamp: A sequential numbering stamp used to number documents such as those produced in discovery or at trial for reference purposes.

Bench (the): The judiciary, an aggregate term for judges.

Bench trial: Trial before a judge only, i.e., there is no jury as finder of fact.

Billable hours: Time during which client services are performed and for which a client may be billed.

Billing cycle: Usually a 30-day period, i.e., one month, at the beginning of which a client bill is sent out. Fees are normally due in 30 days.

Billing rate: The dollars per hour billed for a particular legal professional's time, e.g., paralegal billing rates range from perhaps $55 per hour to as much as $125 per hour. The rate at which a paralegal's time is billed impacts directly on the profitability to the firm of the individual paralegal.

Billing requirements: Many firms require paralegals and attorneys to bill a certain number of hours per year. Meeting the billing requirement may be the criteria for a performance bonus, a step increase on a salary schedule, an annual raise, or other form of compensation.

Blowing a statute: Inadvertently allowing a statute of limitations on a cause of action, appeal, or other matter to expire. This is often a fatal error for a paralegal's career.

Board of directors: Governing board of a corporation or other entity.

Brief: A pleading usually submitted to the court providing an argument for one side's position with regard to a particular issue or issues. Briefs can be limited to one issue or can be as broad as a trial brief, which usually includes the facts of the case, relevant law, and an analysis of how the law applies to the facts of the case.

To brief a case, as for example part of a research assignment, is to draft a summary of the case, an analysis of the issues and findings, and a statement of how those holdings may impact a current matter.

Briefing schedule: A schedule outlining when all briefing in a particular proceeding must be accomplished. Briefing schedules may be voluntarily agreed to or court ordered.

Calendar: The calendar for a particular court refers to the list of cases set to be heard in that court and the order in which they will be heard. See *off calendar*. *Calendar* is also used as a verb, as in *to calendar* something, which means to arrange with the court and parties to have a matter placed on the court's calendar or on the calendars of those involved in the case.

Calendaring: The act of setting things on particular calendars. This term is used not only to refer to setting things on the court's calendar, but also to setting meetings between counsel, setting depositions, settlement conferences, and the like.

Career path: Usually refers to a particular track within a law firm to allow paralegals to move from entry-level to senior positions. Career paths were designed to induce long-term, highly trained paralegals to remain with the firm.

Case management conference: Known as CMCs, these conferences usually occur with the judge in court and are for the purpose of allowing the judge to question the parties on the status of settlement discussions, discovery, and other trial preparation matters as well as to provide the parties with the court's rules for case preparation and trial.

Casual day: Casual days occur almost exclusively on Fridays and are days designated by firm or company management when personnel may dress less formally than on normal business days.

Certificated: A paralegal who has attended and graduated from a paralegal education program usually receives a certificate upon completing all the program's requirements. Such a paralegal is *certificated*. This term should not be confused with *certified* (which see) but often is. Law firms often advertise a position as requiring a certified paralegal when in fact they are looking for someone with a certificate from an educational program.

Certified: This term usually refers to someone who has taken and passed a complex exam administered by a state entity or paralegal organization. NALA administers such an exam and those who pass are entitled to use *CLA*, for *Certified Legal Assistant*, after their names.

CLA: Certified Legal Assistant. A paralegal who has passed the NALA exam (see *certified*).

Claim: Used colloquially to refer to 1) a tort claim that a claimant may be required to file with a public entity prior to filing a lawsuit or 2) what a litigant or other claimant is saying occurred or what the claimant alleges is owed.

CLE: Continuing Legal Education. Ongoing legal education by those legal professionals who have completed their formal education.

Client contact: Contact with the client can be as short-lived and superficial as arranging for meetings or as significant as having the responsibility for maintaining a cordial relationship with a long-term client, perhaps serving as a liaison between the law office and the client and often managing that client's work flow. The importance of client contact should never be underestimated. The opportunity to work personally with clients is usually a sign that the lawyer involved trusts and respects the paralegal assigned client contact duties. Client contact is often cited as a source of job satisfaction by paralegals.

Client lunch: Lunch with a client, which usually includes both social and business aspects. See Chapter 11 for client lunch protocol.

Clips: Red cardboard file clips. Used colloquially to refer to pleadings, as in, "Where's the pleading clip?"

Closed session: That session of a legislative body (such as a city council or board of supervisors) that is not open to attendance by the public.

Closing: The final signing of papers and related exchanges when a financial deal such as a merger or sale is occurring.

Confidential: Subject to special rules and requirements prior to any disclosure, and often not disclosable in any form. See *attorney–client privilege*.

Conflict of interest: Conflicts of interest can arise in many situations, e.g., between co-defendants, between co-plaintiffs, or between attorney(s) in a matter and the party or parties the attorney(s) represents. A conflict of interest is a situation when the interests of one person, group of persons, or entity diverges materially from the interest of others. When undertaking the representation of a new client, attorneys must check for conflicts between the firm, themselves as individuals, and other firm clients and the new potential client. It is an important and complex task to determine whether conflicts exist and some firms have paralegal staff dedicated to the task of checking for conflicts.

In the case of an apparent conflict, an analysis of the facts and legal issues may be necessary for a final determination to be made. If it is determined that a conflict exists it may still be possible for a waiver of the conflict by the affected parties to be made, but in order for such a waiver to be effective stringent requirements must be met regarding disclosure not only of the facts but also of the consequences of the waiver.

The issue of conflicts also arises in the hiring process. Courts have disqualified firms from representation in certain matters after the firm hired personnel whose former employment exposed them to information that did or might create a conflict. In the past this potential or actual conflict has been mitigated by the erection of a Chinese or ethical wall within a firm. Ethical walls are designed to shield certain cases or information from access by certain persons, so that no damage to anyone's interests can occur. However, there are practical difficulties of substantial proportion in making such a wall work and in some states there is a presumption that even if there has been an attempt to avoid a conflict by means of an ethical wall, a disclosure has been made.

Consultant: In litigation a consultant is hired to assist in aspects of analyzing and preparing the case. Unlike expert witnesses' files, consultants' files are not normally subject to disclosure.

Continuance: A continuance is a delay to new date of a deadline or a proceeding. In some cases this may be jointly agreed to: in others you must ask the court to grant a continuance. It is also used in the verb form, to continue.

Corporate law: Business law in which lawyers assist companies and businesspeople with their legal affairs.

Costs: Money expended by and on the behalf of clients is usually broken into fees, which are lawyer's and paralegal's billings, and costs, which are nonfee expenditures required to move a matter forward. Examples of costs are monies paid to court reporters, to consultants, to copying services, and for filing fees.

Counsel: Another word for attorney or lawyer. It is usually used to describe the relationship between an attorney and a client as in, "She's counsel for the Abstract Corporation." Many businesses have a general counsel who is its principal attorney as well as outside counsel who are hired on a case-by-case basis to handle certain matters. Companies and public entities often have a firm as general counsel, rather than one particular attorney.

Counting: Legal deadlines include a lot of counting. Check your local code of civil procedure or other rules for counting details like when you only count court days, when you count business days, etc.

Courier: A service set up to messenger documents and filings between one business and another, to the courthouse, or to other destinations. Many firms have contracts with courier services that include a charge account so you don't have to have checks prepared for each delivery.

Court reporter: A court reporter is trained to take down testimony using a machine and to transcribe from those tapes to generate transcripts if needed. Court reporters are authorized to swear in witnesses so that testimony is given subject to perjury provisions.

Cross-training: A concept rarely put into play in which individuals with different job duties are trained to do each other's job in order to cover for each other in emergencies.

Dark: The term *dark* is used to describe courtrooms that are closed for part of or a whole day during the workweek. Dark days allow judges to read briefs and attend to other matters. A common day for a courtroom to be dark is Friday. If the judge hears trials, those trials would run from Monday through Thursday and resume again the following Monday.

Data processing: The data processing department is usually in charge of doing all the math that keeps the firm running. They produce bills, calculate hours, prepare reports, and maintain archival data.

Dead filing: Dead filing is the storing of files for matters that are closed, usually in an off-site storage facility.

Deliberation: The decision-making process by which a jury reaches a verdict.

Demand: A demand is the amount a party in a lawsuit is requesting in order to settle a matter, or the amount a party is claiming it is owed.

Demand for inspection and copying of documents and things: Sometimes called request for production or request for inspection, a litigation procedure to obtain copies of documents or things from another party during discovery.

Depo prep: A preparatory session with a witness prior to a deposition.

Deposition: A discovery procedure in which sworn testimony is taken outside a court proceeding, usually in the presence of counsel and a court reporter.

Discovery: That portion of the litigation process in which information is obtained by parties to a lawsuit by means of procedures authorized by legislation including depositions, interrogatories, and demands for inspection of documents and things.

Discussion documents: Draft versions of documents, usually circulated to interested parties for comments.

Docket: 1) A record of filings and actions in a lawsuit kept by the court. 2) The calendar for a court.

Docket clerk: Law firm personnel responsible for calendaring deadlines in the firm's matters or court personnel responsible for the court calendar.

Docketing: Placing items on the calendar for the law firm.

Document production: A production of documents by a party in response to a discovery demand.

Draft document: Not the final version. In law offices documents are often stamped "draft" and "final." Drafts are sometimes retained to memorialize changes, but failure to stamp and identify draft versus final documents can lead to confusion.

Dress code: The dress requirement at an office, both official and unofficial. While you don't have to be a slave to an unofficial dress code, there is wisdom in dressing the part, especially early in your career.

Due process: The administration of the law according to rules and procedures designed to protect the rights of the individual. Among the elements of due process are proper service of papers and proceeding on notice to all parties.

E-mail: Electronic mail used to communicate in-house via an intranet and with clients and others in the outside world via the Internet.

Eminent domain: Eminent domain is the power of public entities to acquire property and other things for public purposes. This is a speciality area in litigation and is normally governed by separate statutes regarding discovery cutoffs, the exchange of experts, etc.

Employment law: A legal specialty dealing with personnel issues. Paralegals are very active in benefit administration practices and in firms that deal with workers' compensation law.

Entry-level position: Positions for paralegals with educational background but no (or very little) experience.

Estate planning: Legal speciality to help people draw up wills, create trusts, or otherwise care for and arrange for the disposition of their estates.

Evaluations: A procedure to review the performance of employees, usually involving written evaluations and a face-to-face meeting between the evaluator and the employee.

Execute documents: The signing procedure that usually makes legal documents effective, including contracts, wills, settlement agreements, etc.

Executive committee: A governing committee in some firm management programs, usually made up of senior partners elected by the partnership.

Exempt: Employees who by virtue of job duties and other factors are not paid overtime.

Expert witness: A witness with established expertise in a field that qualifies him or her to offer opinion testimony in legal proceedings regarding matters in that field. Working with expert witnesses requires special knowledge on the part of paralegals.

Family law: A legal specialty assisting clients with adoptions, marriage dissolutions, and other legal matters related to family relations. Paralegals often play important roles in family law practices.

Fax filing: Filing official court papers by way of official fax filing programs adopted by some courts. There are usually strict procedures adopted by the courts that accept fax filings.

Fees: Monies charged for professional legal services, as opposed to *costs* (which are monies charged for copying, telephone, etc.)

Filing: Depositing papers with the court that generally become part of the public record. There are situations in which the court orders filed papers to remain sealed, and some juvenile and other records are also not available to the public.

Firm brochure: Literature developed by firms to acquaint the public with their services, history, etc.

Firm holiday: Day when the firm is closed in observance of a holiday.

Firm roster: The list of attorneys and paralegals in the firm. The rosters usually represent seniority, i.e., those with the firm longest are at the top of the list.

Forms (judicial): Forms promulgated by judicial councils to make filing certain pleadings and other legal documents easier.

Form file: Your personal or the firm's files of pleadings and other documents that can be used as starting points to generate other documents.

Hiring decision: The decision to hire new personnel. Usually the power to make a hiring decision belongs to particular persons. It's helpful in the job search process to identify the person or persons who have the power to actually make hiring decisions.

Hostile witness: A witness called to testify who is hostile to the party that called him or her. If a witness is officially designated by the court as hostile, different rules regarding the examination of the witness apply.

Hung jury: A jury that is unable to come to a decision.

Impeach: Impeaching a witness is offering into evidence testimony or other evidence that contradicts the witness' testimony.

In-house: In-house counsel is counsel, usually corporate or governmental, that is part of a larger organization other than a law firm.

Insurance defense: A legal specialty in which attorneys represent insurance companies against claims.

Intake: Intake is the process by which potential new matters are assessed in a law firm. Paralegals are sometimes involved in taking telephone calls from potential clients, screening out calls by people who need services the firm does not provide, and checking potential conflicts.

Intellectual property: A legal specialty involving copyright and other issues.

Interoffice conference: A conference between people in the same firm regarding a matter, e.g, a litigation strategy conference.

Interrogatories: A discovery device involving written questions promulgated by one party to the other party or parties in order to obtain information about the matter that is the subject of the lawsuit.

Job descriptions: A detailed list of the duties of a particular job position.

Journals: This term can refer to legal magazines or newspapers or to law school or specialty journals.

Judicial profiles: Published profiles of judges that describe their educational background, former legal practices, and history on the bench.

Junior partner: A lawyer who has recently been made a partner in a law firm.

Jury fees: Fees that must be paid, usually in advance, to ensure a jury in a trial. Failure to file these fees on time may be deemed a waiver of a jury trial.

Jury instructions: The instructions the judge reads to the jury after the closing arguments and before the jury retires to deliberate.

Jury service: A professional service that assists trial lawyers in choosing a jury. Jury services often offer a range of services including mock trials, exhibit preparation, and the like.

Jury verdict form: A pleading prepared by counsel prior to trial and submitted to the judge, for provision to the jury in formulating its verdict. Special jury verdict forms often break down the findings the jury must make, thereby helping the jury to stay focused and clear on its work.

Lateral hire: An attorney or paralegal with experience hired from another firm, as opposed to those hired right out of school.

Law clerk: Law clerk can refer to law students hired to do research the over the summer (also called *summer associates* or summer clerks), and also to law school graduates and attorneys who do research for judges.

Legal technician: Currently proposed as the title for independent paralegals, i.e., those paralegals who provide services directly to the public without review or supervision by an attorney.

Legal theory: The legal concept that is the basis for a position of a party in litigation.

Lien: A claim for monies that usually attaches to property and that usually has priority when funds are available from sale or transfer of the property.

Local rules: Rules adopted formally by a particular judicial council that control many practical matters related to filing documents, trial preparation, and the like.

Local local rules: This term refers to the ways a particular judge likes things done in his or her court. Sometimes a judge will provide a written document with the rules and sometimes not. Sometimes a judge issues an order regarding trial matters.

Malpractice: The charge of delivery of substandard care of services by a lawyer, doctor, dentist, accountant, or other professional. Talk to your boss about this.

Managing partner: Usually a senior partner elected by the partnership to assume administrative and managerial duties for the firm.

Mandatory mediation: Mediation is required by the court or by statute in some matters. Check your state code. In family law matters litigants are commonly required to go through the mediation process before having their matter heard in court.

Martindale-Hubbel: This is the standard directory in the legal business. It lists firms and provides information regarding the firm, its lawyers, and sometimes its paralegals. Some firms are rated by Martindale-Hubbel.

Mediation: An alternate dispute resolution procedure, sometimes court ordered.

MIS department: The Management Information Services department, also called IMS (Information Management Services) and commonly known as computer support.

Motion: A motion is an application to the court that a certain order be made.

Net: Colloquial for the Internet.

Networking: For people, a method of providing and obtaining help, contacts, and business opportunities through establishing a network of individuals who learn about and support each other's professional goals. Networking computers means to link computers such that they can share programs and communicate easily.

Nonbillable: Services and other activities for which no one can be billed.

Nonexempt: Employees who are paid an hourly amount and overtime.

Notary public: A person who is state-authorized to attest to the authenticity of signatures on documents.

Numbers: As in "your numbers," the statistics that record your hours, profitability, etc.

Of counsel: A relationship in which a lawyer provides services through a law firm but is neither a partner nor an associate.

Off Calendar: To take something off calendar is to remove it from its calendared status. Unless the matter is continued or rescheduled it will be canceled, so do not confuse taking something off calendar with continuing it (see *continue*).

Office hours: Usually refers to time spent on a regular basis by a contract attorney in the offices of a client. During those hours the attorney is available to answer routine questions employees of the client may have and to review legal documents (e.g., contracts the client is considering entering into). This kind of program allows clients to have the best of both worlds: the expertise of outside counsel and the convenience of in-house counsel.

On advice of counsel: This phrase is used by clients to explain the basis of actions they are taking when that basis is the advice of their attorneys.

Open session: That session of a governing body (such as a city council or board of supervisors) that the public may attend (see *closed session*).

Opposing counsel: The attorney on the other side of a lawsuit. You will hear other phrases, such as "the other side of the table" and "the other side."

Other side: See *opposing counsel*.

Outside counsel: An attorney who contracts with a business entity or public agency to represent it, but who is not an employee of the entity.

Paralegal program: This term usually refers to an officially adopted program of management within a law firm that addresses the firm's paralegals. The program usually includes a ranking mechanism with related salary parameters and duties attached.

Partners: Attorneys who have an ownership interest in the firm.

Percipient witness: A witness who has firsthand knowledge of a matter.

Pro bono: Literally *to the good*, in the legal world this refers to legal services provided at no cost.

Proposal: Usually refers to a proposal to provide legal services from a law firm to a potential client.

Public law: A legal specialty devoted to representing public entities such as cities, counties, or special districts.

Public record: Records that are open to public review, including most documents filed with the court and most of those submitted to public agencies.

Public records request: A request by a member of the public to inspect or copy a public record. In the case of federal documents this kind of request may be made under the Freedom of Information Act. When responding to these requests care must be taken to review all documents for exempt status.

Rainmaker: A term used to refer to someone who is particularly good at attracting and signing up new clients for the firm.

Recordation: Recording a document such as a lien or a notice of pending action with a county recorder or other official recording office.

Recuse: To resign from the hearing of a matter based on reasons of personal knowledge or interest.

Redact: To delete text from a document (usually done with white-out, self-adhesive corrective tape, or opaque black felt-tip pen) usually for the purpose of protecting from discovery material that is privileged or otherwise exempt from disclosure.

Redlining: A process of document creation and development in which changes to text from one version or draft of the document to the next are visible. A usual method is to show strike-out marking through deleted text and underlining of the added text. This procedure is often used when parties are negotiating contracts or agreements and when legislative bodies are amending laws.

Request for admissions: A written discovery device by which a party is required to either admit or deny certain statements or claims.

Request for production of documents: See *demand for inspection and copying of documents and things.*

Request for proposal: A request from potential clients for a proposal to provide legal services.

Reporter: The term *reporter* is used to refer to court reporters who record testimony given under oath both in the courtroom and in discovery depositions, and to refer to certain reports of cases in some jurisdictions, e.g., a state reporter.

Research memo: A memo that communicates the results of research on legal issues and often includes their application to a particular client's matter.

Retain: To retain an attorney is to contract with the attorney to represent you.

Retainer: An amount paid to an attorney by a client, often prior to the rendering of services, from which costs related to a legal matter can be paid or which may be held in reserve.

Retainer agreement: The agreement by which an attorney is retained.

Running (the statute is): See *statutes of limitations.* "The statute is running" means the time during which particular actions must be taken is current and passing. The action must be taken before the time period specified in the statute has passed.

Rush: A rush is a job that requires full-time focus in order to be completed on time.

Service: The provision of notice to parties in court and by legislatively prescribed manner.

Shepardizing: Shepard's Citations, Inc. publishes a series of books and updates that detail the status of case decisions and legislation. The term *shepardizing* is used by lawyers and paralegals to refer to the process of tracing and checking the history and treatment of decisions

Short-timer: Someone who is leaving the office soon; goes with "short-timer mentality," which shows up when employees who are leaving know they won't be around to have to handle problems later. Sometimes their focus and handling of a file is negatively impacted. It's clearly not a professional attitude but you should be aware of it.

Statement of the case: A pleading often required to be filed at the beginning of a trial. The statement is supposed to be nonadversarial and simply state the facts and the nature of the dispute.

Statutes of limitations: Time limits set out in state and federal statutes for various actions.

Strategy conference: A conference to discuss, analyze, and plan the strategy in a lawsuit or other matter.

Subpoena: An order issued by a court or administrative agency compelling a witness to appear and testify, or in the case of a subpoena duces tecum to appear and bring identified documents. Be aware that many states have procedures by which an attorney of record in a matter may issue a subpoena that will have the same efficacy as one issued by the court.

Summer associate: A second- or third-year law school student hired to do research for the firm over the summer months. Sometimes referred to as law clerks, a better term because they are not yet lawyers and hence cannot actually associate.

Support staff: Usually refers to secretaries, copying persons, runners, etc.

Take off calendar: To remove an official court proceeding or a deposition from everyone's calendar. Sometimes the term is used to refer to the cancellation of a meeting between counsel.

Telephone conference: Usually a telephone call for which a client will be billed. These can be calls between counsel or between client and counsel.

Tickler file: A file or other system that serves as a diary device to remind legal professionals of upcoming deadlines.

Timekeepers: Those legal professionals (attorneys, clerks, paralegals) whose work time is billed to clients.

Time sheets: Records of a billing professional's time that show how much time was spent on a certain matter and provide some detail about the work performed.

Track record: Track record refers to the history of a particular person with regard to some matter, e.g., an attorney's track record in trial performance usually indicates what kind of results he or she has obtained in trials. Your track record will indicate how your past performance has been viewed.

Transactional work: Business law. See *corporate law*.

Transcripts: Official recordings of events in legal proceedings made by state or federally sanctioned court reporters.

Travel time: The amount of time it takes to travel to a hearing, meeting, or other place on behalf of a client. Sometimes this time is billable on the theory that if the attorney or paralegal was not traveling on behalf of the client, he or she could be working on other billable matters. However, clients are generally less willing to pay travel time than they once were, and this time is not always billable. You must check with the attorney in charge of the client or matter to find out what arrangement the firm and client have in this regard.

Trial management conference : Many jurisdictions have mandatory pretrial conferences in which issues like exhibit exchange, witness list exchange, and other trial details are addressed. When preparing for a Trial Management Conference (TMC) be sure to check for pretrial orders or trial management orders the judge may have issued regarding this conference.

Trial preparation: A series of activities performed in the weeks before trial in which evidence is pulled together, reviewed, and organized for presentation at trial. This preparatory period often includes witness preparation meetings, exhibit preparation, the drafting of motions in limine, exhibit lists, witness lists, drafting of trial briefs, opening and closing statements, etc., as well as preparation for examining and cross-examining witnesses. It's an intense time during which the attorneys and paralegals involved try to focus on one matter.

Trial setting conference: Many jurisdictions have mandatory conferences in which the judge meets with both sides to a dispute and reviews the status of the case in order to decide when the trial should be set.

Trust: An arrangement in which one person or institution controls property or other assets given by another person for the benefit of a third party. Sometimes the grantor is also the trustee.

Turnover rate: The rate at which employees leave a firm.

Underbilling: The practice of not billing all your professional time.

Variance: The difference between the time a billing professional records and the time billed to the client.

Vendor: An outside consultant or other service provider to the law firm.

Web site: An Internet site maintained by a particular Webmaster on behalf of an entity. It is now common for law firms to have their own Web sites.

Witkins: An authoritative legal encyclopedia.

Witness interview: The interview of a witness to gather facts related to a matter. Paralegals often perform these critical interviews.

Witness list: A list of those witnesses a party intends to call at trial.

Word processor: Some firms hire individuals whose only responsibility is to word process audiotapes and other things for paralegals and attorneys.

Work-in-progress: WIP is work that has been done and for which time has been recorded, but which has not yet been billed to the client. When figuring out how much has been spent on a matter it's important to include WIP.

Writ: A writ of mandate is an order by the court that a certain action occur.

Write-off: The amount of time recorded that is not billed out to the client is described as written off. You must be aware of how much of your time is written off because it impacts your profitability to the firm.

FORMS AND TIME SHEETS

SAMPLE   Request for Firm Contribution

TO: (Executive Committee or Managing Partner or Contributions Committee)

DATE: _____   LAST DAY TO RESPOND: _____

RECIPIENT
ORGANIZATION: _____

_____

MAILING ADDRESS: _____

_____

AMOUNT REQUESTED: _____

PURPOSE: _____

BACKGROUND INFORMATION: (attach information as needed)

_____

_____

_____

_____

_____
Signature of Lawyer

DISPOSITION:

Checked Signed by _____

Decline _____

More Information Needed _____

SAMPLE   Library Acquisition Request

TITLE: _____

COST: _____

PUBLISHER/AUTHOR: _____

DESCRIPTION: _____

_____

_____

Please attach brochure/flyer if possible

REQUESTED FOR (specify whether for the library or for attorney/paralegal) _____

_____

REASON/S FOR REQUEST _____

_____

_____

REQUESTED BY: _____

DATE: _____

DISPOSITION:

ORDERED: _____ DATE: _____

DECLINE: _____ DATE: _____

OTHER: _____

_____ DATE: _____

SAMPLE   Expense Voucher

Mileage

From_____ To_____ Date_____ Miles _____ $_____

From_____ To_____ Date_____ Miles _____ $_____

Total: $_____

Business Entertainment

Establishment   Nature   Persons Present   Date

_____ $_____

_____ $_____

Total: $_____

Out of Town Expenses

Destination _____ Inclusive Dates _____

_____ $ _____   _____ $ _____

Hotel   Taxi

_____ $ _____   _____ $ _____

Meals   Car Rental

_____ $ _____   _____ $ _____

Airline   Parking

_____ $ _____   _____ $ _____

Other   Other

Total: $_____

Miscellaneous

Date_____ Item _____   Total: $_____

Purpose_____ Client File #_____

Client/Case Name_____ Billing Atty_____

Charge Client____ Charge Client ____
I certify that the above items represent actual expenses incurred on behalf of

_____

Date:____ Signature_____ Print/type name_____ Total _____

SAMPLE   Secretarial Assignment Sheet

ASSIGNMENT   DATE & TIME NEEDED   _____

Very important

REVISE DOCUMENT:

_____ Draft   _____ Final   _____ Copy/insert from existing doc # _____

TRANSCRIBE TAPE/NOTES   Client_____ Matter_____

___ Letter   ___ Memo   ___ Pleading   ___ Other   ___ Copy from existing doc # _____

PHOTOCOPY   Charge to _____

_____ Number of copies   _____ Route copies to   _____

_____ Return to you   _____ Hand deliver copies to   _____

PREPARE WORKING FILE/FORM FILE/ ADMINISTRATIVE FILE

Client_____ Matter _____

Label   _____

FILE NEEDS UPDATE/ORGANIZATION

Client_____Matter _____

Section(s) needed   _____

FAX TO _____   FAX/NOTE   _____

CALL TO _____   AGENCY   _____

Purpose   _____

_____

OTHER   _____

_____

SAMPLE   Check Request

____ gen'l acct   ____ not-to-exceed acct   ____ trust acct

____ return to requestor ____ hold for pickup   ____ call X   ____ when ready

Date requested:_____ Date due:_____ Time due: _____

Check Amount: $_____   Not to exceed Amount:_____

PAYABLE TO: _____

CHARGE

___ Client _____ Client No. _____ Atty _____ $_____

- re: _____

___ Client _____ Client No. _____ Atty _____ $_____

- re: _____

____Firm Description_____Acct. #_____ $_____

-re: _____

____Firm Description_____Acct. #_____ $_____

-re: _____

Requested by:_____ Ext._____ Approved by:_____

Special Instructions:_____

SAMPLE   Request to Attend Seminar

TO: _____

FROM: _____

DATE: _____

SEMINAR TITLE:

SEMINAR SUBJECT:

BROCHURE ATTACHED: Yes_____ No_____

DATE OF SEMINAR:

LOCATION:

TIME NEEDED OFF WORK:

ITEMIZATION ESTIMATE OF EXPENSES:

    registration fee

    travel

    hotel

    other (be specific)

REMARKS:

APPROVED BY _____ DATE _____

SAMPLE   ABC Attorney Services

REQUEST FOR SERVICES:

Date:_____   Sec/Paralegal: _____   Firm: _____

Client Name: _____   Attorney: _____

Billing # _____   Case Name: _____

Case # _____

Type of Document_____

File at: _____   Deliver to:_____

Address: _____   Address: _____

City: _____   City: _____

Pick Up: _____   Serve on _____

Address: _____   Address: _____

City: _____   City: _____

Special Instructions: (if personal service please describe individual to be served)

_____

_____

Rec'd by _____   Rec'd by _____

Check attached for fees: _____ (service to sign for fees)

Fees fronted by service: _____

Proof of service req._____   Proof of filing req. _____

Total Fees for services:_____

SAMPLE VOUCHERS/RECEIPT/PETTY CASH FORMS/TAPE SLIPS

VENDOR PAYMENT APPROVAL

TO: _____ DATE: _____

Please review the attached invoice and complete the following

___client _____ client #_____ atty _____

___firm acct # _____ re_____

Approved by _____

Special Instructions: _____

_____

LOST RECEIPT VOUCHER

Date:_____ $ _____

Paid to: _____

Purpose: _____

_____

I certify that the above item represents the actual expense incurred on behalf of _____

Date:_____ Signature: _____

SAMPLE   Vouchers and Tape Slips Con't

PETTY CASH VOUCHER

Date:_____ $ _____

Paid to: _____

Charge:

_____ Client: _____ Client #_____ Atty: _____

Re: _____

_____ Firm: Acct # _____

Re: _____

Requested by: _____ Approved by: _____

Received by: _____

TAPE DESCRIPTION

ATTY:_____   CASE: _____

DUE:_____   SIDE   A   B

MEMO _____ LETTER _____   OTHER _____

DRAFT _____   FINAL _____   SPACING _____

COMMENTS: _____

_____

_____

Here's a sample of one kind of time sheet printout generated by a timekeeping software program. When you click on a day of the month a second page appears on which you can record the details of your work.

TIME SHEETS
Time for BOGEN, DEBORAH
December 1998

SUN	MON	TUE	WED	THU	FRI	SAT
		1	2	3	4	5
6	7	8	9	10	11	12
13	14	15	16	17	18	19
20	21	22	23	24	25	26
27	28	29	30	31		

NAME   Deborah Bogen

DATE   12/3/98

CLIENT NUMBER   _____

MATTER NUMBER   _____

TIME   .8

Description of Activity:

T/CONF/CLIENT RE NEW LEGISLATIVE REQUIREMENTS RE DISCLOSURE; FURTHER RESEARCH; DRAFT MEMO RE SAME

Here's a style of time sheet for those who record their time by hand, as opposed to on a computer program.

DATE: December 3, 1998

TIMEKEEPER: Deborah Bogen

Client Name	Client Number	Description of Services	Time
XYZ Corp		T/conf/client re new legislative requirements re disclosure; further research; draft memo re same	.8

TIME MEMO

This kind of time memo is very helpful if you want to keep track of tasks on a busy day and you can't get to your computer timekeeping program.

client	timekeeper
matter	date
work performed	time
client	timekeeper
matter	date
work performed	time
client	timekeeper
matter	date
work performed	time
client	timekeeper
matter	date
work performed	time
client	timekeeper
matter	date
work performed	time

PROFESSIONAL STANDARDS

Code of Ethics and
Professional Responsibility of
National Association of Legal Assistants, Inc.

Preamble

A legal assistant must adhere strictly to the accepted standards of legal ethics and to the general principles of proper conduct. The performance of the duties of the legal assistant shall be governed by specific canons as defined herein so that justice will be served and goals of the profession attained. (See NALA Model Standards and Guidelines for Utilization of Legal Assistants, Section II.)

The canons of ethics set forth hereafter are adopted by the National Association of Legal Assistants, Inc., as a general guide intended to aid legal assistants and attorneys. The enumeration of these rules does not mean there are not others of equal importance although not specifically mentioned. Court rules, agency rules and statutes must be taken into consideration when interpreting the canons.

Definition

Legal assistants, also known as paralegals, are a distinguishable group of persons who assist attorneys in the delivery of legal services. Through formal education, training, and experience, legal assistants have knowledge and expertise regarding the legal system and substantive and procedural law which qualify them to do work of a legal nature under the supervision of an attorney.

Canon 1 — A legal assistant must not perform any of the duties that attorneys only may perform nor take any actions that attorneys may not take.

Canon 2 — A legal assistant may perform any task which is properly delegated and supervised by an attorney, as long as the attorney is ultimately responsible to the client, maintains a direct relationship with the client, and assumes professional responsibility for the work product. (See NALA Model Standards and Guidelines for Utilization of Legal Assistants, Sections IV and VII.)

Canon 3 — A legal assistant must not (See NALA Model Standards and Guidelines for Utilization of Legal Assistants, Section VI):

a. engage in, encourage, or contribute to any act which could constitute the unauthorized practice of law; and
b. establish attorney-client relationships, set fees, give legal opinions or advice or represent a client before a court or agency unless so authorized by that court or agency; and
c. engage in conduct or take any action which would assist or involve the attorney in a violation of professional ethics or give the appearance of professional impropriety.

Canon 4 — A legal assistant must use discretion and professional judgment commensurate with knowledge and experience but must not render independent legal judgment in place of an attorney. The services of an attorney are essential in the public interest whenever such legal judgment is required. (See NALA Model Standards and Guidelines for Utilization of Legal Assistants, Section VII.)

Canon 5 — A legal assistant must disclose his or her status as a legal assistant at the outset of any professional relationship with a client, attorney, a court or administrative agency or personnel thereof, or a member of the general public. A legal assistant must act prudently in determining the extent to which a client may be assisted without the presence of an attorney. (See NALA Model Standards and Guidelines for Utilization of Legal Assistants, Section V.)

Canon 6 — A legal assistant must strive to maintain integrity and a high degree of competency through education and training with respect to professional responsibility, local rules and practice, and through continuing education in substantive areas of law to better assist the legal profession in fulfilling its duty to provide legal service.

Canon 7 — A legal assistant must protect the confidences of a client and must not violate any rule or statute now in effect or hereafter enacted controlling the doctrine of privileged communications between a client and an attorney. (See Model Standards and Guidelines for Utilization of Legal Assistants, Section V.)

Canon 8 — A legal assistant must do all other things incidental, necessary, or expedient for the attainment of the ethics and responsibilities as defined by statute or rule of court.

Canon 9 — A legal assistant's conduct is guided by bar associations' codes of professional responsibility and rules of professional conduct.

National Association of Legal Assistants
1516 S. Boston, Suite 200 • Tulsa, OK 74119-4464 •
(918) 587-6828 • FAX (918) 582-6772

Adopted May 1975
Revised November 1979;
September 1988; August 1995

NATIONAL FEDERATION OF PARALEGAL ASSOCIATIONS, INC.

MODEL CODE OF ETHICS AND PROFESSIONAL RESPONSIBILITY AND GUIDELINES FOR ENFORCEMENT

PREAMBLE

The National Federation of Paralegal Associations, Inc. ("NFPA") is a professional organization comprised of paralegal associations and individual paralegals throughout the United States and Canada. Members of NFPA have varying backgrounds, experiences, education and job responsibilities that reflect the diversity of the paralegal profession. NFPA promotes the growth, development and recognition of the paralegal profession as an integral partner in the delivery of legal services.

In May 1993 NFPA adopted its Model Code of Ethics and Professional Responsibility ("Model Code") to delineate the principles for ethics and conduct to which every paralegal should aspire.

Many paralegal associations throughout the United States have endorsed the concept and content of NFPA's Model Code through the adoption of their own ethical codes. In doing so, paralegals have confirmed the profession's commitment to increase the quality and efficiency of legal services, as well as recognized its responsibilities to the public, the legal community, and colleagues.

Paralegals have recognized, and will continue to recognize, that the profession must continue to evolve to enhance their roles in the delivery of legal services. With increased levels of responsibility comes the need to define and enforce mandatory rules of professional conduct. Enforcement of codes of paralegal conduct is a logical and necessary step to enhance and ensure the confidence of the legal community and the public in the integrity and professional responsibility of paralegals.

In April 1997 NFPA adopted the Model Disciplinary Rules ("Model Rules") to make possible the enforcement of the Canons and Ethical Considerations contained in the NFPA Model Code. A concurrent determination was made that the Model Code of Ethics and Professional Responsibility, formerly aspirational in nature, should be recognized as setting forth the enforceable obligations of all paralegals.

The Model Code and Model Rules offer a framework for professional discipline, either voluntarily or through formal regulatory programs.

§1. NFPA MODEL DISCIPLINARY RULES AND ETHICAL CONSIDERATIONS

1.1 A PARALEGAL SHALL ACHIEVE AND MAINTAIN A HIGH LEVEL OF COMPETENCE.

Ethical Considerations

EC-1.1(a) A paralegal shall achieve competency through education, training, and work experience.

EC-1.1(b) A paralegal shall participate in continuing education in order to keep informed of current legal, technical and general developments.

EC-1.1(c) A paralegal shall perform all assignments promptly and efficiently.

1.2   A PARALEGAL SHALL MAINTAIN A HIGH LEVEL OF PERSONAL AND PROFESSIONAL INTEGRITY.

Ethical Considerations

EC-1.2(a) A paralegal shall not engage in any ex parte communications involving the courts or any other adjudicatory body in an attempt to exert undue influence or to obtain advantage or the benefit of only one party.

EC-1.2(b) A paralegal shall not communicate, or cause another to communicate, with a party the paralegal knows to be represented by a lawyer in a pending matter without the prior consent of the lawyer representing such other party.

EC-1.2(c) A paralegal shall ensure that all timekeeping and billing records prepared by the paralegal are thorough, accurate, honest, and complete.

EC-1.2(d) A paralegal shall not knowingly engage in fraudulent billing practices. Such practices may include, but are not limited to: inflation of hours billed to a client or employer; misrepresentation of the nature of tasks performed; and/or submission of fraudulent expense and disbursement documentation.

EC-1.2(e) A paralegal shall be scrupulous, thorough and honest in the identification and maintenance of all funds, securities, and other assets of a client and shall provide accurate accounting as appropriate.

EC-1.2(f) A paralegal shall advise the proper authority of non-confidential knowledge of any dishonest or fraudulent acts by any person pertaining to the handling of the funds, securities or other assets of a client. The authority to whom the report is made shall depend on the nature and circumstances of the possible misconduct, (e.g., ethics committees of law firms, corporations and/or paralegal associations, local or state bar associations, local prosecutors, administrative agencies, etc.). Failure to report such knowledge is in itself misconduct and shall be treated as such under these rules.

1.3   A PARALEGAL SHALL MAINTAIN A HIGH STANDARD OF PROFESSIONAL CONDUCT.

Ethical Considerations

EC-1.3(a) A paralegal shall refrain from engaging in any conduct that offends the dignity and decorum of proceedings before a court or other adjudicatory body and shall be respectful of all rules and procedures.

EC-1.3(b) A paralegal shall avoid impropriety and the appearance of impropriety and shall not engage in any conduct that would adversely affect his/her fitness to practice. Such conduct may include, but is not limited to: violence, dishonesty, interference with the administration of justice, and/or abuse of a professional position or public office.

EC-1.3(c) Should a paralegal's fitness to practice be compromised by physical or mental illness, causing that paralegal to commit an act that is in direct violation of the Model Code/Model Rules and/or the rules and/or laws governing the jurisdiction in which the paralegal practices, that paralegal may be protected from sanction upon review of the nature and circumstances of that illness.

EC-1.3(d) A paralegal shall advise the proper authority of non-confidential knowledge of any action of another legal professional that clearly demonstrates fraud, deceit, dishonesty, or misrepresentation. The authority to whom the report is made shall depend on the nature and circumstances of the possible misconduct, (e.g., ethics committees of law firms, corporations and/or paralegal associations, local or state bar associations, local prosecutors, administrative agencies, etc.). Failure to report such knowledge is in itself misconduct and shall be treated as such under these rules.

EC-1.3(e) A paralegal shall not knowingly assist any individual with the commission of an act that is in direct violation of the Model Code/Model Rules and/or the rules and/or laws governing the jurisdiction in which the paralegal practices.

EC-1.3(f) If a paralegal possesses knowledge of future criminal activity, that knowledge must be reported to the appropriate authority immediately.

1.4 A PARALEGAL SHALL SERVE THE PUBLIC INTEREST BY CONTRIBUTING TO THE DELIVERY OF QUALITY LEGAL SERVICES AND THE IMPROVEMENT OF THE LEGAL SYSTEM.

Ethical Considerations

EC-1.4(a) A paralegal shall be sensitive to the legal needs of the public and shall promote the development and implementation of programs that address those needs.

EC-1.4(b) A paralegal shall support bona fide efforts to meet the need for legal services by those unable to pay reasonable or customary fees for example, participation in pro bono projects and volunteer work.

EC-1.4(c) A paralegal shall support efforts to improve the legal system and access thereto and shall assist in making changes.

1.5 A PARALEGAL SHALL PRESERVE ALL CONFIDENTIAL INFORMATION PROVIDED BY THE CLIENT OR ACQUIRED FROM OTHER SOURCES BEFORE, DURING, AND AFTER THE COURSE OF THE PROFESSIONAL RELATIONSHIP.

Ethical Considerations

EC-1.5(a) A paralegal shall be aware of and abide by all legal authority governing confidential information in the jurisdiction in which the paralegal practices.

EC-1.5(b) A paralegal shall not use confidential information to the disadvantage of the client.

EC-1.5(c) A paralegal shall not use confidential information to the advantage of the paralegal or of a third person.

EC-1.5(d) A paralegal may reveal confidential information only after full disclosure and with the client's written consent; or, when required by law or court order; or, when necessary to prevent the client from committing an act that could result in death or serious bodily harm.

EC-1.5(e) A paralegal shall keep those individuals responsible for the legal representation of a client fully informed of any confidential information the paralegal may have pertaining to that client.

EC-1.5(f) A paralegal shall not engage in any indiscreet communications concerning clients.

1.6 A PARALEGAL SHALL AVOID CONFLICTS OF INTEREST AND SHALL DISCLOSE ANY POSSIBLE CONFLICT TO THE EMPLOYER OR CLIENT, AS WELL AS TO THE PROSPECTIVE EMPLOYERS OR CLIENTS.

Ethical Considerations

EC-1.6(a) A paralegal shall act within the bounds of the law, solely for the benefit of the client, and shall be free of compromising influences and loyalties. Neither the paralegal's personal or business interest, nor those of other clients or third persons, should compromise the paralegal's professional judgment and loyalty to the client.

EC-1.6(b) A paralegal shall avoid conflicts of interest that may arise from previous assignments, whether for a present or past employer or client.

EC-1.6(c) A paralegal shall avoid conflicts of interest that may arise from family relationships and from personal and business interests.

EC-1.6(d) In order to be able to determine whether an actual or potential conflict of interest exists a paralegal shall create and maintain an effective recordkeeping system that identifies clients, matters, and parties with which the paralegal has worked.

EC-1.6(e) A paralegal shall reveal sufficient non-confidential information about a client or former client to reasonably ascertain if an actual or potential conflict of interest exists.

EC-1.6(f) A paralegal shall not participate in or conduct work on any matter where a conflict of interest has been identified.

EC-1.6(g) In matters where a conflict of interest has been identified and the client consents to continued representation, a paralegal shall comply fully with the implementation and maintenance of an Ethical Wall.

1.7   A PARALEGAL'S TITLE SHALL BE FULLY DISCLOSED.

Ethical Considerations

EC-1.7(a) A paralegal's title shall clearly indicate the individual's status and shall be disclosed in all business and professional communications to avoid misunderstandings and misconceptions about the paralegal's role and responsibilities.

EC-1.7(b) A paralegal's title shall be included if the paralegal's name appears on business cards, letterhead, brochures, directories, and advertisements.

EC-1.7(c) A paralegal shall not use letterhead, business cards or other promotional materials to create a fraudulent impression of his/her status or ability to practice in the jurisdiction in which the paralegal practices.

EC-1.7(d) A paralegal shall not practice under color of any record, diploma, or certificate that has been illegally or fraudulently obtained or issued or which is misrepresentative in any way.

EC-1.7(e) A paralegal shall not participate in the creation, issuance, or dissemination of fraudulent records, diplomas, or certificates.

1.8   A PARALEGAL SHALL NOT ENGAGE IN THE UNAUTHORIZED PRACTICE OF LAW.

Ethical Considerations

EC-1.8(a) A paralegal shall comply with the applicable legal authority governing the unauthorized practice of law in the jurisdiction in which the paralegal practices.

§2.   NFPA GUIDELINES FOR THE ENFORCEMENT OF THE MODEL CODE OF ETHICS AND PROFESSIONAL RESPONSIBILITY

2.1   BASIS FOR DISCIPLINE

2.1(a)   Disciplinary investigations and proceedings brought under authority of the Rules shall be conducted in accord with obligations imposed on the paralegal professional by the Model Code of Ethics and Professional Responsibility.

2.2   STRUCTURE OF DISCIPLINARY COMMITTEE

2.2(a)   The Disciplinary Committee ("Committee") shall be made up of nine (9) members including the Chair.

2.2(b)   Each member of the Committee, including any temporary replacement members, shall have demonstrated working knowledge of ethics/professional responsibility-related issues and activities.

2.2(c)   The Committee shall represent a cross-section of practice areas and work experience. The following recommendations are made regarding the members of the Committee.

   1) At least one paralegal with one to three years of law-related work experience.
   2) At least one paralegal with five to seven years of law related work experience.
   3) At least one paralegal with over ten years of law related work experience.
   4) One paralegal educator with five to seven years of work experience; preferably in

the area of ethics/professional responsibility.

    5) One paralegal manager.

    6) One lawyer with five to seven years of law-related work experience.

    7) One lay member.

2.2(d)   The Chair of the Committee shall be appointed within thirty (30) days of its members' induction. The Chair shall have no fewer than ten (10) years of law-related work experience.

2.2(e)   The terms of all members of the Committee shall be staggered. Of those members initially appointed, a simple majority plus one shall be appointed to a term of one year, and the remaining members shall be appointed to a term of two years. Thereafter, all members of the Committee shall be appointed to terms of two years.

2.2(f)   If for any reason the terms of a majority of the Committee will expire at the same time, members may be appointed to terms of one year to maintain continuity of the Committee.

2.2(g)   The Committee shall organize from its members a three-tiered structure to investigate, prosecute and/or adjudicate charges of misconduct. The members shall be rotated among the tiers.

2.3   **OPERATION OF COMMITTEE**

2.3(a)   The Committee shall meet on an as-needed basis to discuss, investigate, and/or adjudicate alleged violations of the Model Code/Model Rules.

2.3(b)   A majority of the members of the Committee present at a meeting shall constitute a quorum.

2.3(c)   A Recording Secretary shall be designated to maintain complete and accurate minutes of all Committee meetings. All such minutes shall be kept confidential until a decision has been made that the matter will be set for hearing as set forth in Section 6.1 below.

2.3(d)   If any member of the Committee has a conflict of interest with the Charging Party, the Responding Party, or the allegations of misconduct, that member shall not take part in any hearing or deliberations concerning those allegations. If the absence of that member creates a lack of a quorum for the Committee, then a temporary replacement for the member shall be appointed.

2.3(e)   Either the Charging Party or the Responding Party may request that, for good cause shown, any member of the Committee not participate in a hearing or deliberation. All such requests shall be honored. If the absence of a Committee member under those circumstances creates a lack of a quorum for the Committee, then a temporary replacement for that member shall be appointed.

2.3(f)   All discussions and correspondence of the Committee shall be kept confidential until a decision has been made that the matter will be set for hearing as set forth in Section 6.1 below.

2.3(g)   All correspondence from the Committee to the Responding Party regarding any charge of misconduct and any decisions made regarding the charge shall be mailed certified mail, return receipt requested, to the Responding Party's last known address and shall be clearly marked with a "Confidential" designation.

2.4   **PROCEDURE FOR THE REPORTING OF ALLEGED VIOLATIONS OF THE MODEL CODE/DISCIPLINARY RULES**

2.4(a)   An individual or entity in possession of non-confidential knowledge or information concerning possible instances of misconduct shall make a confidential written report to the Committee within thirty (30) days of obtaining same. This report shall include all details of the alleged misconduct.

2.4(b)   The Committee so notified shall inform the Responding Party of the allegation(s) of misconduct no later than ten (10) business days after receiving the confidential written report from the Charging Party.

2.4(c)   Notification to the Responding Party shall include the identity of the Charging Party, unless, for good cause shown, the Charging Party requests anonymity.

2.4(d)   The Responding Party shall reply to the allegations within ten (10) business days of notification.

2.5   PROCEDURE FOR THE INVESTIGATION OF A CHARGE OF MISCONDUCT

2.5(a)   Upon receipt of a Charge of Misconduct ("Charge"), or on its own initiative, the Committee shall initiate an investigation.

2.5(b)   If, upon initial or preliminary review, the Committee makes a determination that the charges are either without basis in fact or, if proven, would not constitute professional misconduct, the Committee shall dismiss the allegations of misconduct. If such determination of dismissal cannot be made, a formal investigation shall be initiated.

2.5(c)   Upon the decision to conduct a formal investigation, the Committee shall:

1) mail to the Charging and Responding Parties within three (3) business days of that decision notice of the commencement of a formal investigation. That notification shall be in writing and shall contain a complete explanation of all Charge(s), as well as the reasons for a formal investigation and shall cite the applicable codes and rules;

2) allow the Responding Party thirty (30) days to prepare and submit a confidential response to the Committee, which response shall address each charge specifically and shall be in writing; and

3) upon receipt of the response to the notification, have thirty (30) days to investigate the Charge(s). If an extension of time is deemed necessary, that extension shall not exceed ninety (90) days.

2.5(d)   Upon conclusion of the investigation, the Committee may:

1) dismiss the Charge upon the finding that it has no basis in fact;
2) dismiss the Charge upon the finding that, if proven, the Charge would not constitute Misconduct;
3) refer the matter for hearing by the Tribunal; or
4) in the case of criminal activity, refer the Charge(s) and all investigation results to the appropriate authority.

2.6   PROCEDURE FOR A MISCONDUCT HEARING BEFORE A TRIBUNAL

2.6(a)   Upon the decision by the Committee that a matter should be heard, all parties shall be notified and a hearing date shall be set. The hearing shall take place no more than thirty (30) days from the conclusion of the formal investigation.

2.6(b)   The Responding Party shall have the right to counsel. The parties and the Tribunal shall have the right to call any witnesses and introduce any documentation that they believe will lead to the fair and reasonable resolution of the matter.

2.6(c)   Upon completion of the hearing, the Tribunal shall deliberate and present a written decision to the parties in accordance with procedures as set forth by the Tribunal.

2.6(d)   Notice of the decision of the Tribunal shall be appropriately published.

2.7   SANCTIONS

2.7(a)   Upon a finding of the Tribunal that misconduct has occurred, any of the following sanctions, or others as may be deemed appropriate, may be imposed upon the Responding Party, either singularly or in combination:

1) letter of reprimand to the Responding Party; counseling;
2) attendance at an ethics course approved by the Tribunal; probation;
3) suspension of license/authority to practice; revocation of license/authority to practice;
4) imposition of a fine; assessment of costs; or
5) in the instance of criminal activity, referral to the appropriate authority.

2.7(b)   Upon the expiration of any period of probation, suspension, or revocation, the Responding Party may make application for reinstatement. With the application for reinstatement, the Responding Party must show proof of having complied with all aspects of the sanctions imposed by the Tribunal.

2.8   APPELLATE PROCEDURES

2.8(a)   The parties shall have the right to appeal the decision of the Tribunal in accordance with the procedure as set forth by the Tribunal.

DEFINITIONS

"Appellate Body" means a body established to adjudicate an appeal to any decision made by a Tribunal or other decision-making body with respect to formally-heard Charges of Misconduct.

"Charge of Misconduct" means a written submission by any individual or entity to an ethics committee, paralegal association, bar association, law enforcement agency, judicial body, government agency, or other appropriate body or entity, that sets forth non-confidential information regarding any instance of alleged misconduct by an individual paralegal or paralegal entity.

"Charging Party" means any individual or entity who submits a Charge of Misconduct against an individual paralegal or paralegal entity.

"Competency" means the demonstration of: diligence, education, skill, and mental, emotional, and physical fitness reasonably necessary for the performance of paralegal services.

"Confidential Information" means information relating to a client, whatever its source, that is not public knowledge nor available to the public. ("Non-Confidential Information" would generally include the name of the client and the identity of the matter for which the paralegal provided services.)

"Disciplinary Hearing" means the confidential proceeding conducted by a committee or other designated body or entity concerning any instance of alleged misconduct by an individual paralegal or paralegal entity.

"Disciplinary Committee" means any committee that has been established by an entity such as a paralegal association, bar association, judicial body, or government agency to: (a) identify, define and investigate general ethical considerations and concerns with respect to paralegal practice; (b) administer and enforce the Model Code and Model Rules and; (c) discipline any individual paralegal or paralegal entity found to be in violation of same.

"Disclose" means communication of information reasonably sufficient to permit identification of the significance of the matter in question.

"Ethical Wall" means the screening method implemented in order to protect a client from a conflict of interest. An Ethical Wall generally includes, but is not limited to, the following elements: (1) prohibit the paralegal from having any connection with the matter; (2) ban discussions with or the transfer of documents to or from the paralegal; (3) restrict access to files; and (4) educate all members of the firm, corporation, or entity as to the separation of the paralegal (both organizationally and physically) from the pending matter. For more information regarding the Ethical Wall, see the NFPA publication entitled "The Ethical Wall - Its Application to Paralegals."

"Ex parte" means actions or communications conducted at the instance and for the benefit of one party only, and without notice to, or contestation by, any person adversely interested.

"Investigation" means the investigation of any charge(s) of misconduct filed against an individual paralegal or paralegal entity by a Committee.

"Letter of Reprimand" means a written notice of formal censure or severe reproof administered to an individual paralegal or paralegal entity for unethical or improper conduct.

"Misconduct" means the knowing or unknowing commission of an act that is in direct violation of those Canons and Ethical Considerations of any and all applicable codes and/or rules of conduct.

"Paralegal" is synonymous with "Legal Assistant" and is defined as a person qualified through education, training, or work experience to perform substantive legal work that requires knowledge of legal concepts and is customarily, but not exclusively performed by a lawyer. This person may be retained or employed by a lawyer, law office, governmental agency, or other entity or may be authorized by administrative, statutory, or court authority to perform this work.

"Proper Authority" means the local paralegal association, the local or state bar association, Committee(s) of the local paralegal or bar association(s), local prosecutor, administrative agency, or other tribunal empowered to investigate or act upon an instance of alleged misconduct.

"Responding Party" means an individual paralegal or paralegal entity against whom a Charge of Misconduct has been submitted.

"Revocation" means the recision of the license, certificate or other authority to practice of an individual paralegal or paralegal entity found in violation of those Canons and Ethical Considerations of any and all applicable codes and/or rules of conduct.

"Suspension" means the suspension of the license, certificate or other authority to practice of an individual paralegal or paralegal entity found in violation of those Canons and Ethical Considerations of any and all applicable codes and/or rules of conduct.

"Tribunal" means the body designated to adjudicate allegations of misconduct.

National Federation of Paralegal Associations

Post Office Box 33108
Kansas City. Missouri 64114
Telephone: 816.941.4000
Facsimile: 816.941.2725
Email: info@paralegals.org
Technical: webmaster@paralegals.org

ABA Standing Committee on Legal Assistants

Model Guidelines for the Utilization of Legal Assistant Services

The following Guidelines were adopted by the ABA's policy making body, the House of Delegates, in 1991. Lawyers are the intended audience of these Guidelines. The Guidelines, therefore, are addressed to lawyer conduct and not directly to the conduct of legal assistants and paralegals. Both the <u>National Association of Legal Assistants</u> (NALA) and the <u>National Federation of Paralegal Associations</u> (NFPA) have adopted guidelines of conduct that are directed to legal assistants and paralegals.

The Guidelines were developed to conform with the ABA's Model Rules of Professional Conduct, decided authority, and contemporary practice. Lawyers are to be directed to Model Rule 5.3 of the Model Rules of Professional Conduct and nothing in these Guidelines is intended to be inconsistent with Rule 5.3. For more information see, the ABA <u>Center for Professional Responsibility</u>.

Note: The terms "legal assistant" and "paralegal" are used interchangeably. Annotations and commentary to the Guidelines (which were not adopted as official policy in 1991 by the House of Delegates) are not included below. They are currently being reviewed by the Standing Committee on Legal Assistants to see if they should be revised in light of current case law. A copy of the Guidelines with annotations and commentary is available through the ABA Legal Assistants Department staff office. (Phone: 312/988-5616; Fax: 312/988-5677; E-Mail: <u>legalassts@abanet.org</u>).

GUIDELINE 1:
A lawyer is responsible for all of the professional actions of a legal assistant performing legal assistant services at the lawyer's direction and should take reasonable measures to ensure that the legal assistant's conduct is consistent with the lawyer's obligations under the ABA Model Rules of Professional Conduct.

GUIDELINE 2:
Provided the lawyer maintains responsibility for the work product, a lawyer may delegate to a legal assistant any task normally performed by the lawyer except those tasks proscribed to one not licensed as a lawyer by statute, court rule, administrative rule or regulation, controlling authority, the ABA Model Rules of Professional Conduct, or these Guidelines.

GUIDELINE 3:
A lawyer may not delegate to a legal assistant:

(a) Responsibility for establishing an attorney-client relationship.
(b) Responsibility for establishing the amount of a fee to be charged for a legal service.
(c) Responsibility for a legal opinion rendered to a client.

GUIDELINE 4:
It is the lawyer's responsibility to take reasonable measures to ensure that clients, courts, and other lawyers are aware that a legal assistant, whose services are utilized by the lawyer in performing legal services, is not licensed to practice law.

GUIDELINE 5:
A lawyer may identify legal assistants by name and title on the lawyer's letterhead and on business cards identifying the lawyer's firm.

GUIDELINE 6:
It is the responsibility of a lawyer to take reasonable measures to ensure that all client confidences are preserved by a legal assistant.

GUIDELINE 7:
A lawyer should take reasonable measures to prevent conflicts of interest resulting from a legal assistant's other employment or interests insofar as such other employment or interests would present a conflict of interest if it were that of the lawyer.

GUIDELINE 8:
A lawyer may include a charge for the work performed by a legal assistant in setting a charge for legal services.

GUIDELINE 9:
A lawyer may not split legal fees with a legal assistant nor pay a legal assistant for the referral of legal business. A lawyer may compensate a legal assistant based on the quantity and quality of the legal assistant's work and the value of that work to a law practice, but the legal assistant's compensation may not be contingent, by advance agreement, upon the profitability of the lawyer's practice.

GUIDELINE 10:
A lawyer who employs a legal assistant should facilitate the legal assistant's participation in appropriate continuing education and pro bono publico activities.

BOOKS AND WEB SITES TO CHECK OUT

BOOKS TO CHECK OUT

Ethics and Professional Responsibility
    Therese A. Cannon (Little, Brown)

The Paralegal's Desk Reference
    Steve Albrecht (Arco)

How to Land Your First Paralegal Job
    Andrea Wagner (Prentice Hall)

Getting Things Done When You're Not in Charge
    Geoffrey M. Bellam (Simon & Schuster)

Getting What You Came For
    Robert L. Peters, Ph.D. (The Noon Day Press/Farra, Straus and Giroux)

Your First Job
    Ron Fry (Career Press)

Better Resumes for Attorneys and Paralegals
    Adele Lewis and David Saltman (Barron's)

Opportunities in Paralegal Careers
    Alice Find (VGM Career Horizons)

Paralegal
    Barbara Bernardo (Petersons)

Who's Hiring Who
    Richard Lathrop (Ten Speed Press)

MAGAZINES AND JOURNALS TO CHECK OUT

Legal Assistant Today
> James Publishing

National Paralegal Reporter
> National Federation of Paralegal Associations

The Paralegal Educator

Journal of Paralegal Education
> American Association for Paralegal Education

Facts and Findings
> National Association of Legal Assistants

WEB SITES TO CHECK OUT

Nothing's easier than surfing the Net. Once you get your feet wet you'll find links from one site to another all on your own. Here are some cool sites to get you started.

Supreme Court Decisions	http://www.law.cornell.edu/supct/
Federal Publications	http://www.fjc.gov/pubs.html
Law Talk	http://www.law.indiana.edu/law/lawtalk.html/
Legal Resources	http://www.law.emory.edu/LAW/LAW/law.html
Experts	http://wwww.witness.net/
Experts	http://www.expertpages.com
Patents	http://www.uspto.gov/
Law School sites	http://www.law.cornell.edu/
	http://www.law.emory.edu
	http://www.usc.edu/dept/law
	http://www.colostate.edu/depts/LTS/research/legal/
Canadian	http://www.cbsc.org/manitoba/links/law

Organizations:

NALA	http://www.nala.org/
NFPA	http://www.paralegals.org/
AAfPE	http://www.aafpe.org/links.html
ABA	http://www.abanet.org
Job Search	http://www.tcm.com
	http://www.dbm.com/jobguide/
	http://www.jobtrak.com

General Law

General	http://www.corporatebar.org
General	http://www.LawLinks.com
General	http://www.alllaw.com/
General (Legal dictionaries, briefs, self-help)	http://www.nolo.com/
General (Search yellow & white pages, trip info)	http://www.theultiamtes.com/

Other

Public International Law	http://www.ecel.uwa.edu.au/law/links/fauburn
ADR Service Provider	http://www.jams-endispute.com
U.S. Dept. of Labor	http://www.dol.gov
U.S. Congress	http://www.thomas.loc.gov
Federal Express tracking	http://www.fedex/cp,/cgi-gin/track_it
AT&T's directory of 800 numbers	http://att.net/dir800/
Dept. of Motor Vehicles	http://www.dmvlink.com.faq.html

INDEX